The Two Horizons Old Testament Commentary

J. Gordon McConville and Craig Bartholomew, *General Editors*

Two features distinguish The Two Horizons Old Testament Commentary series: theological exegesis and theological reflection.

Exegesis since the Reformation era and especially in the past two hundred years emphasized careful attention to philology, grammar, syntax, and concerns of a historical nature. More recently, commentary has expanded to include social-scientific, political, or canonical questions and more.

Without slighting the significance of those sorts of questions, scholars in The Two Horizons Old Testament Commentary locate their primary interests on theological readings of texts, past and present. The result is a paragraph-by-paragraph engagement with the text that is deliberately theological in focus.

Theological reflection in The Two Horizons Old Testament Commentary takes many forms, including locating each Old Testament book in relation to the whole of Scripture — asking what the biblical book contributes to biblical theology — and in conversation with constructive theology of today. How commentators engage in the work of theological reflection will differ from book to book, depending on their particular theological tradition and how they perceive the work of biblical theology and theological hermeneutics. This heterogeneity derives as well from the relative infancy of the project of theological interpretation of Scripture in modern times and from the challenge of grappling with a book's message in Greco-Roman antiquity, in the canon of Scripture and history of interpretation, and for life in the admittedly diverse Western world at the beginning of the twenty-first century.

The Two Horizons Old Testament Commentary is written primarily for students, pastors, and other Christian leaders seeking to engage in theological interpretation of Scripture.

D1601560

Lamentations

Robin Parry

WILLIAM B. EERDMANS PUBLISHING COMPANY
GRAND RAPIDS, MICHIGAN / CAMBRIDGE, U.K.

Published 2010 by

Wm. B. Eerdmans Publishing Co.

2140 Oak Industrial Drive N.E., Grand Rapids, Michigan 49505 /

P.O. Box 163, Cambridge CB3 9PU U.K.

Printed in the United States of America

16 15 14 13 12 11 10   7 6 5 4 3 2 1

Library of Congress Cataloging-in-Publication Data

Parry, Robin A.
    Lamentations / Robin Parry.
        p.   cm.   — (The two horizons Old Testament commentary)
    Includes bibliographical references and index.
    ISBN 978-0-8028-2714-2 (pbk.: alk. paper)
    1. Bible. O.T. Lamentations — Commentaries.   I. Title.

BS1535.53.P37 2010
224'.3077 — dc22

                                                                2010008906

www.eerdmans.com

In memory of

Alan Hayes (1955-2008)

Steve Jeynes (1951-2008)

Graham Rees (1940-2008)

Meg Mudditt (1938-2009)

Jeremy Mudditt (1938-2010)

"If he afflicts then he will have mercy,
according to the abundance of his loving kindness."

LAMENTATIONS 3:32

Contents

Abbreviations

AB	Anchor Bible
ABRL	Anchor Bible Reference Library
ANCL	*Ante-Nicene Christian Library*
ANES	*Ancient Near Eastern Studies*
ANET	*Ancient Near Eastern Texts Relating to the Old Testament,* ed. James B. Pritchard. 3rd ed. Princeton, 1969.
AOTC	Abingdon Old Testament Commentaries
AS	Assyriological Studies
ATD	Das Alte Testament Deutsch
BDB	Francis Brown, S. R. Driver, and Charles A. Briggs, *A Hebrew and English Lexicon of the Old Testament.* Oxford, 1907.
BEATAJ	Beiträge zur Erforschung des Alten Testaments und des antiken Judentum
Bib	*Biblica*
BibInt	*Biblical Interpretation*
BibOr	Biblica et orientalia
BKAT	Biblischer Kommentar, Altes Testament
BRS	Biblical Resource Series
BSac	*Bibliotheca Sacra*
BZAW	Beihefte zur Zeitschrift für die alttestamentliche Wissenschaft
CBQ	*Catholic Biblical Quarterly*
CTJ	*Calvin Theological Journal*
CTQ	*Concordia Theological Quarterly*
CurBR	*Currents in Biblical Research*
CurTM	*Currents in Theology and Mission*
EgT	*Eglise et théologie*
FAT	Forschungen zum Alten Testament
FOTL	Forms of the Old Testament Literature

GKC	Wilhelm Gesenius, *Gesenius' Hebrew Grammar,* ed. E. Kautzsch, trans. A. E. Cowley. 2nd ed. Oxford, 1910.
HAT	Handbuch zum Alten Testament
HBT	*Horizons in Biblical Theology*
HCOT	Historical Commentary on the Old Testament
HKAT	Handkommentar zum Alten Testament
HTR	*Harvard Theological Review*
IB	*The Interpreter's Bible,* ed. George Arthur Buttrick. 12 vols. New York, 1951-57.
Int	*Interpretation*
ITC	International Theological Commentary
JANESCU	*Journal of the Ancient Near Eastern Society of Columbia University*
JBL	*Journal of Biblical Literature*
Jöuon	Paul Jöuon, *A Grammar of Biblical Hebrew,* trans. and ed. T. Muraoka. 2 vols. Subsidia biblica 14/1-2. Rome, 1991.
JPT	*Journal of Pentecostal Theology*
JSOT	*Journal for the Study of the Old Testament*
JSOTSup	Journal for the Study of the Old Testament: Supplement Series
KAT	Kommentar zum Alten Testament
KHC	Kürzer Hand-Commentar zum Alten Testament
LCC	Library of Christian Classics
LHB/OTS	Library of Hebrew Bible/Old Testament Studies
LXX	Septuagint
MT	Masoretic Text
NCBC	New Century Bible Commentary
NIB	*New Interpreter's Bible,* ed. Leander Keck et al. 12 vols. Nashville, 1994-2004.
NPNF[1]	*Nicene and Post-Nicene Fathers,* Series 1
NPNF[2]	*Nicene and Post-Nicene Fathers,* Series 2
OTE	*Old Testament Essays*
OTL	Old Testament Library
QR	*Quarterly Review*
RB	*Revue biblique*
ResQ	*Restoration Quarterly*
RGG	*Die Religion in Geschichte und Gegenwart,* 2nd ed., ed. Hermann Gunkel et al. 5 vols. Tübingen, 1929.
SBL	Society of Biblical Literature
SBLDS	Society of Biblical Literature Dissertation Series
SBT	Studies in Biblical Theology
SemeiaSt	Semeia Studies

SJOT	*Scandinavian Journal of the Old Testament*
SJT	*Scottish Journal of Theoelogy*
TDNT	*Theological Dictionary of the New Testament,* ed. Gerhard Kittel and Gerhard Friedrich. 10 vols. Grand Rapids, 1964-1976.
TynBul	*Tyndale Bulletin*
VT	*Vetus Testamentum*
WBC	Word Biblical Commentary
WUNT	Wissenschaftliche Untersuchungen zum Neuen Testament
ZAW	*Zeitschrift für die alttestamentliche Wissenschaft*
ZBK	Züricher Bibelkommentare

Introduction

The Two Horizons

Western cultures are notoriously averse to pain and tragedy. We spend an extraordinary amount of money and effort seeking to insulate ourselves against life's vicissitudes. All kinds of precautions are taken to ensure the maximal safety of the environments we must inhabit — our homes, our workplaces, our schools, our social space, our transport, our public places — and, just in case something does go wrong, we are offered just about every type of insurance one could dream of. We do not want sorrow to knock at our doors and, when it does, we do not know what to do with it. Our default mode is to keep it out of sight and pretend that it is not there.

Unlike our Victorian forebears, we are no longer shy about sex, and we have innumerable ways to speak about sexual intercourse but we are hopelessly lost for words when confronted with grief and death. We don't know what to do, where to look, what to say. Increasingly we lack the social practices, words, and concepts necessary to grasp our pain by the horns and stare it in the face. We have been robbed of a vocabulary of grief, and we suffer for it. The book of Lamentations accosts us by the wayside as a stranger who offers us an unasked-for, unwanted, and yet priceless gift — the poetry of pain. We would be wise to pay attention.

Lamentations, like the personified Lady Jerusalem within its pages, often sits alone within the landscape of the Christian Bible calling out to those readers who pass by to take notice but, as with Lady Jerusalem, there is no one to comfort. Lamentations is one of those Old Testament books that have never really attained a place of prominence in Christian spirituality and reflection. This means that when attempting to think theologically about the book one does not have the rich heritage of Christian theological interpretation to draw on that one finds with books such as Genesis, Exodus, Psalms, or Isaiah. Perhaps this is to be expected because Lamentations is only twice alluded to in the New Testament, while a book such as Isaiah seems omnipresent.[1] So when one comes to read Lamentations theologically as a Christian, one has to start with a comparatively slender thread of prior reflection as a guide.

When we reflect theologically on Lamentations, issues of method require some comment. First of all, Lamentations was not written to present a theology. As Adele Berlin notes, "the book does not construct a theology of its own, nor does it present in any systematic way the standard theology of its time. It *assumes* the 'theology of destruction' in which destruction and exile are punishment for sin."[2] So one task of the theological reader is to bring to the surface the theology underlying the text and to seek to clarify its contours.

Second, Lamentations was not written *by* Christians, nor *for* Christians. The theology of Lamentations is not Christian theology. Nevertheless, Lamentations is part of the Jewish Scriptures accepted by the earliest churches as their own sacred Scripture. Jesus and his early followers saw their story as one of continuity with Israel's story recounted in those holy scrolls. Thus while Lamentations is not a Christian text, it was received by the early church as one of the books through which God continued to address his people, even if that people was now composed of both Jews *and Gentiles* united by faith in Jesus the Messiah.

But precisely how should Israel's sacred texts be interpreted by this new community of Jesus? In the same way that Israel had always reinterpreted its own texts — in the light of the current thing that God was doing. For the early Jewish followers of Jesus, God had moved to do something radical in the current situation. In Jesus' life, death, resurrection, and ascension the end of the age had come and a new age had broken in. Jesus was seen as the climax (though not the end) of God's dealings with Israel, and all of Israel's traditions and texts were reread in the light of Christ. Christians reading Israel's Scriptures cannot read those texts as if Jesus had not come. But, and it is an important "but," to allow those texts to challenge and contribute to ongoing Christian reflection there is a critical place for seeking to hear them on their own terms. In other words, part of a Christian theological reflection on Lamentations will require the Christian reader to listen for the text's distinctive,

---

1. Matt 23:35 alludes to Lam 4:13, and Matt 27:39 alludes to Lam 2:15. Webb thinks there are a few more allusions: Lam 1:15 in Rev 14:20 and 19:15; Lam 2:15 in Mark 15:29-30; Lam 3:15 in Acts 8:23; Lam 3:45 in 1 Cor 4:13; *Five Festal Garments*, 79-80.

2. Berlin, *Lamentations*, 18. Emphasis mine.

pre-Christian voice. The danger of considering Old Testament texts only in the light of Christ is that all one hears is what one already knows from the New Testament. But the Old Testament has much to teach Christians that they will not find in the New, often because the New took it for granted but then the later church forgot it.[3] However, for the Christian, once one has heard the distinctive voice of Lamentations one has to bring that voice into dialogue with God's revelation in Christ to discern how God is addressing the *church* through it. This is an art, not a science. So our aim in the first part of the commentary is to hear the distinctive theological voice of Lamentations but, in the second part, it is to hear how the acoustics change when that voice is heard in the Cathedral of Christ.

It ought to be said clearly that there will never be such a thing as *the* Christian interpretation of Lamentations. This is because the meanings to which it gives birth are not so much "in the text" as born out of the interaction of the text and the (hopefully) Spirit-led activity of its readers.[4] Christian readers will be mixing the genes of Lamentations with the genes of other biblical texts, Christian theological reflections through the ages, the experiences of various readers, and so on. The book is simply so pregnant with potential that the meanings to which it gives birth will be diverse even within the constraints imposed by canonical context, the Rule of Faith, and the history of Christian interpretation.

Authorship, Date, and Place of Composition

Issues of authorship, date, and place of composition have been prominent in many scholarly discussions, and I see no value in rehearsing them at any length here. Readers who want a good orientation on such matters will find the overviews in the commentaries of Claus Westermann and Paul House helpful.

The earliest tradition regarding the authorship of Lamentations to which we have access identifies the prophet Jeremiah as the writer, and that identification went more or less unchallenged until the eighteenth century.[5] The Septuagint's Greek translation of the book opens with the words, "And it came to pass after Israel had gone into captivity, and Jerusalem was laid to

3. So Goldingay, *Israel's Gospel*, Introduction.

4. See Parry, "Reader-Response Criticism."

5. Which is why, for instance, Rembrandt's painting based on the book of Lamentations is actually a painting of "Jeremiah Lamenting the Destruction of Jerusalem" (1630). See Thomas, "Lamentations in Rembrandt van Rijn."

waste, that Jeremiah sat weeping and composed this lament over Jerusalem and said. . . ."[6] The Syriac, Targum, and Vulgate have similar headings. In keeping with its identification of the author, the Septuagint places Lamentations immediately after the book of Jeremiah — a location it retains in Christian Bibles. While the Hebrew Bible traditions do not locate Lamentations next to Jeremiah, this was for liturgical reasons and not because they reflect a different tradition on authorship (see "The Canonical Locations of Lamentations" below).

The modern period, beginning with Hermann von der Haardt's commentary in 1712, has seen an almost total rejection of the once universal belief that Jeremiah wrote Lamentations.[7] Many now see the author(s) as connected in some way with the royal court, prophetic circles, or more commonly, the temple.

Some modern authors have argued that while Jeremiah is not the author of the book, he may be one of the voices in it or perhaps even the implied author. This would allow us to see deliberate and conscious allusions to the book of Jeremiah in Lamentations while remaining agnostic about actual authorship. This commentary shares such agnosticism about the question of authorship. Indeed, while it inclines towards the view that Lamentations has a single author, it also admits that multiple authorship is a possibility with different poems penned at different times by different people.[8] What it is uncompromising on is the insistence that the book of Lamentations as we have it, whatever its compositional prehistory, should be read as a single, unified book. Even *if* some of the poems (or parts of them) had different origins, they have been crafted into a new literary whole, and it is *that* which is the primary focus for interpretation. For instance, ch. 3, which is the most plausible candidate for different authorship, is very clearly shaped to fit its context in Lamentations, as the use of the acrostic pattern and the intertextual links with the rest of the book show. Consequently, it will be fundamental to the approach of this com-

---

6. On LXX Lamentations, see Youngblood, "The Character and Significance of LXX Lamentations."

7. See the discussion on authorship in the introduction of House, *Lamentations*. In spite of this we ought to note that the case against Jeremiah as author is not as conclusive as some suppose and that there remain plausible arguments for thinking that he could have been the author, though such arguments indicate, at best, only the *possibility* of Jeremiah as author.

8. Chapters 1 and 2 are so similar that a single author is highly likely, and Chapter 4 also seems to share the same author given the linguistic, thematic, and intertextual connections. Chapter 5 is quite different and may possibly have been composed by a different author. Chapter 3 stands out more strongly both in terms of style and content and is the most plausible candidate for different authorship. However, it is not obvious that any of the differences in genre or content require multiple authors.

mentary that the parts of Lamentations are interpreted in the light of the whole. Almost no attention will be given over to attempting to date the separate chapters beyond locating them at some point during the exilic period.

Clearly, if Jeremiah was the author, then Lamentations would be a response to the cataclysmic events in Judah in 587 B.C. and its aftermath. It remains the case that, in spite of the modern rejection of Jeremiah as author, the vast majority of interpreters of Lamentations continue to see it as literature written during the period of exile in Babylon, some time between 587 and 538 B.C. The internal evidence of Lamentations fits very neatly into this historical context even if it does not unequivocally require it.[9] That, combined with a very ancient and uncontested tradition linking Lamentations with the exile, makes a sixth-century B.C. date likely. Recent linguistic arguments have strengthened this conclusion.[10] This commentary therefore assumes that Lamentations was written in Judah (on the grounds that the viewpoint in the book is Jerusalem-focused) by those who were left behind after the fall of Jerusalem and the exile of its key citizens.[11]

The Exilic Context of Lamentations

The exile was the most cataclysmic event (or serial event) in the history of biblical Israel.[12] The Babylonians besieged Jerusalem for three years until, in 587 or 586 B.C., the city wall was breached and the city taken. King Zedekiah fled and was captured. The temple was destroyed and sacked, as later were the palace and the great houses, and the leading citizens were taken off to Babylonian exile (in 597, 2 Kgs 24:14; and 587/586, 2 Kgs 25:11; and again in 582). The following (slightly modified) chart from Walter Kaiser Jr. draws some of the connections between Lamentations and the historic destruction

---

9. A few, such as Provan, have argued for agnosticism regarding the date(s) of composition and the precise historical background; Provan, *Lamentations*, 11-15; "Reading Texts Against an Historical Background." Provan maintains that the internal evidence of the book does not clearly indicate that it addresses the situation in Palestine after the fall of Jerusalem. While I think agnosticism is unnecessary on this issue, Provan does helpfully highlight how the language of Lamentations can be applied to situations other than those after 587 B.C. and this, in part, explains the ongoing power of the book.

10. Dobbs-Allsopp argues that the Hebrew of Lamentations is transitional between Standard Biblical Hebrew and Late Biblical Hebrew, making a sixth-century date between 586/7 and 520 strong; "Linguistic Evidence."

11. On provenance, see Middlemas, *The Troubles of Templeless Judah*, 177-84.

12. For a detailed historical study on the exile, see Albertz, *Israel in Exile*, 45-138. See also Smith, *The Religion of the Landless*.

of Jerusalem (although the following warnings about poetic language need to be kept in mind).[13]

	2 Kings	Jeremiah	Lamentations
The siege of Jerusalem	25:1-2	39:1-3; 52:4-5	2:20-22; 4:1-18
The famine in the city	25:3	37:21; 52:6	1:11, 19; 2:11-12, 19-20; 4:4-5, 9-10; 5:9-10
The flight of the army and the king	25:4-7	39:4-7; 52:7-11	1:3, 6; 2:2; 4:19-20
The burning of the palace, temple, and city	25:8-9	39:8; 52:13	2:3-5, 7; 4:11
The breaching of the city walls	25:10	33:4-5; 52:7	2:7-9
The exile of the populace	25:11-12	28:3-4, 14; 39:9-10	1:1, 3, 5, 18; 2:9, 14; 4:22
The looting of the temple	25:13-15	51:51	1:10; 2:6-7
The execution of the leaders	25:18-21	39:6	1:15; 2:20; 5:12
The vassal status of Judah	25:22-25	40:9	1:1; 5:2
The collapse of expected foreign help	24:7	27:1-11; 37:5-10	1:2, 19; 4:17

Scholars disagree about much of the historical reconstruction of the event including how many people were deported. Some argue that the archaeological evidence supports a very severe destruction and deportation: "Judah was almost entirely destroyed and. . . its Jewish population disappeared from most of the kingdom's territory."[14] Others maintain that only a minority of the population was deported and that the vision of almost total deportation given in Kings and Chronicles is a theological assessment and very misleading if taken as a strictly historical one.[15] Even *if* that were the case, we must not imagine that the exile was not really that bad. There is no doubt that Jerusalem and the surrounding cities were treated *extremely* harshly.

---

13. Kaiser, *Grief and Pain*, 16.

14. Stern, "The Babylonian Gap," 273. See also Stern, *Archaeology of the Land of the Bible*, vol. 2. Albertz argues that "about 20,000 individuals were deported from Judah"; *Israel in Exile*, 90. He adds that if we assume that about 20,000 were lost in the fight against Babylon, "then Judah lost approximately half its inhabitants between 600 and 580 and was reduced to a population of some forty thousand. In truth, the exile meant a severe bloodletting for Judah" (90). See too D. L. Smith-Christopher, *A Biblical Theology of Exile*, ch. 2.

15. E.g., Noth maintains that the actual number of exiles was not high. See also Barstad, *The Myth of the Empty Land*; Blenkinsopp, "The Bible, Archaeology and Politics."

On top of this, it needs to be appreciated that the poetry of Lamentations, while it may not always reflect clear and accurate historical information, reflects the "emotional, social, and . . . spiritual impact of the disaster."[16] And this trauma was induced as much by the social and theological import of the situation as by the physical pain. This crisis cut right to the heart of Israel's covenant relationship with her God. The impregnable city of God, the joy of the whole earth, had been turned to ruins; the temple, the very dwelling place of YHWH on earth, had been desecrated and destroyed; the king, descended from the Davidic line appointed by God to rule over Israel "forever" (2 Sam 7:14-16), was captured and deported; the people who had been given the promised land as an inheritance had been vomited out of it into Babylon. The theological world of the Israelites was torn asunder leaving questions about the possibility of their ongoing relationship with God. The crisis was so traumatic because it was *experienced as* a total abandonment by YHWH.

Lamentations is to be understood, in the first instance, against this historical and theological background but we need to appreciate that the text makes very few direct references to specific historical persons, dates, and incidents. Even Babylon, the archenemy of the exilic period, is not mentioned by name. Instead the language is poetic, and using it to reconstruct history is a precarious business. As Delbert Hillers notes, the history in Lamentations is "experienced and narrated in conformity to certain pre-existing literary and religious patterns."[17] It is this that has enabled it so easily to transcend its original horizons.

The majority of scholars suggest that the poems of Lamentations were written for liturgical use in public rituals of lament. There was a tradition in the cultures of the ancient Near East of the use of city laments in public rituals, and while Lamentations has many differences from these city laments the connections are suggestive. There is also some evidence in the Old Testament of public laments over Jerusalem (Jer 41:4-5; Isa 61:3; Zech 7:2-7; 8:19). The internal evidence of the book suggests that it was written to call YHWH's attention to the plight of the people so he might act to save them, and this would fit with the idea that the book was used in public ceremonies during the exile. However, we have no direct evidence that Lamentations was used in this way, and all that we can do is speculate. What we do know is that in later rabbinic times it was being used in public laments on the 9th of Ab (the fifth month) for the destruction of Herod's temple and for other national disasters.

---

16. Smith-Christopher, *A Biblical Theology of Exile,* 104. On the issue of using the poetry of Lamentations in historical reconstructions, see esp. Hillers, "History and Poetry in Lamentations."

17. Hillers, "History and Poetry in Lamentations," 160.

The Ancient Near Eastern Context of Lamentations

Scholars have long noted similarities and differences between Lamentations and the five extant ancient Sumerian/Babylonian laments over the destruction of cities.[18] The older city laments are usually considered to be compositions to be used in rituals during which the foundations of old sanctuaries were razed prior to the construction of new sanctuaries. The suggestion is that the laments were offered to the deity of the sanctuary to appease his wrath at its destruction. Some have argued that Lamentations stands in the same literary tradition as these older ancient Near Eastern city laments and is directly dependent on them.[19] It is indeed possible that Babylonian city laments were encountered by Jews in the exilic period.[20] F. W. Dobbs-Allsopp proposes that, while there is a direct dependence of Lamentations on the city lament traditions, "Lamentations is no simple Mesopotamian city lament. Rather, it represents a thorough translation and adaptation of the genre in a Judean environment and is ultimately put to a significantly different use."[21] Others argue that direct dependence is not demonstrable and indeed unlikely. Thomas McDaniel maintained that the similarities between Lamentations and other ancient Near Eastern city laments reflect a *common experience* and not a common literary tradition.[22] A mediating position has been taken by other scholars who propose that, while *direct* literary dependence is unlikely (i.e., the author[s] of Lamentations were not aping specific ancient Near Eastern city laments, and may not even have read them), an *indirect* dependence is possible mediated via a common culture.

Lamentations shares much in common with the Sumerian laments and also has many differences. There is still no unanimity on how best to assess the significance of those similarities and differences. It seems wisest to bear in mind this wider nonbiblical tradition of lament when reading Lamentations but not to make it determinative for interpretation. Whatever the precise re-

---

18. *Lamentation over the Destruction of Ur; Lamentations over the Destruction of Sumer and Ur; The Nippur Lament; The Eridu Lament; The Uruk Lament.* See critical editions of the texts by Samuel Kramer in *ANET.* All are also available in translation online. Some have questioned whether these texts all belong to the same genre (e.g., Michalowski, *The Lamentation over the Destruction of Sumer and Ur*). If they do, it must be a genre with considerable stylistic and structural diversity.

19. E.g., Kramer, *Lamentation over the Destruction of Ur.*

20. So Gewaltney, "Biblical Book of Lamentations."

21. Dobbs-Allsopp, *Lamentations,* 9. He sees nine important features in common between Lamentations and ancient Near Eastern city laments (see *Weep, O Daughter of Zion* for his full development of the relationship).

22. McDaniel, "The Alleged Sumerian Influence upon Lamentations."

lationship between Lamentations and older, non-Israelite city laments, we can see that the experience of loss reflected in the former is not utterly unique but participates in a more general human experience of suffering. This is not to suggest that the suffering reflected in Lamentations lacks particularity and uniqueness. Nevertheless, while the suffering of Judah has unique dimensions, it is not utterly unlike the suffering of wider humanity. Those in Judah, for instance, were hardly the first or the last people in the ancient world to experience the horrors of siege warfare. This point will be of theological significance later in the commentary.

The Poetry of Lamentations

For the most part the poetry of Lamentations is like biblical poetry found throughout the Old Testament.[23] I would simply like to highlight six specific features of the poetry of Lamentations that warrant mention:

The Qinah Meter

The *qinah* meter consists of two cola, the second of which must be shorter than the first. The meter is normally measured by the number of word stresses (not syllables) in each half line (3 + 2, 4 + 3, 4 + 2 etc.). For instance, 1:6a has a 4 + 2 meter in Hebrew,

> And so gone from Daughter Zion
>   is all her glory.

And 1:7d has a 3 + 2 meter in Hebrew

> Adversaries saw and mocked
>   over her destruction.

According to Karl Budde, this produces a "peculiar limping rhythm, in which the second member as it were dies away and expires."[24] It is, according to Budde, a meter often used in funeral dirges because the form seems so appropriate to the content. This assessment of the meter has been very widely ac-

23. See, e.g., Alter, *The Art of Biblical Poetry;* Watson, *Classical Hebrew Poetry;* Berlin, *The Dynamics of Biblical Parallelism,* "Introduction."
24. Budde, "Poetry (Hebrew)," 5.

cepted, even if in refined form, and rarely questioned. It does seem that Budde overplayed the connection between the *qinah* meter and the funeral dirge, for it also occurs outside of dirges (e.g., Isa 1:10-12; 40:9ff.; Jonah 2:3-10) and we possess dirges that do not use that meter (2 Sam 1:17-27).[25] It may be linked to lament more generally rather than just to funeral laments.[26] Hillers suggests that the *qinah* meter communicates meaning by association and its general, if not exclusive, association with laments, combined with its prominence in Lamentations,[27] is enough to direct the audiences' reaction in a manner appropriate to lamenting.

Enjambment

Hebrew poetry typically contains pairs of lines that are marked by a pause between them. These lines parallel each other in some way. For instance, Lam 5:15:

> Our heart has ceased from rejoicing,
>> Our dancing was turned to mourning.

However, Lamentations is full of couplets in which the meaning and syntax run over the end of the first line into the second. For instance, 1:10 has three such couplets:

> An adversary has stretched out his hand
>> over all her precious things.
> Indeed, she saw nations
>> enter her sanctuary
> concerning whom you had commanded,
>> "They shall not enter your assembly."

This phenomenon is known as enjambment. Robert Gordis remarks that "In Lamentations this divergence [between metric pattern and meaning] is so common that it may fairly be regarded as a special characteristic of the poet."[28] Enjambment is most intense in Poems 1-2, decreases in 3-4, and is al-

---

25. Hillers, *Lamentations*, 18-19. I also confess to having reservations about whether the ancient Hebrews saw the meter as communicating the idea of limping and expiring.

26. Freedman, "Acrostics and Metrics in Hebrew Poetry," 392.

27. See Freedman and von Fange, "Metrics in Hebrew Poetry;" Freedman and Geoghegan, "Quantitative Measurement in Biblical Hebrew Poetry."

28. Gordis, *The Song of Songs and Lamentations*, 120.

most absent in 5. Dobbs-Allsopp suggests that the use of this device gives the poems a sense of forward movement. On occasions, he also notes, it can serve to encourage readers to interpret the first line in one way and then to have to reverse that interpretation once they read the second line. For instance, 2:22a:

> You invite, like on a festival day,
>> my terrors from all around.

The first line announces a joyous religious festival, but the second line gives a horrible twist to any expectations that may have been raised in the audience.[29]

Genre

There has been much discussion of the genres of the individual poems in Lamentations. Chapter 5 is the least controversial, being closest to a "pure" type. It is almost universally agreed to be a variation on a communal lament. Chapter 3 is the most difficult to handle as it seems to contain elements from several genres blended into something quite unlike any other poem in the Old Testament. Hedwig Jahnow argued in 1923 that chs. 1, 2, and 4 reflected the genre of the funeral lament.[30] That thesis was influentially developed by Hermann Gunkel in 1929, who saw elements of the communal lament being joined to the dirge genre and this approach has been widely accepted.[31] Westermann has broken ranks and sees the communal lament, not the funeral dirge, as the underlying genre in chs. 1, 2, and 4. These poems have merely been supplemented with motifs from the dirge, but the dirge does not dictate the underlying structure.[32] Whatever the outcome of that discussion, it is widely agreed that elements of both the dirge and the communal lament are mixed in those poems.

Voices

One feature of the poetry of Lamentations is the range of voices employed. Each voice is "the mask or characterization assumed by the poet as the me-

---

29. Dobbs-Allsopp, *Lamentations,* 19-20.
30. Jahnow, *Das hebräische Leichenlied.*
31. Gunkel, "Klagelieder Jeremiae."
32. Westermann, *Lamentations,* ch. 1. See Lee, *The Singers of Lamentations,* for a critique of Westermann.

dium through which he perceives and gives expression to his world."[33] Scholars disagree about the number of voices found within the book. There is wide agreement that in chs. 1 and 2 there are just two voices — those of Lady Zion and the Narrator. There is disagreement about whether the man in ch. 3 is the same Narrator or a new character and how many voices there are in that chapter. There are two voices in ch. 4, but scholars disagree whether either of them should be identified with earlier voices in the book. Chapter 5 has only one voice — that of the community. Depending on one's decisions on these issues one may identify anything from three speakers (the Narrator, Lady Zion, the community) to nine.

These voices do not represent radically different views on the crisis. Nevertheless, the different speakers bring different perspectives, have different foci, and possibly do disagree at times. There is a quasi-dialogical nature to the poetry, especially in chs. 1–3, as one character addresses the audience or God sparks the words of another character. On some occasions one speaker will *directly* address another (e.g., 2:18-19). The meaning of the book is not to be found in the words of just one speaker but in the dynamic of their "conversation." Indeed, even the individual voices do not statically represent one precise perspective but themselves shift. So Lady Zion fluctuates between recognizing YHWH's righteousness in punishing her (1:18) and raging against the apparent injustice of the punishment (2:20). The Narrator's own attitude to Lady Zion softens from ch. 1 to ch. 2 as her grief penetrates his emotions (2:11-13). The man in ch. 3 clearly moves from raging against God (3:1-18) towards trusting in God to save him (3:19-24). The meaning of the book is found in its dynamic interrelationships rather than in the parts taken in isolation.

Stereotypical Language and Grief

The expressions, motifs, and images of Lamentations are usually drawn from a common fund of lament language. We need to avoid the temptation of imagining that the artistry of Lamentations and its use of stock language mean that it does not reflect real pain. In traumatic times people often revert to traditional motifs, expressions, and rhythms — the language of grief that their tradition has bequeathed them.

---

33. Lanahan, "Speaking Voice," 41.

The Acrostic Patterns

The acrostic poem was known in ancient Egypt and Mesopotamia as well as occurring several times in the Old Testament (e.g., Psalm 119; Prov 31:10-31; Nah 1). Chapters 1–4 follow an alphabetic acrostic pattern. In chs. 1, 2, and 4 each verse begins with a subsequent letter of the alphabet (א/*a*, ב/*b*, ג/*g*, etc.). In ch. 3, each *line* begins with the designated letter of the alphabet, thereby intensifying the acrostic considerably. So we have three א/*a* lines, three ב/*b* lines, three ג/*g* lines, etc. The differences can be seen in this chart:

Lamentations 1	Lamentations 2	Lamentations 3	Lamentations 4	Lamentations 5
acrostic	acrostic	acrostic	acrostic	not acrostic
22 verses with 3 lines each	22 verses with 3 lines each	66 verses with 1 line each	22 verses with 2 lines each	22 verses with 1 line each
Each verse begins with the acrostic letter (thus 3 lines per letter)	Each verse begins with the acrostic letter	Each *line* begins with the acrostic letter	Each verse begins with the acrostic letter	——
66 lines	66 lines	66 lines	44 lines	22 lines
ע/ʿ–פ/*p* ʿayin–pê	פ/*p*–ע/ʿ pê–ʿayin	פ/*p*–ע/ʿ pê–ʿayin	פ/*p*–ע/ʿ pê–ʿayin	——

Several observations can be made about this chart. First, apart from switching the order of two letters (ʿ*ayin* and *pê*),[34] Lamentations 1 and 2 follow exactly the same pattern. Chapter 3 intensifies the acrostic by having three acrostic lines per verse instead of just one. Chapter 4 reverts to the earlier model of one acrostic letter per verse but reduces each verse from three to two lines. Chapter 5 drops the acrostic pattern but echoes it in the fact that it retains 22 verses, albeit verses of only one line each. Another *possible* hint of the acrostic is in 5:19-20. Line 1 begins with א/*a* (first letter of the alphabet), line 2 begins with כ/*k* (last letter of first half of the alphabet), line 3 begins with ל/*l* (first

---

34. Lamentations 2 switches the order of the ע/ʿ*ayin*–פ/*pê* sequence of ch. 1 to a פ/*pê*–ע/ʿ*ayin* sequence (Lamentations 3 and 4 follow this new pattern, making Poem 1 the odd one out). The reason for this is not clear. It is likely that the order of the Hebrew alphabet was not in a fixed form at this period and that either alternative was a recognized and legitimate order (contrast Psalm 119 with Proverbs 31). In this case, no significance need be attached to the alternative ordering. Renkema suggests that the change to the order of Poem 1 was simply to avoid the scrolls of Poems 1 and 2 getting mixed up and read in the wrong order (Poems 1 and 2 are the only ones that were liable to be confused in this way as they follow exactly the same literary pattern; Renkema, *Lamentations*, 49).

letter of second half of the alphabet), and line 4 begins with **ת**/*t* (last letter of the alphabet).[35]

Two main questions arise from this. First, what, if anything, is the significance of the acrostic pattern? Second, are the differences between the chapters of significance? We shall briefly consider both questions together. However, we need to declare right at the start that we simply do not know the answers, and the best that scholars can do is to make educated guesses. Among the numerous suggestions that have been proposed are the following:

1. *A mnemonic device?* Some suggest that the acrostic is simply a mnemonic device to aid the oral performance of liturgies. While this could be one *result* of the acrostic technique, it is unclear whether it was a *purpose* of it.

2. *An artistic device?* Some have suggested that the acrostic device was simply used for its aesthetic appeal in the ancient world or perhaps to emphasize the beginnings of the lines.[36] It certainly structures the poems, binding the "otherwise scattered and chaotic lyrics"[37] together as units and guiding readers through from the start to the end. Heath Thomas draws attention to the way in which the acrostic propels the reader forward through the poems.[38] Possibly the variations in the patterns across the chapters are simply for aesthetic variation or to add to the dynamic progression of the book (see below).

3. *A way to capture the breadth of the pain?* The acrostic may connote completeness. Norman Gottwald influentially suggested that the author "wished to play upon the collective grief of the community in every aspect, 'from *Aleph* to *Taw*', so that the people might experience an emotional catharsis."[39] The suggestion that the acrostic implies that we have the A to Z of suffering has merit (especially in chs. 1, 2), although it seems to make less sense in ch. 3, which unites an intensification of the acrostic with a more hopeful message. Gottwald himself suggested that the form also implied complete confession of sin, complete cleansing of the conscience, and complete hope for the future. This begins to address the objection just noted, although it seems to overemphasize the place and nature of confession, cleansing, and hope in the book. Chapter 5 is

---

35. Pete Wilcox suggested this idea to me.
36. So Hillers, *Lamentations*, 27.
37. Dobbs-Allsopp, *Lamentations*, 18.
38. Thomas, "Poetry and Theology in Lamentations," 104-8.
39. Gottwald, *Studies in the Book of Lamentations*, 30.

also an issue because it certainly covers the A to Z of the social humiliation of the people yet there is no acrostic.

4. *A way to structure chaos?* O'Connor thinks that "the alphabetic devices embody struggles of survivors to contain and control the chaos of unstructured pain, and the variations among the poems reflect the processes of facing their deadening reality."[40] It could, somewhat more positively, be seen as an affirmation of an underlying order to life *in spite of* its apparent undermining in the community's experience.[41] There is merit to these ideas.

What are we to make of the way that the acrostic is deployed in different ways across the book? This question leads us into a discussion of the structure of the book.

The Structure of Lamentations

Many scholars are of the opinion that, while the individual poems are structured, there is no pattern to the book of Lamentations *as a whole*.[42] However, a growing number are now reconsidering whether there may be some logic to the overall arrangement.[43] Starting with the acrostic patterns and chapter lengths, we could represent them as in the diagram on page 16. While ch. 4 is a full acrostic like chs. 1–2, the shorter lines in the chapter have the effect of magnifying the acrostic intensity. Similarly, while ch. 5 is not an acrostic, the echoes noted above give it some limited acrostic intensity.

These changes give the book a dynamic feel, even if not a plot. Whether a message is communicated to the audience by the changes is much more difficult to ascertain, and the "meaning" is as much brought by the reader as the text. The patterning does lead us to consider the possibility that ch. 3, with its intensified acrostic, may be pivotal in the book. This would inspire us to ask

---

40. O'Connor, *Lamentations and the Tears of the World*, 12. She combines this view with view 3 above.

41. So Gous, "A Survey of Research," 195.

42. E.g., Rudolph, *Die Klagelieder*; Plöger, "Die Klagelieder"; Kraus, *Klagelieder (Threni)*; Boecker, *Klagelieder*; O. Kaiser, *Klagelieder*.

43. By far the most ambitious attempt to see an overall structure in the book is that of Renkema *(Lamentations)*. While some of the patterns Renkema finds in Lamentations are striking and compelling and do indicate genuine structural clues, it seems to me that at many points he is trying to force the text to fit his structure. One often finds that Renkema's proposed structures for poems cut across what appear to be the obvious surface structures simply to make them fit his overall scheme.

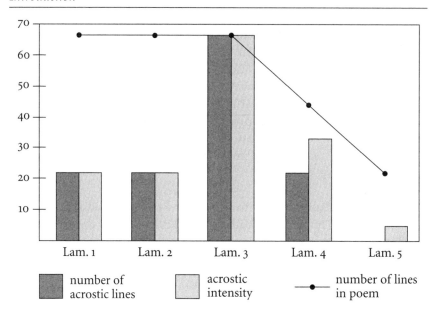

how chs. 1 and 2 progress towards 3 and how 4 and 5 follow on from it. What is the effect of the lack of an acrostic in ch. 5? Does it suggest the abandonment of the attempt to discern order in chaos and the surrender to despair? I will argue that the content of ch. 5 does not support such an interpretation. Alternatively, perhaps the promise of salvation at the end of ch. 4 brings the overt acrostic to an end with the appropriate word "completed." Perhaps in ch. 5 there is a growing confidence such that the pattern and order is still there, but it does not need to be so *conspicuously* asserted? This might fit with the dropping of the lamenting *qinah* meter and the change in poetic style in ch. 5. Whether the content of ch. 5 can be read so positively is a moot point to be considered in the commentary. Alternatively, is dropping the acrostic simply a way to mark off ch. 5 as a climax of some sort?

William Shea suggested that the book as a whole reflects the *qinah* meter of many of the individual verses. Like a 3 + 2 stress pattern in a verse, the book as a whole is 3 + 2 chapters (and chs. 1–3 have a 2 + 1 pattern).[44] This enables the overall pattern of the book to imply lament. I find this idea suggestive and may cast the whole book as a cohesive lament.

There may also be a pattern in the temporal focus of the chapters. Chapters 1 and 5 focus on the current situation in Judah, while chs. 2 and 4 look back to the past calamity — the siege of the city (ch. 4) and its destruc-

44. Shea, "The *qinah* Structure."

tion (ch. 2). This also has the effect of drawing attention to ch. 3, which holds together past, present, and future.

> Chapter 1: *present* situation
>> Chapter 2: *past* devastation
>>> Chapter 3
>> Chapter 4: *past* devastation
> Chapter 5: *present* situation

For my reading of the text the following features are important:

1. *The unity of chs. 1–2.* Chapters 1 and 2 clearly belong together in that they follow the same poetic pattern and contain the same two voices (narrator and Lady Zion) addressing different aspects of the same basic situation in its present and past dimensions.
2. *Intertextual links between chapters.* There are numerous key words, phrases, themes, and images that recur throughout the book which serve to weave it together. These shall be noted in the main commentary. One key result of these links is that the suffering of the man in ch. 3 is linked intertextually to the suffering of Zion and her people in chs. 1–2.
3. *The centrality of ch. 3.* As already argued, ch. 3 seems to be marked out in several respects. It will be argued in the commentary that the man in ch. 3 embodies the suffering of the people as a whole and that he has already *begun* to experience YHWH's deliverance. His experience becomes a source of hope for the people as a whole, even though he also awaits full salvation.
4. *The place of 4:21-22.* Chapters 1, 3, and 4 all end on the note of retributive punishment on the oppressors. In 1:21c-22 Lady Zion asks YHWH to punish her enemies and deliver her. In ch. 4 a voice promises that YHWH will punish Zion's enemies and end her exile (answering Zion's prayer). The end of ch. 4 marks a clear advance in the book and counts against those who see a sinking into despair after ch. 3.
5. *The climactic nature of ch. 5.* Chapter 5 is marked out in several ways. First, the acrostic pattern is dropped. Second, the use of parallelism increases significantly and enjambment virtually disappears.[45] Third, it is much shorter than all the other poems. Fourth, it is the only poem in a single voice. Fifth, it is the only proper communal lament in the book.

---

45. In chs. 1–4 only 59 percent of the lines contain parallelism, while in ch. 5 86 percent do; Hillers, *Lamentations,* 19-20.

Sixth, uniquely in Lamentations, the whole poem is a prayer. In context, the poem can arguably be understood as the natural climax of the book and a tentative response to the words of hope at the end of ch. 4.

6. *The suffering recounted and the fact that salvation has not arrived, nor has YHWH spoken, by the end of the book.*

The majority of modern scholars wish to strongly resist any suggestion that there is a movement towards hope in chs. 1–5. The trend is to see a constant fluctuation between hope and despair (with the latter dominant). While there is some measure of a fluctuating back and forth between hope and grief, I will argue that there is a general, albeit cautious, movement in the direction of hope. I propose that chs. 4 and 5 do not unweave the hope of ch. 3. This is *not* to suggest that Lamentations brings closure — by the end of the book YHWH has neither spoken to nor redeemed his suffering people, and even the prayerful response in the fifth poem is very tentative and still full of lament. While there may not be a move from lament to praise as there is so often in Psalms of Lament, I propose that there is a trajectory from "death" towards hoped-for "resurrection" — a hope grounded in the character of God revealed in ch. 3.

The Canonical Locations of Lamentations

The placing of Lamentations within the biblical canon was not unreflective and was intended to guide Jewish readers in their interpretation of the text. However, Lamentations has occupied various places within the Jewish Bible. The Septuagint places it after the book of Jeremiah. This is clearly because the editors thought that Lamentations was written by Jeremiah, and historically most Jews and Christians read it that way. The Christian Bible has always followed the LXX location of the book.[46]

The Hebrew canon reflected in the Masoretic Text seems to be the ordering of medieval Jewish communities and places Lamentations in a section of the Writings knows as the Megilloth (festival scrolls) right after Psalms and Proverbs. The Megilloth are found in the following order in Codex Leningradensis: Ruth, Song of Songs, Ecclesiastes, Lamentations, Esther. The order reflects the ancient beliefs about chronological order of composition.

---

46. However, certain contemporary French ecumenical translations follow the Hebrew order for the Old Testament as this resolves the question of where to locate the Deutero-canonical books. My thanks to Philip Johnston for drawing my attention to this.

In the Hebrew Bible of the Ashkenazic Jews the order is Song of Songs, Ruth, Lamentations, Ecclesiastes, and Esther. This is a liturgical placing reflecting its use in Jewish festivals: Song of Songs is recited at Passover, Ruth at the Feast of Weeks, Lamentations on the 9th of Ab, Ecclesiastes at the Feast of Tabernacles, Esther at Purim. This order served a *dual* function. On the one hand, it grouped Lamentations with the other festival scrolls. On the other, it placed Lamentations at the head of a group of texts about exile and return which close the biblical canon (Lamentations, Esther, Daniel, Ezra, Nehemiah, Chronicles). What is clear is that Lamentations was linked with the Babylonian destruction of Jerusalem in the later Hebrew canonical order as well as in the LXX, albeit in different ways.

None of these locations for our book are the "right" one, and all can be of profit for theological reappropriation. For instance, all the canonical locations of Lamentations link it with the Babylonian exile. The medieval Jewish location invites readers to take seriously the ongoing relevance of that cataclysmic event in the life of the worshipping community. The LXX can also instruct readers — some commentators now argue that Lamentations itself, while not actually written by Jeremiah, is consciously Jeremiah-like, perhaps even speaking at times in the voice of Jeremiah.[47] This would suggest that the LXX location and superscription rightly pick up on intentional textual indicators. The location alerts readers to this and asks for them to read the book as a lament for the destruction Jeremiah predicted would befall Jerusalem at the hands of Babylon.

The Theology of Lamentations in Key Modern Studies

It will be of some help in orientating readers in advance of reading the book to sketch an overview of some significant studies on the theology of Lamentations that have appeared in recent decades. I will not at this point offer an assessment of the different proposals. Readers will find my engagement with these, and other, scholars throughout the commentary.

Norman Gottwald (1954)

For Gottwald the key to the theology of Lamentations is to see the background as the Deuteronomic theology of total divine control over the world

---

47. So Lee, *The Singers of Lamentations*.

and neat retribution in history: Sinners will suffer and the righteous will be vindicated. After Josiah's great reforms, that righteous king died and the nation suffered more than it had ever done in its history. Why? Lamentations struggles with *that* question. It is "the tension between Deuteronomic faith and historical adversity."[48] The reversal motif is used time and time again to depict the shocking fall from honor into shame. Lamentations is a step towards the unweaving of a *simplistic* Deuteronomic theology, but it does *not* seek to overthrow the basic elements of that theology.

Lamentations has both a theology of doom and a theology of hope. It emphasizes the seriousness of Zion's suffering but also the equal seriousness of the sin that underlies her suffering. As such it preserves the basic approach of Judah's prophets. In Lamentations God *is* in control, he is *angered* by Israel's sin, and so he is *punishing* her. Nevertheless, God is believed to be able to redeem. That hope for salvation is not abandoned is evidenced by the prayers. Indeed, the whole book with its extended depictions of suffering is intended to draw out YHWH's compassion and aid. "In truth, the chief characteristic of the prayers in Lamentations is that they are *motives* calculated to arouse God to action."[49] The high watermark of the theology of Lamentations is the insight that God "does not afflict from the heart" (3:33). Mercy and not anger is the deeper reality about God. Here lie the foundations of hope in the book.

Lamentations is a book of honest theological and spiritual struggle. Like Christ, the people can cry, "My God, My God, why have you forsaken me?" but also, like Christ, they are led to trust in God — "Into your hands I commit my spirit." For Gottwald, while the book takes the act of questioning God and lamenting with theological seriousness, "the whole burden of his message was the indestructibility of Jahweh's purposes of love and justice and, in consequence, the seed of hope in a restored Israel."[50]

Bertil Albrektson (1963)

Albrektson engages in extensive discussion of Gottwald's book and concludes that while Gottwald is right about much, he is mistaken in thinking that the key to Lamentations' theology is the unexpected suffering of Israel after Josiah's successful reforms. Those reforms were not successful, and, in light of

---

48. Gottwald, *Studies in the Book of Lamentations*, 53.
49. Gottwald, *Studies in the Book of Lamentations*, 94.
50. Gottwald, *Studies in the Book of Lamentations*, 56.

Deuteronomy 28, the people had good reason to expect curses not blessings.[51] Alongside the strand of Deuteronomic theology Albrektson sees a critical thread of Zion theology (2:15; 4:12, 20; 5:19). In Zion theology Jerusalem was impenetrable (Psalms 46, 48, 76) — a theme alluded to several times in Lamentations. The theological key to Lamentations is "in the tension between specific religious conceptions and historical realities: between the confident belief of the Zion traditions in the inviolability of the temple and city, and the actual brutal facts."[52] He argues that the anguished questions and cries of pain throughout the book indicate that the people thought their city was inviolable. For Albrektson it is the Deuteronomic theology of covenant-sin-incurring-covenant-curse that was used in Lamentations to explain the failure of Zion theology. Lamentations thus leads Israel away from faith-in-a-place to faith-in-YHWH.

Claus Westermann (1990)

There is quite a consensus among many commentators that Lamentations seeks to explain Zion's suffering in terms of her sin and to help her posture herself rightly before YHWH so as to seek relief. Westermann detects in this majority view a failure to recognize the theological significance of lament. Looking at the book as a whole (rather than taking ch. 3 as the true heart of the book as many do), Westermann, speaking as a form critic, observes that almost all the clauses which speak of God are either accusations against God or complaints addressed to God. This is the fundamental mode of theology in Lamentations. "The 'meaning' of these laments is to be found in their very expression. Questions of a reflective sort arose out of these laments only secondarily; such questions are of subordinate importance to the phenomenon of lamentation itself."[53] The widespread devaluation of lament among Christian commentators is rooted in the suspicion that lament is not a pious response to God. But this animosity to lament says more about the impoverished prayer traditions in the churches than in Lamentations. For Westermann lament has intrinsic value as a mode of relating to the God of

---

51. The chief problem with Gottwald's seeing a simple *tension* between Deuteronomic faith and historical experience in Lamentations was highlighted well by Albrektson, who pointed out that Lamentations describes the affliction as *punishment for sin*. So rather than a contradiction to Deuteronomic theology, "the historic outcome becomes a seal on the truth of the Deuteronomic faith"; Albrektson, *Studies in the Text,* 219.

52. Albrektson, *Studies in the Text,* 230.

53. Westermann, *Lamentations,* 81.

the Bible and it is the primary theological contribution of Lamentations. The biblical God allows sufferers to voice their pain to him with brutal honesty. Such prayer takes place *within* the covenant relationship of God and Israel.

F. W. Dobbs-Allsopp (1997)

Dobbs-Alsopp argues first that the theology of Lamentations is tragic.[54] Identifying the genre as that of a city lament, he observes that unlike the other ancient Near Eastern city laments Lamentations does not have a happy ending. Given the expectations that the genre would raise for a return of the deity, the absence of such a resolution grates against readers. Also, while Lamentations genuinely acknowledges the sin of Israel, its complaint is that her punishment *far exceeds* her crimes (contra Gottwald). This is brought out by the much greater emphasis on the suffering of Judah than on her sins, the lack of specificity of her sins, and the way in which even some of the confessions of sin are undermined contextually (e.g., 1:18; 3:42-43). Ultimately Lamentations calls God to account for the extremity of his abusive punishments.

Lamentations subtly undermines the ethical visions of the Deuteronomic, prophetic, Wisdom, and Zion traditions. It does this by presenting aspects of those ethical visions and suffusing them "with arresting and manifold images of human suffering to make the inability of the ethical vision to contain such suffering strikingly obvious . . . the events of 587/86 explode and finally ironize the ethical vision."[55] For instance, in Dobbs-Allsopp's view, the positive theology in 3:19-39 is undercut by the material that follows it. So rather than it being the theological center of the book it is actually a traditional theology being exposed as unable to handle the reality of the crisis.

The theological value of Lamentations lies in giving "space for the individual's or community's anger to be *faithfully* expressed before Yahweh."[56] It eschews theodicy in favor of affirming the integrity and value of human sufferers. It refuses to accept evil passively but resists it rhetorically. It solicits compassion in response to suffering, and it brings healing through language by giving voice to the suffering.

---

54. He maintains that it shares historical context, trajectory of organizing pattern, setting, treatment of the problem of evil, and the centrality of the tragic hero, with other tragedies.

55. Dobbs-Allsopp, "Tragedy, Tradition, and Theology," 47.

56. Dobbs-Allsopp, "Tragedy, Tradition, and Theology," 53.

Tod Linafelt (2000)

Linafelt focuses on the figure of Lady Zion in chs. 1–2 to shift attention away from an often obsessive focus by commentators on the man in ch. 3. Linafelt suggests that Zion offers an alternative, and more helpful, role model than the "patient sufferer" in ch. 3. He joins Westermann in protesting against the common dismissal of lament spirituality. However, Linafelt criticizes Westermann for failing to recognize the degree of protest against God in chs. 1–2 and falling back on traditional, God-defending interpretations. While Lamentations does offer some *interpretation* of pain, its focus is on the *presentation* of pain. Lamentations is not about God's righteous judgment, sin and guilt, or hope — it is more about the *expression* of suffering than its *meaning*, and it has some *very harsh* criticism to make of God. Even the prayers to God for deliverance do not paint him in a good light: "The notion of an abused and violated woman turning for help to her abuser, and the one who abused her children, should inspire in the modern reader something less than the notion of gracious intervention."[57] Biblical scholars tend to be too eager to focus on the reasons for pain (pain is due to sin, so repentance is called for), but the eye of Lamentations is elsewhere. It aims to solicit horror and compassion from its readers rather than to lead them to repent. It is about survival in the face of unbearable horror. The absence of God throughout the book leaves an open wound for later readers to deal with. Lamentations does not contain the cure to its own wounds — that must come from readers. The bulk of Linafelt's book is a study of how Jewish readers in different periods have sought to survive their assault by Lamentations through seeking such a cure outside of its borders.

Kathleen O'Connor (2003)

The key value of Lamentations, for O'Connor, is the "reverence the book accords to the voices of the afflicted."[58] These voices are multiple and do not reflect a single understanding of the tragedy. Rather, "their testimonies nudge up against each other in disquieting tension and conflict." There is no "right" response, and no voice is allowed to absorb the others and dominate the discussion. The missing voice is the one that the book most longs for — the voice of God. But this literary silence of God is "a calculated choice, a con-

---

57. Linafelt, *Surviving Lamentations*, 55.
58. O'Connor, *Lamentations and the Tears of the World*, 83.

scious theological decision. . . . Any words from God would endanger human voices. They would undercut anger and despair, foreshorten protest, and give the audience only a passing glimpse of the real terror of their condition."[59] By omitting the voice that would trump the other voices, Lamentations "honors truth-telling and denies 'denial.' . . . In this way Lamentations can shelter the tears of the world."[60]

Lamentations also contains the rudiments of a theology of witness. Zion longs for a comforter, someone to stand with her in her desolation as a faithful and empathetic witness to her pain. The narrator comes to fulfill this role of comforter to Zion and, in the process, is himself transformed. He comes to see the plight from her perspective and to feel her pain. "The witness sees suffering for what it is, without denying it, twisting it into a story of endurance, or giving it a happy ending. The witness has a profound and rare human capacity to give reverent attention to sufferers and reflect their truth back to them. And in the encounter with those who suffer, the witness undergoes conversion from numbed or removed observer to passionate advocate."[61] In so doing the witness restores the human dignity of the sufferer. What the narrator is to Zion, the book of Lamentations was to its ancient readers — a witness to their pain: poetry *as* salvation. The book also calls its readers to witness to suffering.

When it comes to God himself, theology proper, while the book moves between justifying God's actions and criticizing him, the dominant image is of a violently abusive God whose punishment far exceeds any crime. We cannot ignore God's violence in Lamentations, and to justify it is immoral. O'Connor suggests that the biblical text, as a human text, participates in both the insights and blindness of the community that produced it. Suffering was explained in terms of divine causality, and the honor-shame culture of ancient Israel created an image of God as punishing and violent. Human suffering was wrongly explained in terms of God's retribution. We can now see natural explanations for what Lamentations saw in terms of divine action. So "we need Lamentations' bracing speech about God for its raw honesty and its iconoclastic power . . . [but its] insistence on God's punishing violence must be critiqued for our time. It is wrong."[62] O'Connor "finds" the slenderest thread of an acceptable vision of God in 3:33, which she sees as hinting at God's powerlessness — a God *unable* to prevent evil.[63]

59. O'Connor, *Lamentations and the Tears of the World*, 85.

60. O'Connor, *Lamentations and the Tears of the World*, 86, 95.

61. O'Connor, *Lamentations and the Tears of the World*, 100.

62. O'Connor, *Lamentations and the Tears of the World*, 120.

63. O'Connor, *Lamentations and the Tears of the World*, 122.

Lamentations is first and foremost an act of worship, and it can teach us how to pray with honesty as we face horror full in the face — how to pray when God is silent and prayer seems one-sided. Prayer must be truth-telling if it is to be faithful. And the fact that they persist in prayer in the face of unrelenting suffering and ongoing divine absence makes the prayer a life-affirming act of hope. The refusal to accept the current situation embodied in lament also makes the book a call for justice — for a new reality. "Without the practice of public lament, collective work for justice is blocked, unable to begin."[64] The powerful gift of tears can serve as a revelation of injury and thus as an act of political resistance. Lamentations validates tears and serves as "a 'sacred bottle' for the tears of the world."[65]

Paul House (2004)

A very different interpretation of the book's theology from that found in Westermann, Linafelt, Dobbs-Allsopp, and O'Connor can be seen in House's commentary. House thinks that other commentators greatly exaggerate the extent to which Lamentations is a protest against God's injustice. On the contrary, the book accepts the guilt of the people and the need for confession. The people have broken the covenant and incurred the just punishment for so doing. The cries of pain and the plea for salvation are not protests against injustice but demonstrate "that those who suffer because of their own sins may cry out to God as readily as innocent sufferers do."[66] Lamentations also offers a theology of hope grounded in the character of God and his covenant relationship with Israel, although exactly how and when God will act to redeem his people is not yet clear.

House summarizes the theology of the book under four centering themes:

1. *God, the people of God, and their suffering:* The Lord is a harsh judge of his perpetually sinful people (and his judgment followed many warnings). This punishing God is also the one to whom Israel must call for salvation.
2. *God and Jerusalem/Zion:* As the capital city, the loss of Jerusalem symbolizes the fall of the whole nation. As the city chosen by God to "in-

---

64. O'Connor, *Lamentations and the Tears of the World*, 128.
65. O'Connor, *Lamentations and the Tears of the World*, 130.
66. House, *Lamentations*, 320.

habit," its loss represents God's departure and a catastrophic fracture in Israel's relationship with him. Jerusalem is significant but not inviolable.

3. *God and the nations:* God is sovereign over the nations and uses them to punish Israel. However, he applies the same standards of justice and punishment to the nations as to Israel. There is no favoritism. To the extent that the book holds out hope for Israel, it also *implies* hope for the nations.

4. *God and Prayer:* There is one God who rules over history and to whom prayer can be made. The prayers are honest, stark, and extreme because the situation is extreme, but "there seems to be no question in the worshippers' minds that God hears and answers prayers, even prayers of lament."[67]

In Lamentations

> the Lord is righteous, just, powerful, kind, severe, compassionate, faithful, and willing to hear and answer prayer. There is no question that the Lord is a thorough, severe, and unstinting judge of thorough, ingrained, consistent sin. At the same time, it is plain that these characteristics are not the primary facets of God's nature. For these are not constant actions derived from that character. God's lovingkindness, faithfulness, and ruling power are the Lord's ongoing traits, so the covenant people have hope for the future.[68]

In a subsequent essay House develops the idea that Lamentations does *not* present the affliction of Jerusalem as the unjust suffering of innocents, but as the just punishment of the guilty. This makes him very cautious about reapplying the text to contemporary situations which may not be analogous. The book of Lamentations, he believes, teaches us that God shows outrageous grace to those who do not deserve it.[69]

Elizabeth Boase (2006)

Boase sets out to analyze how Lamentations picks up motifs from the prophetic traditions (the personification of Jerusalem as female, the Day of YHWH, and the relationship between sin and judgment) and transforms

---

67. House, *Lamentations*, 328.
68. House, *Lamentations*, 329.
69. House, "Outrageous Demonstrations of Grace."

them.[70] She resists the tendency to try to reduce the theology of Lamentations to monologic theological statements. Instead, she maintains that Lamentations contains different perspectives on the destruction of Jerusalem and that, while the prophetic perspective is one of them, it is *only* one of them. This polyphonic expression of unmerged viewpoints is how the book functions theologically. So, for instance, we see in the references to the destruction as Yahweh's punishment for Judah's sin a clear adoption of the prophetic viewpoint, but it is set alongside texts which subvert the prophetic perspective by presenting Jerusalem in a sympathetic and pitiable position and seeking to solicit sympathy for her. The *focus* is very much on her pain and not on her (unspecified) sin. So we find within the book an unresolved, tension-filled dialogue around the motif. This is the dialogic character of Lamentations in which the "viewpoint that questions Yahweh's actions stands alongside the more orthodox view of the just punishment of sin, giving voice to the inherent, unmerged tensions within Lamentations."[71] Consequently, the theology of Lamentations is not neat and reducible to simple propositions. It is in motion, open-ended and unfinished. It invites further theological reflection rather than shutting the discussion with the final word on the fall of Jerusalem.

Carleen Mandolfo (2007)

Mandolfo explores the metaphor of marriage that was used in Hosea, Jeremiah, and Deutero-Isaiah to describe the relationship between God and Israel, and to contrast their presentations with Lamentations 1–2. Mandolfo argues that the prophets describe that relationship from the perspective of the "husband," but that Lamentations 1–2 describes it from the perspective of the "wife." The prophets have objectified the woman and have silenced her voice so she cannot reply to their portrayal of her as wanton and perverse. The prophetic silencing of the "wife" serves to justify God's violence against her.[72] But in Lamentations 1–2 Daughter Zion finds her voice and talks back to the prophets. Zion questions the legitimacy of the degree of violence that YHWH has used and shifts the focus away from her guilt to her suffering. She presents

---

70. She acknowledges the need for a similar study of Lamentations' engagement with Deuteronomic, Wisdom, Zion, and Davidic traditions.

71. Boase, *The Fulfillment of Doom?*, 242.

72. Mandolfo, *Daughter Zion Talks Back to the Prophets*, chs. 2, 5. For an excellent general introduction to feminist interpretations of Lamentations which discusses, among others, both O'Connor and Mandolfo, see Thomas, "Feminist Interpretation(s) and Lamentations."

herself first and foremost as a mother who has lost her children, rather than as a wife.[73] Zion's voice thus serves to disturb the discursive hegemony of the prophetic/divine voice.

Mandolfo aims to highlight the polyvalent nature of the Hebrew Bible and to dethrone notions of biblical authority that see the Bible as speaking with a single voice. The Hebrew Bible allows space, albeit minimal space, for the presentation of subversive countervoices that challenge the dominant speakers. Mandolfo's dialogic, feminist, postcolonial hermeneutical strategy is to bring those sidelined speakers to the front.

Clearly there is much disagreement on how to assess the theology of this book. It will be helpful at this point to sketch out how I see the theology of Lamentations.

Sin and Punishment in Covenant Context

Covenant is the context within which the theology of sin and punishment in Lamentations must be understood. The book presupposes the story of God's covenant relationship with Israel. That the word "covenant" does not appear in the book is beside the point — the *concept* clearly underlies the poems. From all the people of the world God has chosen *this* people as his treasured possession. He had chosen them to walk in his ways in the sight of the nations. He had brought them into the promised land, he had chosen Jerusalem as the city where the ark of the covenant should rest and his temple should be built.

This covenant with Israel was initiated by God, not Israel, and was a covenant of grace. Israel's election was not earned but originated in divine love. It cannot be emphasized too much that the Law was given to Israel *after* God had redeemed them from Egypt, so the question of earning salvation did not arise: "God gives the law to redeemed people not to redeem the people."[74] However, within the context of this relationship there can be no question that obedience and loyalty to YHWH were expected and required. The encounter between God and Israel at Sinai, mediated by Moses, placed a great emphasis on making clear to Israel what her obligations to YHWH were. There can also be no doubt that disobedience to the covenant was liable to divine punishment. This is perhaps clearest in the covenant curses detailed in Lev 26:14-46 and Deut 28:15-68. Lamentations seems to allude to these covenant curses

---

73. Mandolfo, *Daughter Zion Talks Back to the Prophets*, ch. 4.
74. Bird, *The Saving Righteousness of God*, 91.

when describing the plight of the people (e.g., 1:3, 5), thus indicating the covenant context of their sufferings. This covenant framework explains why it is not the Babylonians but God who is seen as the primary assailant. Israel had violated her covenant with YHWH, not her covenant with Babylon, so it is *YHWH* who punishes her.

Lamentations never asks, "*Why* has this happened to us?" This is because the "why" is already known — Israel has broken the covenant law. Rather, the anguished questions behind Lamentations are, "Why punish *so severely?*" and "*How long* until you save?" The book at no point seeks to protest the innocence of the people, and the admission of sin is found on the lips of every speaker: the narrator (1:5, 8-9; 4:13), Zion (1:14, 18, 22), the valiant man (3:39), the speaker of the salvation oracle (4:22), and the community (3:42; 5:7, 16). The sin is not explained in any detail, but it is certainly not underestimated. The narrator says that "Jerusalem sinned *grievously,* therefore she became filthy" (1:8) and speaks of "the *multitude* of her transgressions" (1:5). Zion speaks of her "transgressions" (1:14, 22) and confesses that she "rebelled" against the word of YHWH (1:18). The community admits, "We have transgressed and rebelled" (3:42), and cries, "Woe to us for we have sinned" (5:16). Clearly the community as a whole has violated the covenant, but special focus is placed upon the leadership. In particular the prophets, whose commission involved calling the people back to the covenant when they went astray, are accused of having seen false visions and not exposing the iniquity of the people so their fortunes could be restored (2:14). The fall of the city is attributed, in part, to the sins of the prophets and priests who shed the blood of the righteous (4:13). How literally this blood-shedding is to be taken is unclear, but what is clear is that those who had been appointed by YHWH to guide his people in righteousness are accused of betraying their vocations and "polluting" the city. Instead of leading the people in God's ways, they let them wander from them and they themselves wandered. And the entire book is predicated on the belief that the exilic afflictions of Jerusalem are the direct consequence of this covenant violation (cf. Ezra 9:15; Neh 9:33).

However, having said all that, it is clear that the focus of Lamentations is *not* on the sin of the people but on their terrible suffering. This is clear on two counts. First, consider how much space devoted to the sin of the people and how much to their torment. Even a moment's reflection will make crystal clear that the book is far more concerned with giving expression to their pain than with exploring the depths of their depravity. Second, even on the occasions on which the sin is admitted, it is always in contexts which focus on the suffering. The book aims to solicit sympathy for afflicted Zion *in spite of* her sin. Thus while the sin is manifest, it is not explored at any length. Lamentations seeks out a delicate balance between emphasizing her transgression (which would undermine the audience's sympathy for her) and ignoring it (which would falsify her plight). It does this by forcing the audience to dwell at length on heart-rending descriptions of her decimation but including regular, passing reminders of her iniquity. We will return to this theme later.

Presupposed by the theology of sin and punishment is the righteousness of YHWH. As Zion says, "YHWH is indeed righteous, for against his mouth I have rebelled" (1:18). The book does raise some painful and piercing questions about this righteousness because the severity and duration of the punishment appear to exceed the bounds of what is justified. However, such questions only make sense against a background theology which affirms the justice and righteousness of the Lord. The book is not saying that God is not really righteous because he has done what he has done. Rather, it is seeking to make God feel uncomfortable with what is happening and act to change the situation *precisely because* he is righteous. "Act in accord with the covenant and save us!" is what the people are saying when they draw God's attention to their living hell.

Also presupposed by the theology of sin and punishment is the belief that YHWH is the sovereign Lord who rules not only over Israel but also over all the nations. YHWH is no mere localized deity but the one creator-God who has all power. The disaster has not come about because of God's weakness and inability to defend his people. There is no question that he could have averted the destruction had he chosen to. Rather, the fall of the city was something God himself planned and foretold (1:21; 2:17). While the Babylonians were the immediate cause of the affliction, Lamentations is brutally unflinching in its assertions that God was the ultimate cause. If there is someone to be angry at, it is God. The buck stops with him.

Some scholars seek to maintain a weaker view of God's oversight than that above. They argue that while God commissioned the enemies to attack Jerusalem, those enemies went "beyond the mandate they received from YHWH."[75] As a result they are held accountable and are subject to divine judgment. This view is, I maintain, mistaken on two counts. First, it suggests that God did not intend for the destruction to go as far as it did. Nothing in Lamentations supports this claim. God is held to be responsible for every last part of it. If the punishment went too far, it is *YHWH* as much as the enemy that receives the criticism. Second, it suggests that the enemies are culpable only for the slaughter that went *beyond* the divine commission, while the violence that fell within the limits of their mandate is not liable to punishment.

---

75. Renkema, *Lamentations*, 465.

This, I suggest, is quite wrong. *All* the violence of the Babylonians, Edomites, and others against Zion is culpable and liable to punishment. While God used the evil actions of humans to bring about his righteous judgment, this does not make those human actions righteous. The enemies were not seeking to bring about YHWH's righteous judgment on Zion. Their goal was quite different, and their actions were sinful. No attempt is made in Lamentations to explain how human freedom and responsibility are compatible with God's sovereign rule over human actions. Both genuine freedom and strong sovereignty are affirmed, and it is left to later theologians and philosophers to try to make sense of the resulting tension.

Finally, this strong theology of divine sovereignty over history also underlies the book's affirmative action aimed at securing future hope. There is no one else to turn to for salvation apart from the one who had brought about their damnation — YHWH. No one can deliver from his hand. The *only* hope for the future lies with the very one who has slaughtered them. So it is that throughout the book the voices turn to prayer. We might not like this theology, but if we seek to hear Lamentations on its own terms, then, I suggest, this is how things look.

Hope in Covenant Context

Covenant is also the context within which the glimmers of hope in Lamentations must be situated. God's election of Israel was an election of grace based on God's unwavering commitment to them, and that commitment stood firm despite the ongoing infidelity of the people. Crucial to understanding the hope implicit in Lamentations is the appreciation that *the fire of divine punishment falls within a covenant relationship and does not mean the end of that relationship.*

> Destruction, according to the covenant, is a sign neither of God's abandonment of Israel and his cancellation of His obligations to the people, nor of God's eclipse by competing powers in the cosmos. The Destruction is to be taken, rather, as a deserved and necessary punishment for sin. . . . As a chastisement, the Destruction becomes an expression of God's continuing concern for Israel, since the suffering of the Destruction expiates the sin that provoked it and allows a penitent remnant to survive in a rehabilitated and restored relationship with God.[76]

76. Mintz, Ḥurban, 3; quoted in Berlin, *Lamentations,* 18.

Commentators often miss the fact that the anguished question in 5:20 — "Why do you forget us forever? Why do you forsake us for so many days?" — presupposes God's *ongoing* commitment to Israel. It presupposes that divine abandonment is not supposed to last forever and that, because God is still committed to Israel, he should have brought their sorrow to an end by now. If the speaker thought that God had ended his relationship with Abraham's family, then the question would make no sense. Indeed, all the prayers for divine help throughout the book (1:9, 11, 20-21; 2:19) presuppose that *if* God would take note he would be moved by compassion to redeem his people.

So the hope in Lamentations is grounded in the covenant — or rather, in the *God* who covenants. God is absent in Lamentations, but it is clear throughout the book that this absence is *not* the way things are supposed to be. Lamentations does not presuppose the concept of a distant deity who is ever remote from human lives and sufferings. Quite the contrary, God is *supposed* to be near to his people, to dwell in their midst, and to bless them. Lamentations is describing the very antithesis of God's "normal" mode of engagement with Israel. Scholars often focus on the way God is presented in the book (angry and punishing) but fail to emphasize that this very presentation is so shocking to the speaker and implied audience *precisely because* it is not the way God normally engages with Israel. Thus no appreciation of the view of God in Lamentations would be complete if it did not make clear the assumed nature of God's normal relationship to his people.

God's heart was to bless Judah, and, when she walked according to the covenant, she was blessed. She was majestic (1:6), great among the nations, a princess among the provinces (1:1) at rest in her promised land (1:3; 5:2). She was the head, and her enemies were the tail (1:5; cf. Deut 28:13) because God fought for her and against her enemies. Zion was the perfection of beauty, the joy of all the earth (2:15). Indeed, YHWH protected Zion — it had never fallen to the enemy before, and some believed it impregnable (4:12). At the heart of the holy city stood the temple where YHWH dwelt. There the people celebrated joyfully their covenant relationship with God (1:4; 2:6; 5:15). The temple stood at the heart of the relationship — it was YHWH's footstool, the place where heaven and earth touched (1:10; 2:1, 6-7). There the sacrifices that enabled sin to be dealt with and the relationship to be maintained were made on the altar (2:7). God provided the nation with a king under whose shadow they would be blessed in the midst of the nations (2:6, 9; 4:20). He gave them priests to teach them the holy Law (2:6, 9; 4:13), prophets to speak his word and guide them (2:9, 14; 4:13). God placed a crown upon the head of the nation (5:16), and he held them as his special people (5:21).

The vision of YHWH that the valiant man calls to mind in 3:21-24 is, I believe, grounded in the divine self-revelation to Moses (Exod 34:6-7) and the story of God's relationship with the nation of Israel.

> This I remind my heart,
>   therefore I wait hopefully:
> The loving kindnesses of YHWH are surely not ended,
>   surely his tender mercies are not finished.
> New [signs of favor] every morning!
>   great is your faithfulness!
> "My inheritance is YHWH," says my soul,
>   "therefore I will wait hopefully for him."

The "loving kindnesses" to which the man refers are his acts of covenant fidelity to his people. Though they are not evident in the present crisis, the man reasons that God's relationship with his people (and hence with him) is surely not terminated. This God has shown himself to be full of loving kindness and tender mercy. He is good and faithful. Hence patience is called for.

> For he will not reject forever,
>   the Lord,
> for if he afflicts then he will have mercy,
>   according to the abundance of his loving kindness.
> For he does not afflict from his heart,
>   or bring grief to the sons of man. (3:31-33)

Here is a central theological insight of the book. The man situates the terrible rejection he has suffered within the context of the being of God. Yes, God does reject but he does not do so *forever*. Rejection will be followed by overflowing mercy according to his vast loving kindness. Yes, God does afflict, but it is not something that flows from his heart. There is an asymmetry between wrath and loving kindness. Loving kindness emerges from the very heart of God, but wrath does not. Love is a permanent disposition of YHWH, but anger is a temporary reaction to sin. In the end mercy will always triumph over judgment because of the nature of the God revealed in Israel's story. This vision of God underlies Lamentations.

None of the comments above must allow us to downplay the vivid and disturbing portrayal of God's fierce anger in the book, but it is precisely against this background that the portrayal of God's violence has its full impact.

Presenting Suffering

"The book is not an explanation of suffering but a re-creation of it and a commemoration of it."[77] While it will become clear that I part company with Linafelt on many points, he is surely right to maintain that the book is not primarily about explaining and justifying Jerusalem's suffering (although I do think it has *something* to say about that) but about *presenting* the pain. It is here that the insights of many modern readers like O'Connor (see above) are so helpful. This will be of considerable significance in my later theological reflections.

77. Berlin, *Lamentations*, 18.

Commentary

LAMENTATIONS 1: NO COMFORT

v. 1 א/'ālep

> Alas! She sits alone —
>> the city [once] full of people;
> She has become like a widow,
>> [she who was] great among the nations.
> Princess among the provinces,
>> she has become a forced laborer.

v. 2 ב/bêt

> Bitterly she weeps in the night,
>> and her tears are upon her cheeks.
> [For] her there is no comforter,
>> from among all those who love her.
> All her companions have betrayed her,
>> they have become to her as enemies.

v. 3 ג/gîmel

> Judah has gone into exile after[1] affliction,
>> and after an abundance of servitude.

---

1. There is some debate as to how the prefixed מן/*min* ("from") in 1:3a-b should be translated (on מן/*min*, see Waltke and O'Connor, *Biblical Hebrew Syntax*, 212-14). Some argue that it means that Judah was exiled *because of* (מן/*min*) affliction and servitude. But this makes little sense. The most plausible option here is to suggest that she chose to go into exile *to escape from* harsh conditions at home (so Salters, "Lamentations 1:3"), but this is unlikely, as living in Babylon was just as traumatic as living in Judah and the root גלה/*glh* is never used for voluntary ex-

She sits among the nations,
   she has not found a resting place.
All her pursuers have caught up with her,
   in narrow straits.

v. 4 ד/*dālet*
   The roads of Zion are in mourning,
      from the lack of those coming to the Assembly.
   All her gates are desolate.
   Her priests are groaning,
      her maidens are grieving,
      and, as for her, it is bitter.

v. 5 ה/*hê*
   Her adversaries have become [the] head,
      Her enemies prosper.
   For YHWH brought affliction
      on account of her many transgressions.
   Her children went as captives
      before the adversary.

v. 6 ו/*wāw*
   And so gone from Daughter Zion
      is all her glory.
   Her leaders have become like stags,
      [that] did not find pasture,
   but they went on exhausted,
      before a pursuer.

v. 7 ז/*zayin*
   Jerusalem remembered,
      [in] the days of her affliction and her wanderings,[2]

---

ile. Alternatively, with the Targum, one could suggest that she went into exile because *she af-flicted others*. While possible, it does not convince. Others argue that it means that Judah was exiled *with* (מן/*min*) affliction and servitude. This would make sense, although it is not clear that מן/*min* can function in this way. Most plausibly מן/*min* in this context means "after."

2. There is debate about the word מרודיה/*měrûdêhā* ("her wanderings," derived from the root רוד/*rûd*, "to wander restlessly, to roam"). The LXX renders it as *apōsmos* ("repulsion, driving away"). This would suggest a reference to the exile. The problem is that in this poem Jerusalem is not exiled, her children are. The difficulty of מרודיה/*měrûdêhā* may be resolved in one of

all her precious things
  which were from days of old
until her people fell into the hand of an adversary
  and there was no one to help her.
Adversaries saw and mocked
  over her destruction.

v. 8 ח/*ḥêt*

Jerusalem sinned grievously,
  therefore she became unclean.
All those who honored her despise her,
  for they saw her nakedness.
Indeed, she herself groans,
  and turns away.

v. 9 ט/*ṭêt*

Her impurity was in her skirts,
  she gave no thought to her future,[3]
  and she has declined amazingly!
There is no one to comfort her.
  "See, YHWH, my affliction,
  for an enemy has magnified [himself]."

v. 10 י/*yôd*

An adversary has stretched out his hand
  over all her precious things.
Indeed, she saw nations
  enter her sanctuary
concerning whom you had commanded,
  "They shall not enter your assembly."

---

four ways: (a) by emending מרודיה/*měrûdêhā* to מרוריה/*měrôrêhā* ("her sorrows") on the grounds that a ר/*r* was mistaken for a ד/*d;* (b) by taking it as a reference to Jerusalem's homeless people (her wander*ers*) as opposed to her own wanderings (cf. Isa 58:7). On this view she recalls her own affliction and her homeless people; (c) as derived from the root רדד/*rdd* ("to beat down, subdue") rather than רוד/*rûd* ("to wander restlessly"). Thus she recalls her "oppression" (cf. Isa 45:1; Ps 144:2); (d) by tolerating tensions within the poetry.

3. Gordis translates the line as "she does not remember her children," taking אחריתה/*'aḥărîtāh* to refer to "her children" (cf. Ezek 23:25; Amos 4:2) rather than "her end part/latter part/future part"; *Lamentations*, 156. This seems not to fit the context so well, esp. in light of 1:7 and Isa 47:7 (where the identical words are used of Babylon to suggest that she did not consider the consequences of her actions).

v. 11 כ/*kāp*

    All her people are groaning,
        searching for bread.
    They have given their precious things for food
        to sustain life.
    "See, YHWH, and observe
        for I have become despised."

v. 12 ל/*lāmed*

    May it not happen to you, all you who pass by!
        Observe and see,
    whether there is sorrow like my sorrow,
        which has been severely dealt out to me;
        which YHWH has afflicted me with
        on the day of the burning of his anger.

v. 13 מ/*mêm*

    From on high he has sent fire into my bones,
        and he caused it to descend.[4]
    He spread out a net for my feet.
        He made me turn back.
    He made me desolate,
        all day long faint.

v. 14 נ/*nûn*

    He fashioned a yoke of my transgressions.
        In his hand they were entwined;
    they ascended upon my neck.
        He caused my strength to fail.

---

4. וירדנה/*wayyirdennâ* (MT) from the root רדה/*rdh* ("to rule/to trample"). Thus, "he [YHWH] ruled over it [the fire]" (technically the suffix could refer to "her" [i.e., Jerusalem] — "he/it ruled over/trampled *her*" — but as Jerusalem is speaking this is not likely). The idea would then be that God controlled the fire and he sent it into Jerusalem's bones. Many repoint the Hebrew וירדנה to read *wayyōrĕdennâ* from the root ירד/*yrd* ("to descend"). Thus, "he caused it [the fire] to come down." This makes more sense contextually. Hillers emends the Hebrew to read יורדנה/*yôrîdennâ* and translates it as "and he sank it" (i.e., "he sank the fire into my bones"); *Lamentations*, 72. A different ambiguity arises regarding the referent of the suffix. In the MT it is clearly the fire or Jerusalem ("he caused *it* to descend/ruled over *it*"), but the Syriac and Vulgate have a first person suffix making Jerusalem the referent ("he made *me* descend/ruled over *me*").

My Lord gave me into the hands of
    those I cannot withstand.

v. 15 ס/*sāmek*

He has despised all my mighty men,
    the Lord in my midst.
He called an assembly against me,
    to shatter my young men.
The Lord has trodden in a winepress
    Maiden Daughter Judah.

v. 16 ע/*'ayin*

On account of these things I am weeping.
    My eyes [. . .] are flowing [with] water!
Indeed, far removed from me is any comforter,
    one who can sustain my life.
My sons were desolate
    for an enemy prevailed.

v. 17 פ/*pê*

Zion stretches out her hands,
    there is none to comfort her.
YHWH has issued a command against Jacob
    [that] those surrounding him are his enemies.
Jerusalem became
    as one ritually unclean among them.

v. 18 צ/*ṣādê*

YHWH is indeed righteous,
    for against his mouth I have rebelled.
Listen then, all the peoples,
    and see my sorrow.
My maidens and my young men
    have gone into captivity.

v. 19 ק/*qôp*

I called to my lovers.
    Even they deceived me.
My priests and elders,
    in the city they perish

as they seek food for themselves
  to sustain their lives.

v. 20 ר/rêš

Look, YHWH, for I am in distress!
  My bowels churn.
My heart is turned over inside me,
  for I have indeed rebelled.
Outside the sword bereaved;
  Within the house it is like death.

v. 21 שׁ/šîn

They heard that *I* was groaning.
  There is no one to comfort me.
All my enemies heard of the evil that had befallen me.
  They rejoiced that *you* had done it.
You brought the day that you proclaimed;
  May they become like me.[5]

v. 22 ת/tāw

Let all their evil-doing come before you,
  and deal harshly with it,
  as you dealt harshly with me,
  on account of all my transgressions.
For many are my groans,
  and my heart is faint.

Lamentations 1 has two main speakers — the narrator and Zion — and the poem falls quite neatly into two sections. In the first the narrator speaks (though with an interruption from Zion), and in the second Zion speaks (though with an interruption from the narrator). My exegesis leads me to propose the following structure for the poem:

  I. The Narrator Speaks (1:1-11)
    1. 1:1-6 The tragic reversal of Lady Zion's fortunes
    2. 1:7-11 The sin and humiliation of Zion
      (a) 1:7 Zion looks back to her glorious past, then back to the attack
      (b) 1:8-9b Zion has sinned and so is stripped naked, humiliated, and despised

5. Or, "Bring the day that you proclaimed, and let them be like me."

(c) 1:9c *Zion interrupts:* she calls out to YHWH

(d) 1:10 The rape of Zion

(e) 1:11a-b Hunger in the city

(f) 1:11c *Zion interrupts:* she calls out to YHWH

II. Lady Zion Speaks (1:12-22)

    1. 1:12-17 Zion's first main speech: An "accusation" against YHWH

       (a) 1:12 Introduction to "the day of the burning of his anger"

       (b) 1:13-15 Description of "the day of the burning of his anger"

       (c) 1:16 Zion's pained response to "the day of the burning of his anger"

       (d) 1:17 *The narrator comments* on 1:12-16

    2. 1:18-22 Zion's second main speech: "I have rebelled" and Plea to YHWH

       (a) 1:18-19 Vindication of YHWH and summary of Zion's sorrow

       (b) 1:20-22 Plea to YHWH that he do to her enemies as he has done to her

In 1:1-6 the narrator presents a wide range of disconnected images somewhat like a photomontage, and it would be a mistake to try to find a line of logical progression linking one image to the next. What all the diverse snapshots have in common is a focus on the tragic reversal in Zion's fortunes: she has been reduced from glory to dust.

The narrator opens 1:7-11 with Zion recalling the glories of her past and then the attack which brought disaster. The focus in 1:7-8 is on her social humiliation: enemies laugh at her (1:7d), she has become an object of mockery (1:8a), stripped naked and thus despised by former allies (1:8b). This has happened because of her sin (1:8a, 9a). At this point Zion herself speaks, interrupting the narrator, and calls out to YHWH to see the self-exalting enemy (1:9c). Zion's mention of her enemy leads the narrator to reflect on how she has been raped by her adversaries (1:10) — a thought which leads him to make an implicit complaint to YHWH (1:10c). The narrator then reflects on the famine faced by her citizens (1:11a-b) before Zion interrupts again, pleading with YHWH to see how despised she has become (1:11c).

Jerusalem begins the first of two main speeches in 1:12. Her audience are the passers-by. She describes to them a catalogue of suffering inflicted on her by YHWH (1:13-15) before closing the speech in tears (1:16). The narrator responds by echoing her comments that she has no helper and that YHWH is behind her situation (1:17). Thus, as she ended his second speech, he ends her first main speech.

In 1:18 Jerusalem begins her second main speech, and her tone is quite different. In this speech YHWH is considered to have acted righteously towards Zion by punishing her. She summarizes her sorrows in 18b-19, drawing together themes from across the poem. The climax of the speech sees Zion turn from addressing the nations in 1:18-19 to addressing YHWH in 1:20-22. She pleads again for him to see her pain (1:20) before focusing in on the terrible behavior of her enemies and asking YHWH to punish them for it (1:20-22).

It is almost unanimously agreed among scholars that Lamentations 1 is a combination of different forms. Since the work of Hedwig Jahnow in 1923[6] and Hermann Gunkel in 1933[7] most commentators recognize elements from *the funeral dirge* in the poem. These include the mournful cry איכה/*'êkâ,* "Alas!" (1:1), the description of misery that follows it (2a, 4c), and the presence of the reversal motif (1:1, 6). Clearly the dirge form has been modified because certain elements, such as the announcement that someone has died, are missing while alien elements, such as the plea to YHWH and the confession of guilt, are present. Claus Westermann, on the other hand, argues that Lamentations 1, especially the second section, is primarily a *communal lament.*[8] He sees the following major elements from the communal lament in the poem: (a) the community's direct complaint (1:9c, 11c, 20a), (b) the accusation against God (1:12c-15), (c) the complaint about enemies (1:5a, 9c, 21b). He also thinks that the following minor elements are drawn from the communal lament form: (d) the acknowledgement of guilt (1:14a, 18a, 22b), (e) the plea for YHWH to take heed (1:9c, 11c, 20a), (f) the plea for reprisal on the enemies (1:21-22), and (g) the motif of God's justification (1:18) set over against the accusation against God (1:12c-15). However, there are also elements from the communal lament form, such as the expression of trust, that are missing in Lamentations 1. Also our poem does not always follow the expected order of elements in the communal lament. Westermann sees this as resulting from the pressure of the acrostic form, but even if this were the case, the form is still disrupted. Whether we see Lamentations 1 as a dirge modified by elements from the communal lament or vice versa, we must concede that it is not a pure form. This poem includes some, but not all, elements from both forms and blends them in a unique way. We need to adequately respect the *uniqueness* of the poem as well as what it shares with other poems.[9] Tod

---

6. Jahnow, *Das hebräische Leichenlied.*

7. Gunkel, *Einleitung in die Psalmen.*

8. Westermann, *Lamentations,* 114-19. Eissfeldt, while seeing a dirge in 1:1-11 and 17, maintains that 9c, 11c, 12-16 are in the form of an *individual lament; The Old Testament,* 501-5. See also Re'emi, "The Theology of Hope," 79.

9. Renkema, *Lamentations,* 91-93.

Linafelt proposes that it is not a coincidence that the elements of the dirge form cluster in the narrator's speech while elements of the lament cluster in Lady Zion's speech. The narrator's speech is dominated by the overtones of death even though Zion is not dead. Zion, however, is a survivor, and when she speaks it is in a lament straining towards life, and not a dirge looking back to death, that she employs. Thus the very form of her speech indicates a resistance to her fate not found in the narrator's speech, the form of which suggests a mournful resignation.[10]

The Narrator Speaks (1:1-11)

v. 1 א/*'ālep* Lamentations opens with a cry of exclamation, "Alas!" (איכה/ *'êkâ*). It is a cry of despair, of horror, and of lament often associated with announcements of striking changes from better to worse, especially laments and funeral dirges (Isa 1:21; Jer 48:17; Ezek 26:17). The cry sets the tone for all that follows.

The narrator paints a pitiful picture of a once-great city reduced to nothing. The city is not named, although the book's audience would know that it is Jerusalem. Beginning in v. 1 Jerusalem is personified as a desolate woman.[11] She was once a successful mother: full of people. She was once internationally admired: great among the nations, a princess among the provinces. Now she sits alone. Now she is like a widow without a husband to protect and look after her.[12] Now she is reduced to the status of a slave — forced labor for a conquering enemy. Alas!

The contrast between sitting alone and once being full of people suggests that "alone" here means that her many children (her citizens) are gone. She is childless! The fleeting image of the widow is not pressed, but it could possibly indicate the idea that her husband, YHWH, having abandoned her is *like* a dead husband. She is now in a very vulnerable position as she has no one who can act as her legal protector. The narrator is seeking to elicit the pity of the audience right from the start.

The poetry works to accentuate the contrast between her former glory

10. Linafelt, *Surviving Lamentations*, 35-43.

11. On the personification of Zion, see Heim, "The Personification of Jerusalem."

12. On the precarious position of widows in Ancient Israelite society, see Hiebert, "Whence Shall Help Come to Me?"; Deut 10:18; 16:11; Isa 1:23; Jer 7:6-7; Ps 94:6; Lam 5:3. Cohen, "The Widowed City," argues that the image of a widowed city can be used to describe cities reduced to vassal status. This could suggest a second layer of meaning behind the widow image (so Berlin, *Lamentations*, 49).

and her present lowly status. There are three pairs of contrasting lines, the first two of which consider her current, broken condition and then look back to her previous honored status, and the last of which reverses the order, allowing the audience to end where they began — with her plight. She is alone *though once* was full of people (1:1a-b); she has become a widow *though once* was great among the nations (1:1c-d); she was a princess among the provinces[13] *but now* has been reduced to a prisoner of war forced to work for the enemy (1:1e-f).[14] The poet also links c-d with e-f by means of a chiasm.

> c She has become (היתה/*hāyĕtâ*) like a widow,
> d great (רבתי/*rabbātî*) among the nations,
> e princess (שרתי/*śārātî*) among the provinces;
> f she has become (היתה/*hāyĕtâ*) a slave.

1d and e both describe the past glory in parallel expressions (note also the rhyme in the first Hebrew word in each line). Lines c and f surround this image of the past with the present reality both beginning with the word היתה/*hāyĕtâ*, "she has become."

While the first chapter is not a dirge proper (Lady Jerusalem has not died), the reversal of fortunes theme, the use of the *qinah* meter, and the opening cry, "Alas!" would probably remind the audience of a funeral song and cast the shadow of death over the city. This implicit context invites us to see the image of the woman sitting alone in 1:1a as that of a mourner who sits or lies in the dust.

> The image . . . is that of the persona of the city sitting alone at the site of ruined Jerusalem — an image comparable to that of the city goddess in the Mesopotamian laments sitting and lamenting at the site of her ruined city. Thus, the personified figure of Jerusalem comes to life in the words and phrases which constitute the poetry itself, as if the stone and mudbrick of the destroyed city suddenly by poetic magic metamorphose into the flesh and bones of a woman with blood coursing through her veins.[15]

v. 2 ב/*bêt* The narrator now draws the audience a little closer to the woman. They see her crying out, her tears glistening on her cheeks, and the

---

13. Here we may suppose that Jerusalem did *rule over* the provinces (Renkema, *Lamentations*, 100). The contrast is that she who ruled over others is now herself ruled over.

14. למס/*lāmas* means a tribute, a levy extracted by a superior power, a vassal, or one required to do forced labor. The city is enslaved in a labor gang as part of the tribute paid to the conqueror.

15. Dobbs-Allsopp, *Lamentations*, 55.

treachery of her so-called friends is revealed. The verse is divided into three pairs of lines (strophes or cola). The first pair (1:2a-b) paints a sad image of the woman crying throughout the night. Night is the time when people sleep and one is alone in one's misery (e.g., Ps 6:7). This woman gets no sleep, for she weeps unceasingly.

The second pair (1:2c-d) introduces a tragic theme: that from all those who profess to love her, this woman can find none who will comfort her in her loss. She must weep *alone*. It was customary for friends and relatives of those in mourning or sorrow to stand in solidarity with them and offer comfort (e.g., Gen 37:35; 50:21; Ruth 2:13; 2 Sam 10:2-3; Eccl 4:1). For Jerusalem there is no one to stand with her in her pain. The expressions "those who love her" (1:2d) and "her companions" (1:2e) refer to the cities or states surrounding Judah that in the past she had been on good terms with. Now they disgracefully abandon her to her fate. As Adele Berlin points out, "A nation was obligated to mourn the loss of an ally, and to provide comfort to his survivors."[16] Jerusalem's political allies provide no such support.[17]

The third pair (1:2e-f) accentuates the wicked behavior of her "friends." It is not that they are merely indifferent to her plight (1:2c-d). Worse than that, they have acted treacherously (בגדו/*bāgĕdû*) towards her and treated her as enemies would! It may be implied by the use of בגדו/*bāgĕdu* that formal agreements between Judah and her allies have been broken — perhaps "promises of mutual assistance in the event of a Babylonian aggression."[18]

v. 3 ג/*gîmel* The focus shifts in 1:3 from the desolate city to her exiled daughter, a personification of Judah. The verse is divided into three sets of paired lines. The first focuses on the exile of Judah, the second on her state of restlessness in exile, and the third on her capture by the enemy.

After suffering a period of affliction and harsh servitude under Babylon, Judah's situation got even worse as she went from the frying pan of servitude into the fire of exile.[19] The terms עני/*ʿōnî* ("affliction") and עבדה/*ʿăbōdâ* ("work, service, labor") are used elsewhere with reference to Israel's enslave-

---

16. Berlin, *Lamentations*, 50.

17. On a first reading there is no reason for the audience to suppose that the expression "those who love her" is an implicit criticism of Lady Jerusalem (i.e., illicit lovers). This way of reading 1:2d as critical of Jerusalem has an ancient pedigree and can be found in modern commentators also. However, there is a case for saying that on a *second* reading of the poem, once the audience has read 1:19a, they would hear another level of meaning with implicit criticism of Jerusalem's infidelity.

18. Renkema, *Lamentations*, 105-6 (cf. Jer 25:1-38).

19. Rightly Westermann, *Lamentations*, 126.

ment in Egypt (Exod 1:14; 2:23; 3:7, 17; 4:31; 5:11; 6:6). The possibility of an allusion to the exodus story is strengthened by the use of the word מצרים/*mĕṣārîm* ("narrow straits") in 1:3c, which sounds and looks very similar to the word מצרים/*miṣrayim* ("Egypt"). "The vassalage of Judah to Babylonia is likened to the enslavement in Egypt in that it returned the people to their preexodus state. But unlike the Egyptian experience, the servitude to Babylonia led not to freedom but to exile."[20]

1:3c continues the story of Judah. Now, after her exile, she dwells in the midst of the nations instead of in the land that YHWH had given to her. There are two links with 1:1 in this line. First there is a link with her city-mother: Jerusalem dwells (ישבה/*yāšĕbâ*) alone (1:1) because her daughter dwells (ישבה/*yāšĕbâ*) among the nations (1:3).[21] The mother weeps for the loss of her child, and the daughter laments being snatched from her mother and her home. Second, in 1:1 Jerusalem was said to have once been greatly esteemed "among the nations" (בגוים/*baggôyîm*), but now in 1:3 her daughter lives in captivity "among the nations" (בגוים/*baggôyîm*). This is a tragic reversal as the nations who honored her now hold her dear child captive. Among these nations Judah cannot settle, for God has given her another land which is home. So she finds "no resting place." The theme of Israel's "resting" from enemies in the promised land is strong in biblical literature (e.g., Exod 33:14; Deut 3:20; 12:9; 25:19; Josh 1:13, 15; 22:4; 2 Sam 7:1, 11), and the removal of this "rest" indicates divine punishment. Indeed, there is a clear allusion here to the curse of Deut 28:64-65: "Then the Lord will scatter you among all nations, from one end of the earth to the other. . . . Among those nations you will find no repose, *no resting place for the sole of your foot.*" The readers would recognize the signs of the divine curse in Judah's homelessness.

The third pair of lines takes us back in time and focuses on the futility of Judah's flight from the pursuing enemy, probably those who attacked the nation and its capital before exile. All her pursuers caught up with her as she passed through narrow straits. The image conjured up indicates a situation in which no escape to the left and the right is possible.

v. 4 ד/*dālet* In 1:4 the narrator brings his audience back from the brief glance at the exiles in v. 3 to their lost home: Jerusalem, here identified clearly for the first time. But the focus in 1:4 is on the results of the catastrophe for the Jerusalem *cult*, so the city is called "Zion," the name that identifies it as the center of worship. The verse divides up into two sets of three lines. In the first

---

20. So Berlin, *Lamentations*, 51.
21. So Provan, *Lamentations*, 39.

set, we see the roads to Zion and the city gates (or perhaps the temple gates), which are normally crowded with pilgrims heading up for religious festivals. They are now empty of pilgrims, and no one passes through the gates into the temple. At the hands of the poet the inanimate routes to Zion come alive and lament the death of worship. The roads mourn and the gates are desolate, both in the objective sense that they are ruined or empty and, more particularly, in the subjective sense that they are in despair. This loss is so great that the *very architecture* of Zion joins in with her inhabitants to lament.

The second half of the unit takes us to the people who serve in the courts of YHWH. But the priests can no longer celebrate the great feasts or make the sacrifices — their very reason for being is gone! Instead, joined by young maidens, they add their own lamentations with the roads and gates. The women were public singers who had a part in festal celebrations (Judg 21:19-21; Ps 68:25; Jer 31:13; Lam 2:10). Now their role is reversed, and instead of singing with joy they grieve. The destruction of the temple with the consequent loss of the divinely-appointed festivals and sacrifices was a catastrophic blow for Israel. Johan Renkema points out that the Babylonians normally left temples intact but the place that the Jerusalem temple had come to occupy in Zion theology made it a threat to the stability of Babylonian dominion. The belief that the Lord, dwelling in Zion's temple, would protect the city against all attacks was partly behind the rebellion against Nebuchadnezzer.[22] It is interesting that, while this verse presupposes the loss of the temple, it *does not refer to it directly.* It is as if it is too dreadful a thing to utter aloud at this stage, so the verse instead describes only the mourners gathered around the unmentioned temple-corpse. Israel's relationship with God was lived out through the cult, and the implications of its loss for that relationship were unclear at best. And what of Lady Zion herself? Her bitterness is not that of another character on the stage. Rather, it contains within it all the mourning, desolation, groaning, and grieving of the other characters expressed throughout the verse.

v. 5 ה/hê In 1:5 attention is directed to the triumph of Zion's enemies, and for the first time it is made explicit that YHWH lies behind her suffering. The first two lines allude again to the divine curse in Deuteronomy. Moses says to Israel that, if they break the covenant, then the alien in their midst "will become the head [i.e., the master], and you will become the tail [i.e., the servant]" (Deut 28:44). The image is not merely that of defeat by one's enemies but also of humiliation.

The reason for the triumph of Zion's enemies is spelled out in the next

---

22. Renkema, *Lamentations*, 114-15.

two lines, although it has been implicit in the allusions to Deuteronomy 28. *YHWH himself* is the one who has caused her to suffer on account of her many sins. The word used to describe Zion's sin is פֶּשַׁע/*peša'*, which refers to rebellion against an overlord. That is a fitting term to describe Israel's numerous violations of her covenant with YHWH. Up until this point the focus has been on Zion's suffering, but now, for the first time, her sin comes into focus. The narrator tells us that Zion is being punished for her "*many* rebellions." As Paul House comments, "Zion's rebellions were not sporadic, rash acts that disrupted a general pattern of obedience."[23] However, we also need to note that the reference to her sin is brief, general, and in a context designed to elicit compassion from YHWH and the implied readers. The narrator does not want the focus to be on her sin, nor does he wish to minimize or ignore it.

The verse ends by considering again the image of Zion's children being taken off into exile (cf. 1:3), yet another of the covenant curses in Deuteronomy 28 (vv. 58-63).

> What a heart wrenching scene this paints! The word for children comes from the Hebrew word for suckle, suggesting the intimate bond that exists between the city and her inhabitants. In the past she nourished them from the substance of her own being. They were suckling infants, totally dependant upon her. Snatched from her embrace and her protection and forced into exile, they are now captives of the enemy. This loss of children is not only a present tragedy, but it also signifies the forfeiture of the city's future.[24]

The word for "adversaries" (צָר/*ṣār*) begins and ends the verse, "linguistically surrounding and capturing Zion and her suffering children just as the foes surround the city."[25]

v. 6 וְ/*wāw* Following on from the mention of Zion's children taken as captives,[26] the narrator focuses on some of those children in particular: the rulers.[27] The "splendor" or "glory" that has departed from Zion refers, in this context, to her leaders. These "children" are her treasure — a glory bestowed

---

23. House, *Lamentations*, 351.

24. Bergant, *Lamentations*, 34-35.

25. O'Connor, *Lamentations and the Tears of the World*, 21.

26. The verse opens with a וְ/*wāw* ("and"), linking it to the previous verse. Even if the acrostic pattern forced the use of וְ/*wāw*, it still has the effect of linking the two verses.

27. שַׂר/*śar* is a general term designating a ruler of *some variety*. It can refer to a military captain, a royal official, a tribal chief, a religious official, etc. Its referent in this case is general.

by YHWH.[28] The point being made is that the ruling classes in Zion have departed the city and without them "it seems unlikely that the city will be able to regroup effectively and rebuild any time soon."[29]

Zion is referred to as בת־ציון/*bat-ṣîyyôn*. Many English Bible translations render it "daughter of Zion." But "it is not Zion's daughter who is being addressed (Zion has no daughter) but Zion herself, who is classified as a 'daughter.'"[30] So "Daughter Zion" is our preferred translation.[31]

The image of stags, creatures that symbolized elegance and swiftness, is used of the rulers. But here it is subverted as the poet paints the picture of a stag hunt to depict the defeat of Jerusalem's rulers. "The stags, once swift and elegant, can no longer find pasture and are left breathless and weak."[32] Delbert Hillers draws attention to one of the curses in Esarhaddon's vassel treaties: "Just as a stag is chased and killed, so may your avengers chase and kill you, your brothers, your sons."[33] The weakened leaders, lacking the strength to evade their hunters, cannot even save themselves, let alone the city.

v. 7 ז/*zayin*   The focus now moves from the present to the past, and for the first time the name "Jerusalem" is used. We are told that "she remembers" — but what does she remember? At face value it looks as if she recalls "the days of her affliction and homelessness." But this is problematic on several counts. For this reason many commentators and translators suppose that there is an implicit ב/*b* ("in") in v. 7a. Thus they render line 1 as "Jerusalem remembered/ [*in*] the days of her affliction and her wanderings." So *in the midst of present pain* she recalls the recent past when the wound was inflicted.

Jerusalem remembers her glorious past. The "precious things" are not spelled out, and the audience are left to fill in the details. Perhaps she remem-

---

28. Isaiah 5:13-14 speaks of the exile of Israel's leaders as the exile of her glory (כבד/*kbd*) and her majesty (הדרה/*hdrh*).

29. House, *Lamentations*, 352.

30. Berlin, *Lamentations*, 10. Dobbs-Allsop disagrees and sees בת־ציון/*bat-ṣîyyôn* as a normal construct chain — "Daughter of the City Zion." This, in the ancient Near Eastern context, would refer to the city goddess as an inhabitant of the city. Obviously for a biblical author this is only a metaphor, as there could be no actual city goddess ("Syntagma," 469-70). For a cautious objection to Dobbs-Allsopp, see Berlin, *Lamentations*, 11-12.

31. Whose daughter is Zion? The text never seeks to answer that question, and it may be that seeking an answer is to push the personification of the city too far. On the other hand, it *may* be implied that Zion is YHWH's daughter.

32. Renkema, *Lamentations*, 124. Is the mention of the starving and weakened stags a reference to the hunger from the siege?

33. Citing lines 576-78 in *ANET*, 540.

bered the stories of David and of Solomon, perhaps the riches that were once hers, perhaps her precious children, perhaps the wonderful buildings such as the palace and temple, perhaps the presence of YHWH himself. There were many "precious things" Jerusalem could remember which were hers "until her people fell into the hand of an adversary." In that day of doom nobody was there to help Jerusalem. Maybe she would have expected help from her political allies (cf. 1:2) or perhaps from YHWH, the city's protector (Ps 22:11; 46:5). The reality was that she faced the foe alone.

Mocking by enemies is a common motif in individual (e.g., Ps 37:13; 52:6) and communal (Ps 44:14; 79:4; 80:6) laments, and we encounter it here for the first time in Lamentations. What the enemies laugh at derisively is her downfall. "In a society where matters of honor and shame play such a major role in both self-identity and social status, derision itself is often more deplorable than the actual reasons for the derision. The city has collapsed and now her enemies gloat over her. It is possible that at the heart of the city's lament over her defeat is a more pointed lament over her humiliation."[34]

v. 8 ח/*ḥêt* The theme of social shaming is intensified in 1:8. The verse opens with a return to the topic of Jerusalem's grievous sin. That sin is the root cause of the humiliation she has subsequently experienced. In 1:5 the word פשע/*peša'* ("transgression") was used with its focus on the breach of covenant stipulations. Here we find the root חטא/*ḥāṭā'*, which, according to Renkema, "points more towards a breach of community relationships."[35] This sin, he says, is a breach of Jerusalem's relationship with God by virtue of the fact that the community relationships that have been violated by Jerusalem were established by YHWH.

The result of Jerusalem's sin is that she became a נידה/*nîdâ*. What is a נידה/*nîdâ*? The word appears only in this verse, but the following possibilities present themselves. (1) Many see the root as נדה/*ndh*. In its nominal form it can refer to the ritual uncleanness of menstrual discharge (Lev 12:2, 5) and the ritually unclean state of a menstrual woman (Lev 15:19-33). The suggestion is that Jerusalem's sin makes her unclean like a menstrual woman (or like her menstrual blood). As a consequence she is shunned. While a menstruating woman was not considered morally "unclean," in Ezekiel the concept of ritual impurity was *metaphorically extended* to cover moral "uncleanness" (Ezek 36:17). Many suggest that this is what is going on here also. This interpretation could link with the next verse if the words "her impurity was in her skirts" re-

34. Bergant, *Lamentations*, 40.
35. Renkema, *Lamentations*, 132.

fer to ritually defiling menstrual blood. The parallel with v. 17c could further reinforce this interpretation. The problems with it are (i) that it requires either changing the text from נִידָה/*nîdâ* to נִדָּה/*niddâ* or accepting the former as an otherwise unattested variant of the latter, (ii) that the link between her menstrual state in 1:8a and her nakedness in 1:8b-c is not clear.[36] (2) Others see the root as נוּד/*nûd*, and this is certainly how 4QLam, a fragment of Lamentations found among the Dead Sea Scrolls, takes it. Now נוּד/*nûd* can mean one of two quite distinct things.

(a) "Wanderer." This is how the LXX translated the Hebrew. The idea is that Jerusalem is exiled for her sin. Thus "she has been banished." The basic problem with this view is that Jerusalem is *not* sent into exile in this poem but remains sitting where she is and *her children* are banished.

(b) "To shake." It can refer to the shaking of the head in mockery, scorn, or horror (Jer 18:16; 48:27; Ps 44:14). Perhaps Jerusalem is the object of head-nodding. Thus the NRSV's "she has become a mockery" and Hillers's "Because Jerusalem sinned so great a sin, people shake their heads at her."[37] This interpretation certainly fits well with the reference to mocking laughter at the end of the previous verse and with the following reference to her humiliation. I tentatively incline towards this option.

Those foreigners who used to hold Jerusalem in high esteem (cf. 1:2) now despise her as something worthless. Why? Because she has been publicly humiliated by having her naked body exposed for all to stare at. In the ancient world to have one's naked body exposed, especially the genitals, was an utter disgrace. She has been stripped and left bare by those who attacked her. Her nakedness points towards the city "stripped" of its walls, its palaces, and riches by the foe.[38] Two contexts possibly inform this image: first, the social practice of punishing a woman guilty of sexual impropriety by exposing her genitalia

---

36. Some commentators *support* the menstruant interpretation by the reference to her "nakedness" in this verse (Renkema, *Lamentations*, 133), but the link is not an obvious one. Menstrual women did not strip naked. Appealing to Lev 18:19, in which it is forbidden to uncover a woman's nakedness (i.e., to have sex with her) during her menstrual uncleanness, does not support the link between menstruation and nakedness in Lam 1:8. While the words "nakedness" (עֶרְוָתָה/*ʿerwātâ*) and "mentrual uncleanness" (בְּנִדַּת טֻמְאָתָהּ/*běniddat ṭûm'ātâ*) occur together in Lev 18:19, the link between them there is *not* what is in view in Lam 1:8.

37. Hillers, *Lamentations*, 62.

38. Other Old Testament texts see the metaphorical stripping of a city as divine judgment (Nah 3:5f; Jer 13:26; Isa 47:2-3; Lam 4:21).

in public (Hos 2:3; Ezek 16:35-39; 23:29). Second, the action of an invading army stripping their captives naked to humiliate them (Isa 20:3-4). The two images could be combined here: YHWH strips Jerusalem as punishment for her infidelity, and to do that he uses the adversary who attack and "strip" her as a defeated foe.[39]

Her enemies look on in disgust, and she groans from the depths of her being and turns her face away so her eyes do not have to meet those of the people staring in horror! The social shame and humiliation of Jerusalem is painful, and the audience have to consider the experience *from her perspective.* Does the poet want his audience to stare in disgust at Jerusalem with those who used to honor her? He clearly wants his readers/hearers to judge Jerusalem as a sinner suffering divine punishment, but his poem so far has also worked to elicit considerable sympathy for this lonely, suffering woman. It is inconceivable that he would wish his audience to be among those who despise her.

v. 9 ט/*têt* The verse opens with the comment that "her impurity was in her skirts," that is to say, in the lower part of her garments. This expression has been taken in different ways. Those who take the נידה/*nîdâ* in 1:8 as a menstruant often maintain that it is a reference to menstrual blood staining her robes.[40] If we follow this line, then "it may suggest that Jerusalem's moral impurity was obvious for all to see, as visible as a bloodstain on the skirt of a menstruating woman."[41] I tentatively follow Berlin in taking the phrase to refer to the impurity of Jerusalem's sexual immodesty. The skirts of a robe were sometimes associated with one's modesty, and one punishment for a woman's sexual infidelity was her public humiliation by having her skirts "lifted up" to

---

39. Modern readers will find the cultural practices on which this imagery draws disturbing. See Guest, "Hiding Behind the Naked Women." However, while Guest is sensitive to the violence-against-women motif (She got what she deserved!), she fails to perceive that violence against men (He got what he deserved!) is also prominent in Lamentations and consequently wrongly suggests that Lamentations has the effect of transferring guilt away from male readers and locating it in women (429).

40. Hillers, *Lamentations,* 86; Provan, *Lamentations,* 45; Westermann, *Lamentations,* 129; Bergant, *Lamentations,* 41.

41. Berlin, *Lamentations,* 54. Renkema thinks that Jerusalem "paid no attention to the purity of her clothing," allowing defiling menstrual blood to soak through it; *Lamentations,* 136. But that seems unlikely. Even more unlikely is O'Connor's claim that the blood is proof of sexual intercourse (*Tears of the World,* 22). Jerusalem is no virgin! She is, after all, a mother! Also unlikely is Dobbs-Allsopp's suggestion that the blood on her skirts might possibly be there from an attack; *Lamentations,* 64. But the text doesn't mention blood on her skirts: it speaks of "uncleanness" in her skirts which *may* be menstrual blood.

expose her genitalia for all to see (Nah 3:5; Jer 13:22, 26). Berlin thus suggests that "she is not a menstruant; she is a whore."[42] Jerusalem did not consider the consequences her behavior would have for her future. She went ahead with reckless abandon, never expecting her actions to catch up with her, but they did, and when they did her reversal of fortunes was breathtaking.

In 1:9c Lady Jerusalem speaks for the first time, breaking into the narrator's speech. Thus, "there is no one to comfort her" (1:9b) serves to introduce the words of Lady Jerusalem in 1:9c. This repeat of the complaint in 1:2 serves to underline the tragic isolation of Jerusalem but also adds a further dimension in this new context — the absence of *YHWH* as comforter implied by the juxtaposition of the complaint and the woman's call for YHWH to "Look!"

Jerusalem is not satisfied to accept her fate and her isolation. She needs a comforter, and so she cries out to God, "Look, YHWH, at my affliction!" The narrator has thus far spoken *about* YHWH, but it is Jerusalem herself who first speaks *to* him. It is YHWH who has abandoned her and punished her, but it is to YHWH also that she looks for help. When the speakers in Lamentations call on YHWH to see, we must not suppose that they think that God does not know about the situation — after all, he himself inflicted it! What is being requested is that YHWH pay attention to it *by acting to remove it*. God may know about her situation in the abstract, but he seems to be acting *as if* he was unaware of her plight. The gloating self-exaltation of the enemy over her is a motive for YHWH to pay attention. Presumably Jerusalem is appealing to God's own loss of honor that accompanies the loss of honor of his people, his city, and his house. "For the sake of your name," she implies, "stop these enemies mocking me."

It is interesting that her first words are not words of confession or repentance but of calling for deliverance. In good Israelite tradition she calls out to the God who answers the cries of his afflicted people — even when their affliction is the result of sin (Judg 2:18; 3:9, 15; 10:10ff.; Ps 81:7; 107, etc.). God does not reply.

v. 10 ʾ/yôd Jerusalem's words that her enemy has exalted himself over her (1:9) are given a horrible, metaphorical explication in this verse: Jerusalem has been raped by her Gentile enemies. The verse opens by picking up threads from 1:7: an adversary (צר/ṣār) has stretched out his hand (ידו/yādô) over her precious things (מחמדיה/maḥămaddêhā). Here the precious things are likely to be the treasures of the temple now plundered by the enemy (cf. 2 Kgs 25:13-15; Jer 52:17-23) or a reference to the temple sanctuary itself, desecrated by the

---

42. Berlin, *Lamentations*, 55.

invaders.[43] The image of sexual molestation, given the following line, may well be present.

To her horror Jerusalem watched Gentile nations enter her sanctuary. The sexual allusions are clear. The word "enter" (בא/*bāʾ*) is often used to describe the act of a man "entering" a woman in sexual intercourse.[44] In this image the temple sanctuary is pictured as her vagina, Jerusalem's most holy place, entered by the enemy. The image is of her being raped; indeed the plural "nations" may suggest that she is gang-raped. In the ancient world, as often today, the honor of a group was decimated if the group was unable to protect its women. Consequently, in war the rape of women was used as a psychological tool of terror not only against the women but against their men, who were disgraced by their inability to protect their wives and daughters. The integrity of women's bodies represented the integrity of the community.[45] Rape was thus used to demonstrate the power of one group over another. If earlier verses have alluded to Jerusalem's sexual infidelity, then here we may see a horrible image of reversal in which "what began as unwitting, voluntary promiscuity, suddenly turned into unwished for, forcible defilement."[46]

The narrator turns to prayer for the first time at this point, perhaps inspired by Jerusalem's prayer in 1:9c,[47] and reminds the Lord that it was by YHWH's *own* command that the nations be kept away from the sanctuary. There seems to be an implicit objection against YHWH here: *You* forbade these nations to enter your assembly, and yet *you* have allowed them to force their way in! The command in question is Deut 23:3-6, in which Moabites and Ammonites are forbidden from entering the assembly of YHWH. Here that prohibition is seen as having a broader application to other nations (Ezek 44:9; Neh 13:1-3). What is interesting is that this verse seems intended to arouse God to act for Jerusalem's salvation. If YHWH's wife has been raped, then not only is she dishonored, *he is also!* It looks to the nations as if their gods have triumphed over Jerusalem's God, so not only Lady Jerusalem but YHWH also is the object of mockery. The narrator's prayer reminding YHWH of his command seems intended to provoke a response. It should be

---

43. Perhaps treasures from the royal palace are also intended. Dobbs-Allsopp points to a Sumerian parallel in which the clothing and treasures of a city goddess are torn from her by an enemy and used to dress his own wife and daughter (*Weep, O Daughter of Zion*, 48; *Lamentations*, 66).

44. The word "her precious things" (מחמדיה/*maḥămaddêhā*) can be used in a sexual context (Song 5:16: the woman's lover is "altogether lovely").

45. So Keefe, "Rapes of Women."

46. Mintz, "The Rhetoric of Lamentations," 3.

47. So Linafelt, *Surviving Lamentations*, 39.

noted that while the narrator does not avoid the fact that Jerusalem has sinned grievously, he reacts to her rape with horror, anger, sympathy, and prayer. If readers feel distinctly uncomfortable with the image of Zion's rape and shocked at YHWH's complicity in it, then they can stand with the narrator. Such a reaction is *precisely* that which the text seeks to solicit.[48]

v. 11 כ/*kāp* The narrator focuses attention on the food crisis faced by the citizens of Jerusalem. During the siege there would have been a famine (cf. 2 Kg 6:25), and now, in the destroyed remains, food would have proven hard to come by.[49] The famine causes the people to groan as they search for what few scraps of bread remained.[50] "The circle of those who groan enlarges. First it was the priests (v. 4), then the city (v. 8), now all of the inhabitants."[51] Their primitive instinct to survive drives them to exchange their precious things for whatever food they can get hold of. This is a matter of life or death, so "daily life turns around one single obsession: food."[52] The precious things (cf. 1:7, 10) in this case are presumably privately owned objects of great value, *possibly* even children.[53]

48. Contra Guest, who goes too far by suggesting that the text seeks to *justify* the rape ("Hiding Behind the Naked Women"). Dobbs-Allsopp and Linafelt are right in seeing a critique of YHWH, although they go beyond the text in saying that the poet thinks that YHWH's actions can *never* be justified ("The Rape of Zion in Thr 1,10"). I think that the text retains an unresolved tension between theodic and antitheodic elements. Thus the rape metaphor is presented to be deeply disturbing and perplexing. Interestingly the narrator pictures the enemies, *not YHWH*, as raping Zion, thus putting some distance between God and the act. Nevertheless, YHWH allows it to happen and is thus complicit. Yet while the narrator is seeking to offer some criticism, he does not take a stance of rejecting YHWH and neither, we must add, does Zion.

49. Renkema explains that during the siege "the economic life of the countryside was also brought to a standstill," making food hard to come by even after it was possible to exit the city. He explains why this situation would have lasted for quite some time, extending the duration of the famine; *Lamentations*, 148.

50. Hunger is a central theme of the book also found in 2:11; 3:16; 4:10; 5:9-10 (see also the famine texts in 1:19; 2:19; 4:3-5; 4:7-9; 5:6).

51. Bergant, *Lamentations*, 42.

52. Renkema, *Lamentations*, 148.

53. Hos 9:16 uses the same word to refer to the slaying of their children. Hillers argues that children are in view here. He notes a parallel in the Atrahasis Epic in which family members are sold in times of famine (*Lamentations*, 87-88). Berlin objects that in a besieged city human beings had little value as commodities. Her alternative is to see parents giving their children away to people as free laborers in exchange for food *to feed the children* (*Lamentations*, 56-57). While it is possible to read the verse in this way, it is not the most natural reading. On top of that, it is far from certain that children are referred to at all (Renkema argues against "children"; *Lamentations*, 149), nor that this text refers to the famine *during* the siege.

"*All* her people are groaning." It is interesting to consider how the poet has used the word "all" so far in the poem. Dianne Bergant writes,

> The scope of this pitiful situation is seen in the repeated use of the inclusive word "all." All [those who love her] have abandoned her, all of her friends have been treacherous (v. 2), and all who once honored her now despise her (v. 8); all of her pursuers have overtaken her (v. 3), and all of her gates are desolate (v. 4); she has lost all of her majesty (v. 6), and all of her precious things (vv. 7, 10).[54]

Once again Lady Jerusalem interrupts the narrator, perhaps prompted by his portrait of her starving people. This time her cry to get YHWH's attention is intensified. She not only cries, "Look, YHWH!" (cf. 1:9), but "Look, YHWH, *and see!*" (or "*and consider!*"). The reason she wants him to look is that she has become זוללה/*zôlēlâ*. It is not certain what this means. It is probably derived from זלל/*zālal*, which can mean (a) to shake or to quake ("I have become shaken [i.e., distressed]");[55] (b) to waste/to dissipate ("I have become ruined"); or, most likely in this case, (c) to be worthless ("I have become despised/worthless"). Virtually all English translations translate the word as "despised" (cf. 1:8).[56] The social shaming once again comes to the forefront.

Lady Zion Speaks (1:12-22)

v. 12 ל/*lāmed* Lady Jerusalem opens her first main speech (1:12-16) by turning from addressing YHWH to addressing those passing by. Calling on those passing by is a common motif in a destruction scene.[57] Passers-by play the conventional role of witnesses to disaster and often of mockers (Ps 89:41). The audience is cast in the role of passers-by and drawn in by this address as Jerusalem's words to onlookers reach out of the page to the readers. She invites the readers to look at her but not to mock her. Has she given up on YHWH, and is she now looking for solace in those gawping at her? It is not clear at this point, but what is clear is that she needs a comforter to stand with her, and thus she calls out to bystanders.

"May the pain that has befallen me not befall you," she says to them, re-

---

54. Bergant, *Lamentations*, 42.

55. It seems to bear this meaning in the *nip'al*, but the word here is a *qal* participle.

56. Alternatively, it may be connected with the Akkadian *zilulû* meaning "tramp," hence Berlin's "see what a beggar I have become."

57. So Berlin (*Lamentations*, 57), who refers to Zeph 2:15.

minding them not to look on her with smug self-assurance for they may one day find themselves in the gutter as she does now. Then she calls out for their attention with the same word pair that she has just addressed to YHWH ("*See,* YHWH, and *observe,*" v. 11), but this time in reverse ("*observe* and *see,*" v. 12). She asks them, and implicitly the readers also, to consider the situation *from her perspective.* Has there ever been mental anguish or sorrow like that which she has experienced? The question is rhetorical, and the implied answer is No, never.

> In the face of trauma, catastrophe, and radical suffering, claims of incomparability and uniqueness do not function as equations of measurement. They serve, instead, to express the vastness of pain that overcomes individuals and groups, suffering that defies containment, that blasts away at the imagination, that has no words to express its depth and totality. From her position inside the pain, no one has suffered as much as she because there is no way she could imagine more suffering.[58]

The rhetorical question is an urgent plea for understanding and sympathy.

The surpassing grief she has suffered was inflicted by YHWH himself. That fact is what makes the mental anguish so acute. Most commentators point out that 1:12c echoes 1:5a in that in both YHWH makes Jerusalem "grieve" (הוגה/*hôgâ,* a *hipʿil* of יגה/*yāgâ,* "to afflict/to grieve"). In 1:5 the narrator explains that YHWH did this because of her many sins, but Jerusalem makes no mention of her sin at this point, only of YHWH's burning anger. The mention of the "day of the burning of his anger" probably draws on the Day of YHWH theology found in some of the prophets (Amos 5:18-20; Isa 2:12; Jer 46:10; Joel 1:15; Zeph 1; Ezek 7:19): a day of terrible divine judgment. There is no other way to envisage the world-shattering experience Jerusalem has undergone.

v. 13 מ/*mêm* While Zion does not *explicitly* charge God with wrongdoing, she may *imply* that he has not acted appropriately. Jerusalem now expresses in metaphorical language what it felt like to experience the day of fiery wrath. Like Sodom she experienced burning fire from on high (Gen 19:23-29). This fire enters into the very depths of her being and hence cannot be put out or avoided. The bones, the seat of health and vigor (Job 20:11; Prov 16:24), are ravaged by the fire that burns within. Possibly the image was inspired by the actual fires lit by the Babylonians in the city when they plundered it — but

---

58. O'Connor, *Lamentations and the Tears of the World,* 26.

from Jerusalem's perspective the Babylonian fires were lit by YHWH and sent from on high.

The image then changes from God-the-military-arsonist to God-the-military-hunter. The use of nets in battles was not uncommon in the ancient Near East, and here God spreads a net to trap Jerusalem and take her prisoner. Iain Provan explains that "elsewhere in the OT the image of 'spreading the net' is often used of the enemy's assault on the righteous (e.g. Ps 35:7) or of Yahweh's action against his enemies (Hos 7:12). That Jerusalem should be the object of Yahweh's attention in this respect is a shocking reversal of the norms, emphasizing the dire plight in which the city finds itself."[59]

The expression "he made me turn back" probably means that he caused Jerusalem to turn her face away in shame (cf. 1:8-9). The consequences of the fire within and the net without are that Jerusalem feels shamed, desolate,[60] and faint/sick all day long. She has lost hope.

v. 14 ב/*nûn* The description of the day of the burning of his anger (1:12) continues. From being caught in YHWH's net (1:13), Jerusalem is now, like a prisoner of war, constrained in a yoke.[61] The yoke symbolized servitude (Jer 27:8; cf. Lam 1:1, 3). It has been constructed by YHWH not from wood but out of her rebellions (on "rebellions," see 1:5).[62] The image suggests an organic relationship between Jerusalem's sins and her current suffering. It is not simply that her sins motivate YHWH to punish her in response, although that idea is clearly present. The image goes further, suggesting that as punishment for her rebellions *YHWH has taken those very sins and woven them into a weapon against her* — a yoke that binds her and weighs down heavily on her neck. Possibly this indicates the way in which Jerusalem's illicit affairs with foreign nations have recoiled against her and those nations now become her yoke. But we must also note that the image is not one of some kind of "natural justice" built into the fabric of the world — it is YHWH who *personally actualizes* the effects of Jerusalem's sin. Throughout the verse it is emphatically

---

59. Provan, *Lamentations*, 49.

60. The word is often used to describe devastated land or cities (Lev 26:33; Isa 54:3; Jer 12:11; Amos 9:14).

61. O'Connor sees in this sequence "a scene of domestic violence in which a powerful, angry man beats his wife, hurls her about, and leaves her for dead"; *Lamentations and the Tears of the World*, 26. But this is to misread the metaphors which all depict Yahweh as a military opponent and not as an angry husband. The scene painted by the metaphors is *not domestic* (husbands did not catch their wives in nets and put them in yokes).

62. Contra Renkema, who sees the many sins bound together *and attached to the yoke* for Jerusalem to pull along; *Lamentations*, 165.

YHWH who is behind the pain: "*He* fashioned a yoke . . . ," "*he* caused my strength to fail," "*my Lord* gave me into the hands. . . ." The last reference is the most poignant as she describes her oppressor as "*my* Lord."

With all her rebellions bound together and placed on her at once, she crumpled, weighed down under YHWH's yoke. Handed over to the enemy, it is no wonder she could not withstand them.

v. 15 ס/*sāmek*   The account of the day of the burning of YHWH's anger (1:12) draws to a close with a lament for the military defeat and its implications for Jerusalem's fighting men. So far we have heard of no attempted resistance to the enemy, but here we see that there was indeed a fight. However, Jerusalem's **אבירים**/'*abbîrîm,* her "strong/valiant men," were no match for YHWH, who treated them with disdain. The **אבירים**/'*abbîrîm* here may refer to the warrior or perhaps the noble leaders of the city. The one who despised the strong men is designated as "the Lord *in my midst*" — an expression which in times past would have indicated YHWH's dwelling with his people to bless and protect them. But YHWH's holy presence in Jerusalem now becomes a devastating curse, for he has turned against them. In the normal order of things the Lord in Jerusalem's midst called holy assemblies (מועד/ *mô'ēd*) of worship and sacrifice. Now, in a painful twist of the temple traditions, Adonai-in-her-midst calls an assembly (מועד/*mô'ēd*) *against* her. This is not an assembly of joyous pilgrims (such assemblies are no more, 1:4) but an assembly of enemy troops who shatter her young men (lit., "my chosen ones"). This is a dreadful exchange of the joyful Zion festivals for a "festival" in which the pilgrims are an enemy army.[63] Possibly, in this context of cultic imagery, the choice of the word **אבירים**/'*abbîrîm* for the warriors has sinister overtones. It is a word that can also mean "bulls," and one wonders whether these "bulls" are the grisly sacrifice at the "festival."[64]

The picture of the festival is possibly expanded on in the image of wine. But the reversal of the image is grotesque. The wine for this feast is the blood of Daughter Judah crushed under the feet of the Lord in his winepress! The title "Maiden Daughter Judah" is probably not synonymous with "Daughter Zion" but refers to the whole land beyond the bounds of Jerusalem itself. That would explain why Jerusalem refers to her in the third person and not the first person. So Jerusalem herself suffers the same fate as the rest of Judah.

Westermann points out that the language and imagery employed to de-

---

63. House compares this assembly to Zeph 1:7-8, in which the Lord calls a sacrificial meal for Judah but it is a meal of judgment in which *she is the sacrifice; Lamentations,* 359.
64. So Dobbs-Allsopp, *Lamentations,* 69.

scribe the "day of burning anger" in 1:12-15 is drawn from the traditional accusation-against-God section of the communal lament form. The clauses, both literal and metaphorical, are piled upon each other to create what would be understood to be an accusation against God, albeit somewhat muted in that God is not directly addressed and Zion's sin *is* acknowledged.[65]

v. 16 ע/ʿayin Jerusalem has now finished telling about the day of the burning of God's anger (1:12) and explains to the by-passers how she has reacted to the end of her world. Since the beginning of the poem she has been in tears (1:2). Now she cries out, "On account of these things I am weeping. My eyes are flowing [with] water!" She is crying incessantly and uncontrollably because of what YHWH has done on the day of his wrath. There is no end to her suffering, so there can be no end to her sorrow.

The pain might be more bearable if there was one to stand alongside her and comfort her. This is the third time Zion's lack of comforter has surfaced (1:2, 9), and the readers begin to see how central the no-comfort theme is in the poem. The presence of a comforter is *not even on the horizon for her* — he is "far removed." That said, the possibility of a comforter is not *altogether* obliterated by this observation. Thus her calling out to YHWH (1:9) and the by-passers (1:12) may not be in vain.

The verse climaxes with Jerusalem looking helplessly on at her suffering children. An enemy has prevailed, and they are desolate, appalled, or horrified (cf. 1:4, 13). As a mother she longs to help her children in their despair and is heartbroken that she can do nothing but look on.

v. 17 פ/pê Now the narrator breaks into Jerusalem's speech to the passersby. This interruption divides Jerusalem's first and second speeches. He paints a pathetic portrait of her stretching out her hands (cf. 1:10) in the hope that someone will notice her and help. But, for the fourth time we are told there is no one to comfort her (1:2, 9, 16). She is *still* suffering alone. Indeed, far from comforting her, YHWH has decreed (cf. 1:10) that all Jacob's neighbors in the surrounding cities and nations should be enemies (cf. 1:2, 8-9). "Jacob" probably refers to *all* Israel and not simply Judah or Jerusalem. Jacob, and thus by implication Jerusalem, is surrounded by those hostile to him. This may provide the ultimate explanation of why Jerusalem's pleading to the by-passers has fallen on deaf ears — God ordained that it would! So not only does YHWH fail to comfort Zion, but he stops others fulfilling that role by turning them against her.

65. Westermann, *Lamentations*, 132-35.

From their own perspective the reason the surrounding nations do not respond to Zion's pleas is that she has become like a ritually unclean menstruant in the midst.[66] They would defile themselves by having contact with her.

> Menstruation . . . renders a person impure and thereby unable to come into contact with the *sancta* (Lev 15:19-24). It does not, however, mean that the woman is disgusting or that she must physically separate herself from others. . . . *Niddâ* can [occur]. . . in the context of moral impurity. Having sex with a *niddâ* is listed among prohibited sexual relationships. . . . Leviticus 18:19, "Do not approach a woman in her menstrual impurity," is what is behind our verse. . . . She has become like a *niddâ* among them, in that no one wanted to have relations with her. Judah's erstwhile "lovers" do not want to have "sexual" relations with her because she is in a state of [ritual] "impurity."[67]

That Zion (Jerusalem-as-cultic-center) has become ritually unclean is a shocking situation, and it negates her role as the dwelling place of YHWH. It also alienates her neighbors.

v. 18 צ/ṣādê Jerusalem begins her second main speech (1:18-22), directing it to the nations.[68] She says that YHWH has indeed been righteous to punish her in this way because she rebelled against his mouth.[69] There *may* be an allusion to rebellions of the exodus generation by the choice of the word מרה/*mārâ* ("rebellion"). The rebellion in the wilderness is often referred to in this way (Num 20:10, 24; 27:14; Deut 1:26, 43; 9:7, 23-24); indeed, several references use the very expression found here — "to rebel against the mouth" (Num 20:24; 27:14; Deut 1:26, 43; 9:23). The likelihood of an exodus allusion is increased by the presence of other such exodus allusions in Lamentations.[70] If

66. Here, unlike 1:8, we *clearly* have נדה/*niddâ*. The parallel with 1:8 may lead us to interpret נידה/*nîdâ* in 1:8 as an alternative spelling of נדה/*niddâ*, or we may reason that 1:17 shows that if this poet meant נדה/*niddâ* in 1:8 he would have written נדה/*niddâ*. We cannot be dogmatic.

67. Berlin, *Lamentations*, 58-59.

68. Is this audience of "nations" broader than the audience of "passers-by" in the first speech? Possibly.

69. Westermann sees 1:18a as the climax of the chapter and the conclusion of the accusation against God in 1:12-15; *Lamentations*, 135-36. However, he has allowed form-critical parallels to override the actual structure of the poem we have. 1:18a begins Jerusalem's second speech rather than concluding her first. Westermann's way of dealing with the awkward 1:16-17 does not do them justice.

70. On such, see Dobbs-Allsopp, *Lamentations*, 75-77.

such an allusion is intended, we may see that God's people have not changed at all since the days of the exodus and rebel now as they did then. Against which of YHWH's words has she rebelled? Is this just a general reference to the covenant stipulations that he had given at Sinai? Perhaps, although Renkema argues that the expression to "rebel against (the) mouth" "is always used for resistance to a particular command given in a particular situation, but never with respect to commandments which have eternal validity."[71] Thus he suggests that it may be the words of the prophets such as Jeremiah that Jerusalem rebelled against. Either way, Jerusalem again admits that she has sinned (cf. 1:14), and, as such, she concurs with the narrator's assessment in v. 5 and v. 8.

However, instead of developing the theme of her guilt, she returns to the matter of the pain that God's punishment has brought. It seems best to take line 2 as a warning to the nations to learn from her mistake. "Listen then," she says before spelling out again the awful consequences of this rebellion — her sorrow (cf. 1:12) at the captivity of her children (cf. 1:5): both maidens (cf. 1:4) and young men (cf. 1:15). The loss of the young men and young women of childbearing age is the loss of the city's future.

F. W. Dobbs-Allsopp makes the interesting suggestion that by shifting the focus again back to her pain Zion is transforming the declaration of God's innocence ("YHWH is indeed righteous") retrospectively into an appeal to God in his capacity as righteous judge. "The images of suffering that come here and in the succeeding stanzas are intended, as in similar passages (cf. Ezra 9:15; Neh. 9:8, 33; Dan. 9:14) to move the just judge, regardless of the offence, to compassion."[72] In effect, YHWH's righteousness has been manifest in punishment, but now may it be manifest in salvation. Given the dominance of positive and salvific overtones to the word צדיק/ṣaddîq ("righteous") in the Hebrew Bible, this is possible.

v. 19 ק/qôp Jerusalem calls out to her lovers. The word מאהבי/mĕ'ahăbay refers to *illicit* lovers (Jer 22:20-22; 30:14; Ezek 16:33, 36; 23:5, 9, 22; Hos 2:5-13). These would be the Gentile nations with which she had improper alliances. Such alliances involved religious duties to idols that would have compromised her sole devotion to YHWH. Thus the political alliances would have led to "adultery" against Israel's God. These alliances would have been moti-

---

71. Renkema, *Lamentations*, 181. He cites Num 20:24; 27:14; Deut 1:26, 43; 9:23; Josh 1:18; 1 Kgs 13:21, 26.

72. Dobbs-Allsopp, *Lamentations*, 71. He cross-references Ps 7:9, 11; Jer 20:12; Zeph 3:5 and sees Jer 12:1 as the closest parallel.

vated, among other things, by the desire for increased security, but in this case such security was not forthcoming. The comment that the lovers deceived her may suggest that their promises of military support were not fulfilled. While now acknowledging that her relationship with the "lovers" was wrong, she still feels terribly betrayed by them (*"even they* deceived me"). The readers will immediately be reminded of v. 2, where the narrator told us that from among "all those who loved her" there was none to comfort and that her friends betrayed her. In v. 2 there was no strong reason to think that the expression "those who loved her" was intended to suggest that her relationship with them was improper. However, the reader cannot but now revisit that earlier verse and see it in a new light.

Having spelled out in the previous verse the exile of her young men and young women, Jerusalem speaks of the hunger of the priests and elders who remain. The high civil position of the elders and priests would have offered them more social protection against the famine than most, and yet even they are dying of hunger. The elders and priests would have had food provided for them, but now suppliers are gone and everyone must fend for themselves. Thus the priests leave the temple and the elders leave the city gate to seek food with the rest of the citizens (cf. v. 11).

v. 20 ר/*rêš* If the audience have been wondering whether Jerusalem has given up hope in YHWH when she turned from him to the passers-by (1:12), they need wonder no longer. For the third time she cries, "Look YHWH!" (cf. 1:9; 1:11) and the remaining three verses of the poem are a prayer directed to God. Even though she has no one to comfort her, there is nowhere else she can turn if she wants to see a reversal in her situation. House points out the play on words in the poem in which the Hebrew word used here for "distress" (צר/*ṣar*) sounds and looks almost identical to the word used elsewhere for "adversary" (צר/*ṣār*): "one is reminded that the foe and the pain are nearly identical."[73] The psychological impact of the trauma is depicted in graphic expressions: her bowels churn or boil, and her heart is overturned within her. The word מעה/*mēʿeh*, here translated "bowels," is a general word that can refer to the stomach, the womb, the inner parts, and is sometimes conceived as the seat of the emotions. Her bowels are in an agitated state — they ferment (Ps 75:8), boil, or foam (Ps 46:3). The picture is of extreme emotional distress. This is reinforced by the image of the heart (the seat of the understanding but also used to indicate emotions) turned upside down inside her.

The reason for her psychological suffering is said to be her rebellion

---

73. House, *Lamentations*, 363.

against YHWH (if we take כי/*kî* as causative). We should not suppose that she feels the inner pain because the thought of her sin so grieves her, but rather that her sin led to the divine punishment of military defeat which in turn led to her deep pain. In *that* sense her rebellions cause her to feel distressed. House points out that the Hebrew for "I have been very rebellious" (מרו מריתי/*mārô mārîtî*) sounds like that just used to describe her foaming/fermenting/churning (חמרמרו/*ḥŏmarmārû*) bowels.

Line 3 returns to the human plight during the siege: there seems no place to escape the shadow of death. Outside the sword bereaves, and inside it is like death. The word שכלה/*šikkělâ* ("bereaves") is often used to designate the loss of children through death or miscarriage. Here Jerusalem's children are slaughtered by the enemy sword. The contrast between "outside" and "in the house" may mean "outside the city" and "inside the city," or "outside in the streets" and "inside in the house." There are parallel biblical and extrabiblical texts which contrast distress inside and outside of a city. Thus Ezek 7:15 speaks of the sword outside the city and famine inside the city. Jeremiah 14:18 also contrasts death by the sword for those outside the city and death by famine for those inside (see also Deut 32:25). The *Lamentation over the Destruction of Sumer and Ur* says, "Ur — inside it is death, outside it is death, Inside it we die of famine, outside it we are killed by the weapons of Elamites."[74] These parallels suggest that this verse in Lamentations depicts the siege in which death by the sword faced those outside the protection of the city, but even within the walls death (in the form of famine or plague?) also ravaged the people.

v. 21 ש/*šîn*–v. 22 ת/*tāw* Someone has heard her groaning (cf. the groaning priests in 1:4 and the groaning, hungry people in 1:11) and realized that she had no comforter. This fifth and final repeat of the no-comforter theme (cf. 1:2, 9, 16, 17) ensures that it is seared onto the readers' consciousness. It is not clear from line 1 who the hearers are, but could it be that now "they" will take on the role of comforter? If such hopes have been raised, they are dashed in line 2. The "they" who heard her distress turn out to be her enemies, and their response was to rejoice at what YHWH had done (which need not suggest that they were aware that it was YHWH who did it). Rejoicing at the misfortune of others was reprehensible (Prov 17:5; 24:17; Job 31:29). In situations like this, rejoicing in God's powerful works is grossly inappropriate. Zion has been clear throughout her speech that her calamity, that in which her enemies rejoice, is *YHWH's* work and indeed a day that he had announced with advanced warnings. She had not heeded God's warnings, so now she acknowl-

---

74. *ANET*, 618, lines 403-4.

edges before the Lord that he did indeed bring about the day he announced. This again refers to the Day of YHWH theology alluded to in 1:12 and drawn from the prophetic literature (Isa 2:12; Amos 5:18; Zeph 1:14-18, etc.). But the agents of God's wrath are not acting in righteousness, and by their cruel behavior they themselves become subject to divine anger. Thus Zion, perhaps recalling the universal scope of the Day of YHWH (Isa 13–23; Jer 46–51; Amos 1:3–2:3), either declares that "they will become as I am" or, more likely in this context, prays, "May they become like I am." This is more than a cry for vengeance — it is a call for justice; for evil people to be punished for their sin. Renkema writes, "her prayer . . . is an appeal to YHWH's just and righteous behaviour. Secondly, she does not call for punishment on the enemy detached from the context of her own situation. The true intention of her prayer is not revenge against the enemy but her own liberation. She longs to be set free from the unbearable distress in which her enemies have submerged her."[75]

Having explained that her enemies heard of her "misfortune" (רעתי/ $r\bar{a}\hat{a}t\hat{i}$), now the same word (רעה/$r\bar{a}\hat{a}$) is used to ask YHWH to pay attention to their evil (רעתם/$r\bar{a}\hat{a}t\bar{a}m$). This suggests that their evil is organically linked to her calamity. Justice demands that YHWH deal with the enemies according to their deeds, just as he dealt with Jerusalem according to her deeds. And as Jerusalem's deeds merited harsh treatment, so too do the deeds of her enemies. Notice that there is no attempt to plead her innocence. Rather, she calls for God to notice *all* evils and not merely *her* evils.

But this is a prayer for the future. For now the enemies seem to have prospered, and Jerusalem cannot stop groaning (cf. 1:21); indeed her heart is sick (cf. 1:20). It is worth noting that there could well be a subtle link with v. 1 here. The city was once "great with people" and "great among the nations" (1:1), and now she is literally "great with groans" (1:22). This groaning has been a constant noise throughout the poem (1:4, 8, 11, 21, 22), perhaps reminding readers of Israel's groaning when in Egyptian captivity (Exod 2:23). But while God heard the groaning of those in Egypt, this poem ends without any assurance that he has heard Jerusalem's groaning. The כי/$k\hat{i}$ ("for") that introduces "many are my groans, and my heart is faint" indicates that if YHWH was to punish her enemies it would bring relief to her. The poem then simply stops without any closure, any comforter, or any answer from YHWH. "In the silence that follows the final taw of the alphabet . . . the powerful and haunting presence of Jerusalem ultimately remains unrelieved and unvanquished, as if immune to all forms of incantation."[76]

---

75. Renkema, *Lamentations*, 198.
76. Dobbs-Allsopp, *Lamentations*, 75.

LAMENTATIONS 2: WRATH

v. 1 א/'ālep
> Alas! The Lord, in his anger, covers in cloud
>> Daughter Zion.
> He cast from heaven [to] earth,
>> the splendor of Israel,
> and did not remember his footstool
>> in a day of his anger.

v. 2 ב/bêt
> The Lord swallowed up without compassion
>> all the countryside of Jacob.
> He smashed in his fury
>> the fortifications of Daughter Judah.
> He brought down to the ground [and] defiled
>> the kingdom and its princes.

v. 3 ג/gîmel
> He cut down in the heat of anger
>> every horn of Israel.
> He turned back his right hand
>> from the face of an enemy.
> And he burned in Jacob like a flaming fire,
>> burning up all around.

v. 4 ד/dālet
> He bends his bow like an enemy.
>> He poised his right hand like a foe.
> And he killed all who were precious to the eye
>> in [the] tent of Daughter Zion.
> He poured out like fire
>> his anger.

v. 5 ה/hê
> Adonai was like an enemy:
>> he swallowed up Israel,
> he swallowed up all her[1] citadels,

---

1. Presumably "her" refers to Zion and "his" refers to the whole land of Israel.

he destroyed his fortifications,
and he multiplied in Daughter Zion,
    moaning and mourning.

v. 6 ו/*wāw*

He acted violently against his booth like [in] the garden;[2]
    He destroyed his assembly/festival.
YHWH caused to be forgotten in Zion
    festival and Sabbath.
And he has spurned in his cursing anger
    king and priest.

v. 7 ז/*zayin*

The Lord rejected his altar,
    he destroyed his Sanctuary.
He handed over to an enemy
    the walls of her citadels.
They gave voice in the house of YHWH
    like on a festival day.

v. 8 ח/*ḥêt*

YHWH planned to destroy
    the wall of Daughter Zion.
He stretched out a line,
    he did not draw back his hand from consuming.
And he caused rampart and wall to mourn;
    together they were exhausted.

---

2. 2:6a literally says that "he has demolished his booth like the garden" but this is problematic. The point is that God destroyed his tent as easily as one may destroy a garden. It may be that God destroyed the temple and thus it became like a garden (flattened and not lived in). Berlin suggests a reference to the garden of Eden with all its temple associations and Sodom, which was "like the garden" (Gen 13:10). Thus, "God destroyed his once lovely temple (= Eden) as he destroyed the once gardenlike (or Eden-like) Sodom"; *Lamentations*, 70. However, all these explanations are awkward — it is difficult to make sense of the MT as it stands. Albrektson, followed by Renkema, suggests that a ב/*b* ("in") has dropped out of the text so the original was כבגן/*kĕbaggan*, "like *in* the garden," meaning that God has destroyed his temple just as if it were a temporary garden hut. Berlin suggests that there was a second "booth" which has dropped out of the text: "he destroyed his booth like the garden *booth*"; *Lamentations*, 66.

v. 9 ט/ṭêt

> Her gates sank down into the ground,
>> He destroyed and smashed her bars.
> Her king and her princes are among the nations,
>> there is no instruction.
> Even her prophets could not find
>> a vision from the Lord.

v. 10 י/yôd

> They are sitting down on the ground in stunned silence,
>> the elders of Daughter Zion.
> They put dust on their heads,
>> they dressed in sackcloth.
> They (fem.) press their heads to the ground,
>> the maidens of Jerusalem.

v. 11 כ/kāp

> My eyes were worn out from tears,
>> My stomach churned,
> My liver bile was poured out on the ground
>> because of the destruction of the daughter of my people,
> When a child and a suckling baby grow weak
>> in the town squares.

v. 12 ל/lāmed

> To their mothers they are saying,
>> "Where is grain and the wine?"
> As they faint like those fatally wounded
>> in the city squares;
> as they are pouring out their lives
>> in the bosom of their mothers.

v. 13 מ/mêm

> What can I testify to you? What can I liken to you,
>> Daughter Jerusalem?
> What can I compare to you so that I can comfort you,
>> Maiden Daughter Zion?
> For as vast as the sea is your destruction.
>> Who can heal you?

v. 14 נ/*nûn*

> Your prophets prophesied to you
>> falsehood and folly,
> and they did not reveal your iniquity
>> to reverse your captivity;
> and they prophesied to you false oracles
>> and deceptions.

v. 15 ס/*sāmek*

> They clapped hands against you,
>> all those who passed by.
> They whistled and shook their heads
>> because of Daughter Jerusalem.
> "Is this the city of which they said, 'Perfection of beauty,
>> the joy of all the earth?'"

v. 16 פ/*pê*

> They opened their mouth against you,
>> all your enemies.
> They whistled and they ground teeth.
>> They said, "We consumed.
> Indeed, this is the day that we hoped for.
>> We have found [it]! We have seen [it]!"

v. 17 ע/'*ayin*

> YHWH did what he had purposed;
>> He carried out his utterance,
>> what he commanded from days of old.
> He broke down and did not have compassion.
>> And an enemy rejoiced over you;
>> He exalted the horn of your foes.

v. 18 צ/*ṣādê*

> Their heart cried out to the Lord:
>> Wall of Daughter Zion,[3]

---

3. Is "Wall of Daughter Zion" a parallel expression for "the Lord" (i.e., they called to the Lord, [who is] the wall of Daughter Zion), or is it the actual wall, representing the whole city, which is called to weep because they (whoever "they" are) cried out to the Lord? I tentatively follow the latter route.

Pour down tears like a torrent,
    by day and by night!
Do not give yourself rest!
    Do not let the daughter of your eyes be still!

v. 19 ק/*qôp*

Arise! Cry aloud in the night
    at the beginning of night watches!
Pour out your heart like water
    in front of the presence of the Lord!
Lift up your hands to him
    for the life of your children
    fainting from hunger
    on every street corner!

v. 20 ר/*rêš*

See, YHWH, and observe
    who it is that you have dealt with severely here.[4]
Should women eat their offspring,
    the children of [their] care?
Should, in the sanctuary of the Lord, be killed
    priest and prophet?

v. 21 שׁ/*šîn*

They lay down on the ground outside,
    young and old.
My maidens and my young men
    fell by the sword.
You have killed in a day of your anger,
    You have slaughtered without mercy.

v. 22 ת/*tāw*

You invite, like on a festival day,
    my terrors from all around.
And there was not, on a day of YHWH's anger,
    an escapee or a survivor.
Those whom I nursed and reared,
    my enemy consumed.

4. Or "Who have you dealt with harshly here?" or "Who have you ever treated like this?"

Structure

The second poem falls neatly into thee main sections as the subsequent exegesis will show: the narrator's description of God's demolition of Zion (2:1-10), the narrator's emotional reaction to Zion's calamity (2:11-19), and Zion's protest against God (2:20-22).

I. The Narrator Describes God's Destructive Anger Against Zion (2:1-10)
   1. 2:1-5 A collage of "the Day of his Anger"
      (a) God's violence against the temple (2:1)
      (b) God's violence against the countryside of Jacob (2:2a)
      (c) God's violence against the fortresses of Judah (2:2b)
      (d) God's destruction of the kingdom and its officials (2:2c)
      (e) God's destruction of Israel's army and Jacob (2:3)
      (f) God the enemy archer (2:4)
      (g) God's violence against the palaces and strongholds of Zion (2:5)
   2. 2:6-7 God's violence against the temple in Jerusalem
   3. 2:8-9a God's violence against the walls and gates of Jerusalem
   4. 2:9b-10 The desolation of Jerusalem's people (king, rulers, [priests], prophets, elders, maidens)
II. The Narrator Reacts to Zion's Destruction (2:11-19)
   1. 2:11-12 The narrator expresses his grief at the suffering of Zion's children
   2. 2:13-17 The narrator speaks to Zion of her pain
      (a) 2:13 His astonishment at the incomparable depth of her pain
      (b) 2:14 The failure of the prophets to expose her sin and thus avert disaster
      (c) 2:15-16 The cruel mockery of the passers-by and the enemy
      (d) 2:17 YHWH has done this as he purposed to
   3. 2:18-19 The narrator calls Zion to cry out to YHWH in prayer
III. Zion's Prayer of Protest (2:20-22)

The same two speakers (the narrator and Jerusalem) reappear as the voices of the second poem,[5] but the focus shifts from Zion's calamity to *YHWH as the*

---

5. Not all concede that theirs are the *only* two voices. The narrator certainly speaks in 2:1-10 and Jerusalem in 2:20-22. The questions concern (a) whether the speaker that expresses sorrow at Jerusalem's suffering (2:11-12) is the narrator (the majority view), Lady Jerusalem herself

cause of that calamity. The poem opens (2:1c) and closes (2:22b) with reference to the day of YHWH's wrath. These references form an inclusio, and the rest of the poem fills out the meaning and implications of that dreadful "day." If one word could sum up YHWH's disposition to Zion in chapter 2, it is "anger" (2:1, 2, 3, 4, 6) — an anger which motivates violent destruction.

Like Lamentations 1 and 4, chapter 2 opens with "Alas!" (איכה/'êkâ), and like chapter 1 it employs the *qinah* meter. Chapter 2, like chapter 1, does not conform to a pure form but is composed of elements from the dirge (e.g., the cry איכה/'êkâ, the reversal motif) and the lament (e.g., the accusation against God, the complaint about the enemies).

2:1-10 is *akin to* the "accusation against God" element found in laments.[6] This implicit "accusation" seems to align the narrator's speech here with Zion's first main speech in chapter 1 (1:12-16).[7] In Lamentations 1 the narrator was most reluctant to speak of God as Zion's attacker, leaving such talk to Zion herself. Now he makes up for that with a vengeance! There is a subtle but clear shift in his stance towards Jerusalem's plight in this poem. The first ten verses make God the subject of a "litany of anti-praise"[8] that designates him as Israel's brutal aggressor. Indeed, YHWH is the only actor on the stage in vv. 1-8. While the narrator does not explicitly accuse God of wrongdoing in 2:1-10, the tone of the language here seems to teeter upon the edge of such an accusation.[9] In its final form this poem is to be read in the light of the first, and so her sins are presupposed but they are not in focus.

The physical buildings of Jerusalem form a major focus of 2:1-10: the outer and inner walls, the palaces, the fortifications, the gates, the dwellings, and the temple itself. These beautiful, strong and towering structures are brought crashing to the earth. God is the great demolisher of Jerusalem, deconstructing his city piece by piece as the verses progress. The movement throughout the verses is a downwards one — YHWH brings everything from buildings to people down *towards the ground.*

(Renkema, *Lamentations*, 267), or YHWH (Gerstenberger, *Psalms, Part 2*, 487-88), and (b) whether the speaker who addresses Jerusalem directly (2:13-19) is the narrator or a new speaker. House sees three speakers: the narrator (2:1-10), the prophet Jeremiah (2:11-19), Lady Jerusalem (2:20-22); *Lamentations*, 375. There is no good reason not to take the simplest view: that the Jeremiah-like narrator is speaking throughout 2:1-19.

6. Westermann sees 2:1-9a as an accusation against God; *Lamentations*, 149. The section differs from the conventional "accusation" in that it is *about* God and not directed *to* God.

7. Rightly Linafelt (*Surviving Lamentations*, 49, 52) and O'Connor (*Lamentations and the Tears of the World*, 35-41), although both, in my view, overplay the shift.

8. O'Connor, *Lamentations and the Tears of the World*, 33.

9. Against House, who sees 2:1-10 as purely "theological description" with no overtones of accusation; *Lamentations*, 373.

The Narrator Describes God's
Destructive Anger Against Zion (2:1-10)

v. 1 א/*'ālep*   As with chapter 1, this poem too opens with the mournful cry, "Alas" (איכה/*'êkâ*)! The verse begins and ends with references to YHWH's anger, the reason for the cry. If we have understood the verb in line 1 aright, then Daughter Zion is covered in darkness as YHWH wraps her in a cloud.

> As a storm god, God's theophany is manifested amidst the dark clouds associated with thunderstorms (Exod. 13:21-22; 19:16-19; 1 Kgs. 8:10-11; Ps. 78:14) and as warrior God either is enwrapped in clouds (2 Sam. 22:12, 13; Ps. 97:2; Lam. 3:44), rides upon clouds through the skies (2 Sam. 22:11-12; Ps. 68:4, 33; 104:3), or is otherwise associated with clouds (Judg. 5:4). And thus aptly, Joel (2:2) and Zephaniah (1:15) refer to the "Day of the LORD" as "a day of densest cloud," . . . and Ezekiel (30:18) envisions it as a time when "the city shall be covered by a cloud."[10]

The image may symbolize God's awesome presence in judgment and also God's severing of the link between heaven and earth by hiding himself from Zion behind the cloud (cf. Lam 3:44).[11] This breakdown in the link between heaven and earth is developed in the following images with probable reference to the temple. "The splendor/beauty of Israel" most likely refers to the sanctuary in Jerusalem.[12] The text says that this splendor has been cast out of heaven, but in what sense was the Jerusalem temple ever in heaven? In the ancient Near East temples were perceived as the link point between heaven and earth, the visible and the invisible dimensions of reality. The ancient mythology of the holy mountain with its temple peak, the dwelling place of the gods, in the heavens was appropriated by Israel and applied to Mount Zion (Ps 48:1). Temples were seen as holy space where the dividing wall between heaven and earth blurred and thinned. As such it seems from this verse that the Jerusalem tem-

---

10. Dobbs-Allsopp, *Lamentations*, 80.

11. Alternatively, it may be that the cloud symbolizes YHWH's presence, but, unlike with the exodus generation, it is his presence in anger.

12. Other suggestions for the referent of the "splendor of Israel" include the ark of the covenant, the *whole* city (cf. Isa 13:19), the *king* of Israel, and Israel as a nation. The parallel with God's footstool would suggest either the temple (Ps 99:5; 132:7; Ez 43:7) or the ark (1 Chr 28:2). The ark, however, was possibly gone by 587 B.C. (Jer 3:16, though see Renkema, *Lamentations*, 219-21) and focus in this chapter on the destruction of the temple suggests that it is the referent. The mention in the first line of Daughter Zion with its focus on Jerusalem-as-cultic-center reinforces the temple focus. Even if the footstool is the ark, it functions to represent (by synecdoche) the temple as a whole.

ple was pictured as, in some sense, coexisting *in heaven itself.* Perhaps we are to envisage the temple on earth as linked with a temple in heaven such that rituals taking place in the Jerusalem temple are mirrored in the heavenly temple. That is, until YHWH hurled it out of heaven and down to the earth breaking the connections. There could also be echoes of a mythical fall motif here such as we find in Isa 14:12 and Ezek 28:14-17. Perhaps we could even say that Israel itself, in the person of its high priest, has been cast out of heaven because the temple link has been broken. It is no longer the place where YHWH's presence dwells, no longer the link point between heaven and earth. The dirgelike reversal motif from the first poem is with us again.

God is pictured as a king sitting on his throne in heaven with his feet resting on a stool. This stool is the ark of the covenant or the temple where his feet touch the earth (Ps 99:5; 132:7). This image was one way of trying to grasp the idea that God truly dwells in the temple but the temple cannot contain him (cf. 1 Kgs 8:27). It also communicates the idea of the temple as a place where heaven and earth meet and where YHWH reigned (Ps 11:4). The shocking point in 2:1 is that this king has disregarded his own footstool! This all happened on "a day of his anger," an allusion to the Day of YHWH theology that we have already encountered in the first poem.

v. 2 ב/*bêt* Each of the lines in verse 2 opens with a verb with Adonai as its subject ("he swallowed up," "he smashed," "he made to touch") and ends with an identification of the object of his aggression. The three lines set out the wide-ranging impact of God's anger against his people and the focus becomes more narrow with each one. The first target is "all the countryside of Jacob" which perhaps represents the rural population (the majority of people in Israel and Judah). The second target is the "fortifications of Daughter Judah" which would be all the fortified cities down in the Southern Kingdom (e.g., Lachish and Azekah) including Jerusalem. The third target is more specific still — the royal house and leadership of Judah. Against all these targets Adonai has acted violently. He *swallowed up* the countryside, he *smashed* in his fury the fortifications, he has *defiled* (Ps 89:39) and *brought to the ground* the rulers. Indeed he acted "without compassion" sparing none from the destruction. The focus is clearly on the manifestation of wrath and its impact and not on the reasons for it.

v. 3 ג/*gîmel* The horn symbolized the strength, power, and pride of a people (e.g., Jer 48:25; Ps 75:10; 112:9; 1 Sam 2:1). God, in his wrath, now chops off all that was strong and mighty about Jacob. Perhaps the Israelite military forces or the Davidic king (Ps 89:24; 132:17) are in mind. Line 2 clarifies that this was done through the work of an enemy. YHWH, in days gone by, had protected his people in battle by "stretching out his hand" against the enemy (e.g., Ps 10:12; 17:13-14; 89:13). Now this protection is removed and YHWH's right hand is pulled back, allowing the enemy to triumph. The focus then shifts away from the enemy back to YHWH again, who burns with theophanic flames (Exod 19:18; 2 Sam 22:9, 13), devouring all that surrounds him in Jacob. Paul House suggests that the imagery in 2:3 may draw on the covenant curse language in Deut 29:22-23, which describes a land burned out by YHWH's wrath.[13] Iain Provan suggests a reversal of the exodus story in which God was present in fire for Israel's blessing (Exod 13:21-22) and his right hand was much in evidence for their salvation (Exod 15:6, 12). Now his hand is withdrawn and the fire consumes.[14]

v. 4 ד/*dālet* YHWH now takes on the role of an enemy archer (Ps 7:13) — he is twice named as enemy in this verse. F. W. Dobbs-Allsopp comments, "That a Judean poet could call God 'enemy' is a telling sign of the deep distress and unparalleled suffering brought on by the catastrophe."[15] Picturing a deity with a bow and arrow was not uncommon in the ancient Near East. YHWH, the divine warrior, now fights *against* Israel. First, he readied himself by putting the arrow in place and bending his bow (2:4a). Then, he took aim, setting his right hand — the hand that held the arrow — in place (2:4a). Then he fired the arrow and killed "all who were precious to the eye" (2:4b). Ready ... Aim ... Fire![16] YHWH has not merely withdrawn his protective hand but actually turns his hand against his people. For the first time in Poem 2 it becomes clear that people, and not simply buildings, have been destroyed by God. Those "precious to the eye" are presumably people who are valued (cf. 1 Kgs 20:6; Ezek 24:16), but it is no longer clear *precisely* who they were (apart from the fact that they were among God's people) or to whom they were precious (God? the people? Zion?). Most likely they are the people beloved by the citizens of Zion, possibly the children. The location of this slaughter is "the tent of Daughter Zion."[17] This may refer to Jerusalem (Isa 33:20; 54:2) or to the temple (Ps 15:1; 27:5; 61:4; 78:60).

Johan Renkema connects the archer image with the final line about God's anger poured out like fire by means of the theophanic tradition in

---

13. House, *Lamentations*, 378.

14. Provan, *Lamentations*, 62.

15. Dobbs-Allsopp, *Lamentations*, 83.

16. Pham, *Mourning in the Ancient Near East*, 123.

17. Assuming that "in the tent of Daughter Zion" does not belong with the following line instead.

which YHWH's arrows are bolts of lightning (2 Sam 22:15; Ps 18:14; 144:6; Hab 3:11; Zech 9:14). Thus YHWH's fire-arrows set Zion ablaze.[18] Alternatively, perhaps this image of pouring out fire is unconnected to the archer image. Perhaps the literal fires lit in the city by the Babylonians inspired the image. God is the ultimate source of the flames that consumed Jerusalem.

v. 5 ה/*hê* The focus of 2:5 is that the *whole* of Israel has been "swallowed up" by the Lord, and the verse acts as a summary of vv. 1-4, reusing several key words and phrases ("like an enemy" in 2:4a, "he swallowed up" in 2:2a, "fortifications" in 2:2b). House points out that in the covenant curses in Leviticus 26 and Deuteronomy 28 God says that he himself will fight against his disobedient people through their enemies (Lev 26:17, 25, 34, 36-41; Deut 28:25, 31, 68). He says, in effect, that *he* will become their enemy if they persist in covenant violation. This is exactly what has now happened. God was the sure defense of Zion's citadels (Ps 48:3), but now he himself destroys them. Zion's citadels and the fortified cities across all Israel are totally decimated. The defensive walls of the cities were no match against YHWH. Thus God has multiplied sadness and mourning across Judah.

v. 6 ו/*wāw* YHWH destroyed *his own* booth (i.e., the temple). Just as one may tear down a temporary booth set up in the fields[19] after the harvest is over, so YHWH has violently demolished his tent. By so doing he has brought worship to an end. The choice of the word שכו/*śukkô*, "his booth," may serve a dual purpose. On the one hand, it refers to the temple (an allusion to the tent of meeting from the wilderness years; Ps 27:5; 76:2); on the other, it may suggest that the Festival of Booths has been brought to an end. A similar wordplay is found in the dual usage of מועד/*mô'ēd*. In line 1 it probably means "appointed place" (i.e., the temple). God has destroyed the place where his people met to worship. In line 2 it refers to the religious festivals that took place at the temple (Deut 16:1-17). By destroying his assembly place (מועדו/*mô'ădô*) God has caused festival (מועד/*mô'ēd*) and Sabbath (Lev 26:34-35) to be forgotten. They cannot be observed in the current crisis. In these ways the verse ties the loss of the temple very closely to its implications for worship and hence for Israel's ability to maintain its relationship with God. The loss of the temple and the loss of worship threatened Israel's covenant life with YHWH.

18. Renkema, *Lamentations*, 233-35.

19. The booths allowed people to watch over crops and guard them from theft or rain (Isa 1:8; Jonah 4:5; Job 27:18).

Not only the temple but king (the representative of the nation) and priest (the temple personnel) have also been spurned by YHWH. It is implied that YHWH's rejection of king and priest is consequent upon their prior rejection of him. In context the king is probably referred to because of his links with the temple.[20] The holy city of Jerusalem, the temple that God established for his worship, the divinely-appointed festivals and Sabbaths, the Davidic king God had set in place, the Levitical priests the Lord commanded to serve him — all rejected! This was the end of the world.

v. 7 ז/*zayin* The altar was a fundamental part of the temple, perhaps the most fundamental part. Here the sacrifices were offered to YHWH. But this altar with its atoning sacrifices is now rejected and the whole sanctuary complex is destroyed. To many in the ancient world the destruction of YHWH's temple was proof that he was not as strong as the gods of the invaders. But the poet is emphatic that weakness on God's part was not the reason for the loss of the sanctuary — *Adonai himself* lay behind the destruction of his temple.

The palaces mentioned by the poet probably, in this context, refer to the royal palaces that were linked to the temple complex. As priest and king were connected in the previous verse, now the temple and the royal palace are linked. Both theologically and architecturally, temple and palace were conjoined. The walls of the palaces are handed over to the enemy. This enemy then entered the house of YHWH and uttered cries of joy just like on a festival day. But this was a cruel parody of a festival. These pagan invaders are forbidden to enter the temple (1:10), and they enter to desecrate and destroy. This pseudofestival is what brought the genuine festivals in Zion to a halt (1:10b). It was, in a cruelly ironic sense, the festival to end all festivals.

v. 8 ח/*ḥêt* This destruction was no sudden divine loss of temper. God had made *a plan* (חשׁב/*ḥāšab*) at some point in the past to destroy the wall of his city. This decision was not inflexible, for, according to Jeremiah, God's destructive plan could have been averted if the people had repented (Jer 26:3; 36:3). They did not, and it was not.

Most commentators take קו/*qāw* to refer to a measuring line used in building work. Whatever God measured in the city with the line was consumed (lit., "swallowed up" — the same word used in 2:2a, 5a-b) by his hand.

---

20. David brought the ark to Jerusalem and offered sacrifices before it. It was his plan to build the temple in the first place. Solomon, his son, built and dedicated the temple. Renkema also points out that the "temple in Jerusalem was a state sanctuary and the priests were in the king's service. . . . Priests could be appointed or removed by the king (cf I Kgs 2₂₇, ₃₅), indeed the king bore responsibility for the sanctuary (cf II Kgs. 12₄*ff*; 22₃*ff*)"; *Lamentations*, 243.

Presumably the measuring line found the walls of the city wanting and hence marked for destruction by the hand of God (cf. 2 Kgs 21:13; Amos 7:7-9).[21] God is pictured here not as a builder but as a demolition man. The idea of the hand swallowing up things is a way of picturing the sheer (metaphorical) size of God's hand — it encompasses whole sections of the city and crushes them to rubble. The consuming hand caused the personified city defenses (the outer rampart wall and inner wall) to loudly mourn and collapse together in exhaustion. With the loss of the walls comes the loss of protection against the foe.

Dobbs-Allsopp sees an allusion to ancient Mesopotamian sanctuary-razing ceremonies. When an old temple was due for a rebuild or renovation, the old walls had to be demolished. A ceremony was held, offerings were made, and the city laments were sung in front of the old temple. All this was done to pacify the god whose temple was being destroyed. The walls were then pulled down.[22] In this city lament it is *the god himself,* YHWH, who destroys the walls, and his anger is certainly not placated! Mesopotamian city laments looked forward to rebuilding and restoration after the demolition. It is not at all clear whether 2:8 holds out such hope.

v. 9 ט/*ṭêt* The lament over the destruction of the city walls concludes in 2:9a, where the gates of the city sink down into the ground, along with the exhausted walls. The bars that locked the gates have been smashed to pieces by God (presumably by means of the battering ram of the foe). With the loss of the gates, not only is a key focus of the life of the community gone but also the last defense against the foe.

2:9b moves on to consider the exile of the king and the princes, who now dwell among the nations (cf. 1:3). In 1:6 the princes were on the run from their pursuers, but escape was impossible. Now they have been taken captive. It is possible that the comment that "there is no instruction/law" is intended to refer to the nations where the king and leaders have been exiled. The point would then be that they are forced to live in a place where God's law is not honored. However, in the light of 2:9c it is more likely that the loss of leadership has led to a loss of *tôrâ* instruction in Judah. While it was not the king's place to provide *tôrâ* instruction, the king was closely associated with the priests (cf. 2:6c), whose task that was. It was the loss of the temple that crippled the priests' ability to teach people God's law because it removed the place where people gathered to hear such instruction. The He-

21. Or perhaps YHWH was measuring the walls so as to destroy them properly.
22. Dobbs-Allsopp, *Lamentations*, 86.

brew indicates the *ongoing* nature of the leaders' exile and the ongoing lack of *tôrâ* instruction. Even the prophets did not get visions from YHWH. There is a loss of both civic (king and rulers) and religious (implicitly priests, and explicitly prophets) leadership. It is theologically interesting that the divine judgment manifests itself *in divine silence.* The God who speaks to his people through *tôrâ* and through prophet becomes quiet, and it is a deathly quiet. This judgment of silence is manifest in the book of Lamentations as a whole, in which YHWH is the one actor that the implied reader is desperate to hear speak, and thus YHWH's lack of voice is very conspicuous. In this way Lamentations embodies the ongoing judgment by means of the words it does *not* contain.

v. 10 י/yôd The first section of chapter 2 closes with an image of the elders of Daughter Zion lifting the earth up to their heads while the maidens of Jerusalem bring their heads down to the earth. Here we see old (elders) and young (maidens), men and women stricken by grief. The poet quite likely intends these groups to represent the whole population remaining in the city. The elders show their grief in the time-honored way — sitting on the ground (like Zion in 1:1), wearing sackcloth, pouring dust on their heads (Josh 7:6; 1 Sam 4:12; 2 Sam 1:2; 15:32; Ezek 27:28-31; Job 2:12-13; 16:15). It is possible that sitting on the ground and putting dust on the head are symbolically linking the mourners with the dead buried in the dust of the earth. They sit in stunned silence (cf. Job 2:13): like the priests and prophets in the previous verse, they have no word of wisdom to offer. The maidens who have not been exiled (cf. 1:18) lower their heads to the ground in mourning — a reversal of their cultic function of joyful praise (cf. 1:4c). The verse emphasizes a theme which has run through the chapter — that of descent to the earth: the "splendor of Israel" has been hurled "from heaven *[to] earth*" (2:1b), the kingdom and its rulers have been "brought down *to the earth*" (2:2c), Zion's gates have "sunk down *into the earth*" (2:9a). Now the elders sit down (lit.) "*to the earth*" (2:10a), and the maidens lower their heads "*to the earth*" (2:10c). In this way, as Dobbs-Allsopp notes, Zion's citizens suffer the same fate as the city: they are humiliated and brought low.

The Narrator Reacts to Zion's Destruction (2:11-19)

v. 11 כ/kāp–v. 12 ל/lāmed The poem now moves from describing Jerusalem's crisis in the third person to first person comments directed at the reader (2:11-12). Nancy Lee has argued that the language here, being so very close to language in Jeremiah, must be intended to identify the narrator *as* Jeremiah.[23] She points out that (a) the personal expression of weeping is typical of Jeremiah (Jer 9:1; 13:17; 14:17); (b) in Jeremiah's weeping passages in 8:19–9:1 and 14:17 he uses the terms "eyes," "weep," and the expression "daughter of my people"; (c) he uses the expression "my inward parts" in Jer 4:9. House also points out, following Carl F. Keil, that (d) "the destruction of the daughter of my people" is also a phrase found in Jeremiah 6:14; 8:11, 21.[24] This case is plausible and, at very least, readers should understand the narrator as Jeremiahlike.

The narrator has moved from a more detached observer role to a fully engaged one where he emotionally identifies with Jerusalem.[25] This emotional turmoil at the fate of the people as the covenant curses are inflicted by YHWH is akin to Jeremiah's. The grief he feels at Zion's destruction impacts him at a deep psycho-physical level. He weeps and weeps (like Zion in 1:16) until he is exhausted, his bowels churn (like Zion's in 1:20), and liver bile is poured out "towards the earth" (perhaps he is vomiting).[26] In this way he participates in the earthward movements discussed in the comments on 2:10. The narrator laments with the personified city itself: "The scream of Zion has, almost literally, become the scream of the poet."[27]

The new element introduced at this point in Lamentations is the suffering of the children, who are clearly growing weak through starvation. They request food and drink[28] from their mothers but they have empty hands and empty breasts (starvation has meant that their own breast milk has dried up). The older children fall like the slain in the city plazas, and the babies die in the arms of their mothers, the place they should find succor and protection. The heart-rending image of mothers helplessly watching the slow deaths of their children is what moves the narrator so much.

v. 13 מ/*mêm*   Now the poet speaks *to* Lady Jerusalem (2:13-19) for the first time in the book. His words echo her words in 1:12, "Observe and see, whether

---

23. Lee, *The Singers of Lamentations*, 147-48.

24. See Keil, *Jeremiah, Lamentations*, 392.

25. So much so that Renkema thinks it *is* Lady Jerusalem (not the narrator) who speaks in 2:11-12; *Lamentations*, 268. Gerstenberger thinks that it is YHWH himself (*Psalms, Part 2*, 487-88) in a manner akin to Jer 4:19-22 and 6:11-12!

26. The bowels and liver were conceived of as the seat of the emotions.

27. Linafelt, *Surviving Lamentations*, 52.

28. On grain and wine, see Berlin, *Lamentations*, 72. Berlin argues that the request was for food that was stored for provisions rather than food that would not last (grain as opposed to bread and wine as opposed to juice). Such provisions had run out. It would not have been uncommon for children to have drunk diluted wine.

there is sorrow like my sorrow, which has been severely dealt out to me." His heart has increasingly opened up as he has observed her grief, and now "his words mirror back her reality to her and validate her own perceptions of her pain. . . . Perhaps if the narrator could find a comparable reality to her suffering, he would be able to limit it, contain it, somehow make it manageable, put limits around it, bind it off from infinity, and offer her comfort."[29] But he has come to perceive that Zion's sorrow is too vast to be compared with other sorrows. "What can I testify to [i.e., memorialize] [about this]?" Nothing. "What can I liken to you?" Nothing. "What can I compare to you?" Nothing. Language fails. Nothing this cataclysmic has *ever* happened before, and so it is beyond any such comparisons. The destruction is as vast as the sea — something which, for the poet, has no visible end and represents enormity of the decimation. The audience may recall Jer 19:10-11, in which YHWH says, "I will shatter this people" and "no one will be able to heal." The same vocabulary and concept are found in our text. When the narrator says that he wishes to comfort Zion in 2:13b, readers will also recall Zion's repeated calls for comfort in the first poem. Now those calls have at last found a willing response, but alas the poet *cannot* console Jerusalem and cannot serve as the comforter she needs because her shattering has gone beyond such things. It is implied that only God can act as her comforter now.

v. 14 נ/*nûn* The narrator has already told us that "her prophets could not find a vision from the Lord" (2:9c). He now returns to that theme and laments the failure of the prophets to expose Zion's iniquity. Instead, they prophesied "falsehood and folly [or, 'whitewash']," "false oracles and deceptions." The nature of the falsehood is not made clear, but it may indicate that the prophets did not warn Judah of the devastation that would follow their persistent disobedience. Had they done so they may have avoided the disaster. The reader may recall the very prominent theme in Jeremiah of the false prophets who say, "'Peace, peace,' when there is no peace" (Jer 6:14; 8:11; 14:13-22; 23:9-40; 27-29).[30] Alternatively, it may refer to the *present* failure of the prophets in the midst of the sorrow: they do not point Judah to the covenant way of living that could reverse their current plight. The verse may cover both past and present prophetic failures. What is clear is that, instead of exposing sin so that it could be dealt with, they just painted over it to hide it from view (cf. Ezek 13:10-16). It is important to mention that while the narrator's focus

---

29. O'Connor, *Lamentations and the Tears of the World*, 39, 38.

30. It is also clear that our verse is influenced by Ezek 13:10-14 in terms of content and vocabulary.

in the second poem is not Jerusalem's sin but her suffering, this verse makes clear that he has not withdrawn his earlier assessment of her behavior.

v. 15 ס/sāmek In the first poem Lady Jerusalem had called out to "all you who pass by" (1:12), presumably the surrounding nations, to observe and see her sorrow. In a disappointing twist we now learn that "all those who passed by" have indeed looked and have indeed seen, but instead of offering comfort they strike a shocked, and possibly even a hostile, mocking pose. In horror, and perhaps also derision, they "clap their hands against her" (Job 27:23), shake their heads, and whistle.

Psalm 48:2 says that Jerusalem, "beautiful in elevation, is *the joy of the whole earth.*" It is the presence of YHWH that gives Jerusalem this mythic and glorious status. The psalm then goes on to invite the hearers to walk about Zion, to number her towers, consider her ramparts, and go through her citadels (Ps 48:12-13). In Lamentations 2 those citadels lie in ruins, and the ramparts languish so the passers allude to Psalm 48 in amazement and perhaps in scorn: "Is this the city of which they said, 'Perfection of beauty [cf. Ps 50:2; Ezek 27:3, 4, 11; 28:12], the joy of all the land/earth' [cf. Jer 51:41]?" Jerusalem, the glory of the land of Israel and (eschatologically) of the whole earth, is reduced to rubble, and the old songs of Zion now serve to taunt her.

v. 16 פ/pê From the failure of the prophets and the lack of help coming from the shocked and possibly taunting passers-by, the narrator moves on to consider the overt hostility of the enemies who destroyed the city. His focus is on their mouths: they open their mouths against Zion in scorn (Ps 22:13; Job 16:10), they whistle (like the passers-by) in mockery, gnash their teeth in anger (Ps 35:16; 37:12; 112:10; Job 16:9), and celebrate their "swallowing" (בלענו/ billāʿĕnû) of Jerusalem. The swallowing is attributed to YHWH in 2:2, 5, 8, 16, but they do not realize that they have been his instrument for harm and attribute their victory to themselves. Destroying the city was, it seems, a long hoped for and eagerly anticipated ambition now finally realized and celebrated.

v. 17 ע/ʿayin The narrator steps back from observing the joyous taunts of the enemy to observe their deeds in theological perspective. They have been God's instruments in bringing about the judgment he planned (cf. 2:8) and spoke of from "days of old." This destruction is no unanticipated loss of temper by YHWH but a long prepared-for plan (Amos 5:18-20; Jer 4:28; 51:12). The narrator probably has the Mosaic covenant curses and the ongoing warnings of the preexilic prophets in mind. We need to appreciate that this divine plan for destruction was always conditional upon Israel's covenant rebellion and failure to repent. Repentance and obedience on Israel's part could have averted it. Repentance did not come, so YHWH implemented his plan: he "broke down and did not have compassion" (cf. 2:2a). It was *God* who not only "cut down in the heat of anger every horn of Israel" (2:3) but who also "exalted the horn of [Zion's] foes." The narrator asked in 2:13, "Who can heal you?" In 2:14 we saw that the prophets did not, in 2:15 that the passers-by could not, in 2:16 that the enemy would not, and now, in 2:17 that YHWH is himself the very one who inflicted the wound.

v. 18 צ/ṣādê–v. 19 ק/qôp   In vv. 18-19 the narrator's words to Zion reach an emotional climax as he urges Lady Jerusalem to call out to YHWH in prayer. The Lord who inflicted her deep wound is the only one able to heal it.

The first line of v. 18 is difficult because it is not clear whose heart cried out to the Lord. For this reason all sorts of emendations have been suggested. If we stick with the MT, then we need a candidate for those praying. Some suggest that the line refers to the collective people of Jerusalem and others that it refers to the suffering children of Jerusalem — *their* heart cried out to the Lord. צעק/ṣāʿaq means to cry out in distress, and the Hebrew Scriptures often portray YHWH as the one to whom such cries are directed (Exod 2:23; 3:7; Ps 107:6, 28). For instance, Exod 22:22 reads, "If you mistreat them [the sojourner], and they *cry out* to me, I will surely hear their cry." Because the citizens in general, or the suffering children in particular, are crying out, the narrator calls the city itself, represented by its wall, to weep without ceasing and without resting.[31] This is just too important to let God ignore it, so the narrator employs a chain of seven imperatives: pour down tears, do not give yourself rest, do not let the daughter of your eyes (i.e., your pupils) be still, arise, cry aloud, pour out your heart, lift up your hands to him. The sheer urgency and intensity of the call is unmistakable.

The night was divided into three four-hour watches, so the narrator urges Zion to cry out to God throughout the night at the beginning of each watch. She must set aside sleep and do whatever it takes to get the Lord's at-

---

31. House suggests that 2:18aii-c represents the words that the children cry out to the city and their parents; *Lamentations*, 391-92. I think this unlikely, not least because 2:18ai says that they cried to *the Lord*, not to the city or to their parents.

Some have suggested that the wall of Jerusalem in 2:18 *is* God himself (Zech 2:5) and not the physical wall (e.g., Gottwald, *Studies in the Book of Lamentations*, 11; Provan, *Lamentations*, 76). Indeed, Renkema sees 2:18aii as the words of the children's prayer to God — they cry out, "Rampart of daughter Zion!"; *Lamentations*, 311. This is possible, although elsewhere in this chapter the "wall" refers to the actual wall of Jerusalem (2:8). Either way, we need to read 2:18b-19c as addressed to Zion.

tention, and she must do it without ceasing. She must lift up hands in prayer (Ps 63:4; 141:2) and pour out her heart in his presence. The reason for the narrator's urgency is that the lives of the children in the city are at risk. They are already fainting from hunger on every street corner (Lam 2:11-12; cf. Jer 6:11; 9:20).

Zion's Prayer of Protest (2:20-22)

v. 20 ר/*rêš* Now Lady Jerusalem speaks for the first time in this poem, and her words form its explosive climax (2:20-22). She responds directly to the narrator's urgent call to prayer by repeating her cry of 1:11c, "See, YHWH, and observe!" The prayer that follows is not a prayer of confession (though she would not deny that she has sinned) but the strongest protest against God in the entire book. The undertone of anger and of accusation is hard to miss. However, we should not see the poem as a whole, nor this prayer in particular, as a rejection of God. Yes there is anger, and yes there is protest, but the narrator knows that Zion's only chance of salvation is with God and so he implores her to intercede. Zion herself does not abandon Adonai but continues to speak to him, trying to shock him into action. He may be her enemy at present, but she also knows that he is her only hope.

First Zion asks the Lord to consider *who it is* that he has dealt with so severely. The identity of the ones punished is not irrelevant to how she feels God should act. It is *his own* holy land, *his own* glorious city, *his own* sacred temple, *his own* Davidic king, *his own* priests and prophets, *his own* covenant people. Jerusalem's prayer does not spell all this out for God; she simply asks him to consider *whom* he has hurt so badly. She hopes that if God is compelled to recall his special relationship with this bleeding city he will be moved to heal. There is also an implicit accusation that to treat his people in this brutal way was not right and that the punishment has crossed a line that should not have been crossed.

Lady Zion then picks up on two specific examples of those YHWH has dealt with harshly: the children, and priests and prophets (1:4, 19; 2:6, 9, 14). She wants him to see the full consequences of his actions by highlighting these two situations. The narrator has asked her to plead for the children, so she does: Should women eat their own children? In a time of severe famine the natural order has broken down and people resort to terrible behavior to survive (Lev 26:29; Deut 28:53-57; 2 Kgs 6:26-30; Jer 19:9; Ezek 5:10). Whether we are to imagine that the women killed their children so as to eat them or, more likely, were forced to eat their dead children so as to survive themselves,

Zion's rhetorical question strikes home. Of course, they should not! The image is grotesque and shocking, and that is precisely what she intends it to be. The second example of the Lord's harsh treatment is the shocking scenario of YHWH's own priests and prophets killed in the holiest place in Israel, desecrating it. Zion asks, "Should this happen?" No!

v. 21 ש/šîn The death in Jerusalem has not discriminated between young and old (1:19; 2:10), female (1:4, 18; 2:10) and male (1:15, 18). Zion identifies YHWH as the one who has slaughtered without mercy on his day of anger. The motif of movement towards the earth is recapitulated yet again in the downward movement of young and old who lay down (lit.) "towards the earth" (cf. 2:1, 2, 9, 10a, 10c, 11). Again the motifs of YHWH's day of anger (cf. 1:12; 2:1, 6) and his lack of mercy (2:2, 17) reappear. This time he is said to have "slaughtered," a word used for the butchering of animals (e.g., 1 Sam 25:11). This may echo the cannibalism theme from the previous verse[32] — the mothers eat the children that YHWH has slaughtered for the "feast," and/or it may be that the people are sacrificial victims.

v. 22 ת/tāw Lady Zion now picks up the recurring theme of the enemies being like antipilgrims coming to celebrate an antifestival in Zion. In 1:15 YHWH has called a parody of a festival against Zion to break her young men, and in 2:7 the enemy shout in the temple as pilgrims shout at an appointed festival. Just as YHWH invited pilgrims to his feasts in Jerusalem, he now invites Zion's fears (i.e., the enemies that terrify her) from all around. The *genuine* religious festivals have ceased and the roads are empty of *real* pilgrims (1:4; 2:6), but to Zion's dismay YHWH has replaced them with aggressive substitutes and the sacrifices are her own populace (2:21)! The Jeremianic expression "terrors from all around" suggests that her worst nightmares have come true (Jer 6:25; 20:3; 20:10; 46:5; 49:29).

The reference to YHWH's day of anger (2:22b) serves to end the poem as it began (2:1a), enclosing the whole within the embrace of divine wrath. Zion now speaks of the utter devastation wrought by this heavenly anger in hyperbolic terms: there were *none* who escaped or survived. Her children have been utterly *consumed* by the enemy. The poet leaves it ambiguous whether the "enemy" referred to is YHWH or the human enemy. Either or both would be appropriate. With that comment on the death of the children that she "nursed and reared," Zion ends her prayer. God makes no immediate response.

---

32. Renkema, *Lamentations*, 326; Berlin, *Lamentations*, 76.

LAMENTATIONS 3: HOPE

vv. 1-3   א/ʾālep.

I am the man who has seen affliction
    from a rod of his fury.
[It was] me he drove and made to walk
    [into] darkness and not light.
Surely against me again and again he turns
    his hand all the day long.

vv. 4-6   ב/*bêt*

He made my flesh and my skin waste away,
    He shattered my bones.
He has besieged me and encircled [me]
    [with] poison and adversity.
In dark places he made me dwell,
    like those long dead.

vv. 7-9   ג/*gîmel*

He walled me up so I cannot get out,
    He made my chains heavy.
Even though I cry out and plead,
    He shut out my prayer.
He has walled off my ways with hewn stones,
    My paths he has twisted.

vv. 10-12   ד/*dālet*

A bear lying in wait is he to me,
    A lion in hiding places.
He forced me off my ways and tore me to pieces,
    He made me desolate.
He bent his bow and set me up,
    as the target for the arrow.

vv. 13-15   ה/*hê*

He has shot into my kidneys
    arrows from his quiver.
I was a laughingstock to all my people,[1]

---

1. A minority of Hebrew mss and the Syriac have "all peoples."

[the object of] their taunt songs all the day long.
He fed me full of bitterness,
He "satisfied" me with wormwood.

vv. 16-18 ו/*wāw*

He ground my teeth in gravel,
He pressed me into the dust.
My life was cast away from peace,[2]
I forgot everything good.
And I said, "He destroyed my future,
and my hope from YHWH!"

vv. 19-21 ז/*zayin*

Remember[3] my affliction and my wandering,
Wormwood and poison.
I recall [them] well[4]
and am downcast.[5]
This I remind my heart,
therefore I wait hopefully:

vv. 22-24 ח/*ḥêt*

The loving kindnesses of YHWH are surely not ended,[6]

2. תזנח/*tiznaḥ* could be (a) a qal impf 3 fs (with "my life" as the subject) or (b) a qal impf 2 ms (with God as the subject). Thus, "You [God] cast my life away from peace." The former is more in keeping with the rest of the passage.

3. זכר/*zĕkār* could be (a) qal impv or (b) qal inf cons ms. If (a), then the poet addresses God ("*remember* my affliction . . ."). The Peshitta and the Vulgate take it in this way. If (b), then the poet is himself recalling his trouble ("[I am] *remembering* my affliction"). The LXX takes it thus ("I remember").

4. Lit., either (a) "remembering she [i.e., 'my soul' from the next line] remembered" or (b) "remembering you [i.e., God] will remember." It depends on whether we take תזכור/*tizkôr* as (a) a qal impf 3 fs, or (b) a qal impf 2 ms.

5. Lit., "she-is-bowed-down on-me my-soul," meaning that the soul itself is enduring "oppression by sorrows or enemies" (Albrektson, *Studies in the Text*, 142, n. 4) or that the soul is lamenting *on account of* the man's suffering (Renkema, *Lamentations*, 381).

6. The MT reads תמנו/*tāmĕnû*, "*we* are ended/consumed." Provan sees the logic of the section as follows: "But this I call to mind, and therefore have hope: the steadfast love of the LORD! For we are not consumed because his mercies never come to an end: they are new every morning"; *Lamentations*. The grammar could suggest such an interpretation. Traditional Jewish readers however read the נ/*n* in תמנו/*tāmĕnû*, as a dissimilation for the double מ/*m*: תמו/*tāmmû* ("they [i.e., God's loving kindnesses] ended"). The chiasm in 3:22 supports taking the verb in this way.

surely his tender mercies are not finished.
New [signs of favor] every morning!
Great is your faithfulness!
"My inheritance is YHWH," says my soul,
"therefore I will wait hopefully for him."

vv. 25-27 ט/*ṭêt*

Good is YHWH to those who hope,
to the soul that seeks him.
Good it is to wait hopefully[7] in silence
for the deliverance of YHWH.[8]
Good it is for the man,
that he carries a yoke in his youth.

vv. 28-30 י/*yôd*

Let him sit alone and be silent
for he[9] lifted [it] upon him.
He should give his mouth to the dust,
perhaps there is hope.
He should give a cheek to his smiter,
He should eat his fill of scorn.

vv. 31-33 כ/*kāp*

For he will not reject forever,
the Lord,
For if he brings grief then he will have mercy,

---

7. ויחיל/*wĕyāḥîl* is an unfamiliar verb form and may be an imperfect of the rare verbal root חול or חיל ("to be strong/to be firm"). The meaning would then be something like "it is good to endure silently." Perhaps the original was יוחיל/*yôḥîl* (a hiph impf 3 ms of יחל/*yāḥal*, "to hope") and the ו/*w* and the י/*y* were accidentally swapped around; Renkema, *Lamentations*, 395. It is possible that the ו/*w* at the start of ודומם/*wĕdûmām* actually belongs at the end of the previous word. Thus the text should be יוחילו דומם/*yôḥîlû dûmām* and not ויחיל ודומם/*wĕyāḥil wĕdûmām*. This yields a translation like, "it is good [that] they hope in silence." See Albrektson, *Studies in the Text*, 146-48 for a discussion.

8. Renkema, following Gottlieb and Wiesmann, translates "Good is he [i.e., YHWH]. May one quietly wait/for YHWH's help." Renkema's translation of 3:25-26 has the attraction of having three statements that all begin with a parallel, "Good is [YHWH]." However, 3:26 is *not* most naturally taken in this way, and this undermines the scheme.

9. With most commentators, taking the "he" as YHWH. However, LXX, Peshitta, and Targum all take the subject to be the suffering one and not YHWH ("when such a one bears the yoke").

according to the abundance of his loving kindness.
For he does not afflict from his heart,
    or bring grief to the sons of man.

vv. 34-36 ל/*lāmed*
    To crush underfoot
        all the prisoners of [the] land . . .
    to deny a man justice
        before the presence of the Most High . . .
    to subvert a man in his lawsuit . . .
        does the Lord not see?

vv. 37-39 מ/*mêm*
    Who is this that spoke and it came to pass?
        Did the Lord not command it?
    From the mouth of the Most High does not go forth
    [both]
    calamity and the good?
    Why should a living man complain,
        a man on account of his sin-punishment?

vv. 40-42 נ/*nûn*
    Let us investigate our ways and examine [them],
        and let us return to YHWH.
    Let us lift up our heart along with our hands
        to God in the heavens.
    We transgressed and were rebellious,
        You have not forgiven.

vv. 43-45 ס/*sāmek*
    You have covered [yourself][10] in anger and you pursue us.
        You have killed without mercy.
    You have covered yourself in a cloud,
        so prayer cannot pass through.
    You have made us filth and refuse
        in the midst of the peoples.

---

10. No object is provided. What is the implied object then? Is it "us" or "yourself"? Either option makes sense in the context.

vv. 46-48 **פ**/*pê*

> They opened their mouth against us,
>> all our enemies.
> A terrifying pit was ours,
>> decimation and destruction.
> My eyes will flow with streams of water
>> on account of the destruction of the daughter of my people.

vv. 49-51 **ע**/*ʿayin*

> My eyes pour down [tears] and will not stop,
>> without weakening,
> until YHWH will look down and see
>> from heaven.
> My eye[s] afflict me
>> because of all the daughters of my city.

vv. 52-54 **צ**/*ṣādê*

> They hunted me like a bird,
>> my enemies, without cause.
> They destroyed my life in the cistern
>> and they placed a stone over me.
> Waters flowed over my head.
>> I said, "I am cut off!"

vv. 55-57 **ק**/*qôp*

> I called your name, YHWH,
>> from the deepest pit.
> You heard my voice, "Do not cover your ear
>> to my [cry for] relief, to my cry of anguish!"
> You drew near in the day I called to you,
>> You said, "Do not fear!"

vv. 58-60 **ר**/*rêš*

> You took up, Lord, my soul's lawsuit,
>> you redeemed my life.
> You have seen, YHWH, the wrong done to me;
>> judge my case.
> You have seen all their vengeance,
>> all their plots against me.

vv. 61-63 שׁ/*šîn*

> You have heard their reproach, YHWH,
> > all their plots against me,
> the lips of those who rise against me and their murmuring
> > against me all the day.
> [In] their sitting and their standing up — Look —
> > I am [the object of] their taunt song.

vv. 64-66 ת/*tāw*

> You will cause[11] recompense to return to them, YHWH,
> > according to the deeds of their hands.
> You will give to them dullness of heart
> > [as] your curse to them.
> You will pursue[12] in anger and destroy them
> > from under the heavens of YHWH.

It seems that there are as many proposed structures and interpretations of Lamentations 3 as there are commentators. Every suggested outline of structure and meaning requires the interpreter to make numerous interpretative decisions, some of which are the most difficult that have to be made in reading the book. The issues that need to be settled include:

1. Can the chapter be read as a unity, or is it a somewhat incoherent patchwork of several earlier poems?
2. If the chapter can be read as a unity, how do its different parts relate to each other?
3. How does chapter 3 relate to the rest of the book of Lamentations?
4. How many speakers are there in the poem?
5. How do we translate the very ambiguous Hebrew in 3:34-39?
6. How do we translate the perfect verbs in 3:56-66?

Our poem certainly combines elements from several literary genres, but it is not clear how much can be read off from this about the prehistory of the parts. I maintain that whether or not the poem was composed from scratch as a unit or "sewn" together from parts of various preexistent poems, the finished result

---

11. The verbs in 3:64-66 are all imperfect and are most naturally translated as "you will cause," "you will give," and "you will pursue." However, contextually, they could be functioning as imperatives ("cause," "give," and "pursue"), and this is how most contemporary commentators take them (see Waltke and O'Connor, *Biblical Hebrew Syntax*, 31.5b).

12. LXX "pursue them."

was intended to be understood as a coherent unity. My interpretation presupposes that whether the poem was composed by the same author as poems 1–2 or 4 and 5 or by a later author, it is now to be read in the context of the whole book of Lamentations. I attempt to interpret Lamentations 3 in the light of chapters 1 and 2 and will later attempt to read chapters 4 and 5 in the light of it.

Employing Occam's razor, I prefer not to multiply speakers beyond what is necessary to make sense of the poem. Consequently, I am inclined to find only one voice, that of the valiant man, throughout the poem. The possible exception to this is 3:42-47, which is a corporate prayer. This may be a prayer led by the valiant man, or it may be the response of the community to his call to repentance. If it is the latter, then we have a second voice — that of the suffering community. This suffering community is, so I maintain, the implied audience of the valiant man's words throughout the poem.

Chapter 3 has been taken by many past interpreters to be central for the interpretation of Lamentations as a whole. One current tendency is to react against this prioritizing of the third poem, but, while this reaction has played a helpful role in redressing the balance, I think that it has often led to an unhelpful *underplaying* of chapter 3. The motivation for the current trend to downplay chapter 3 is the desire to make sense of Lamentations as a book of despair with no hope on the horizon. Chapter 3 seems much too positive and is felt to threaten the integrity of the protest against God. The modern reaction against the hope in chapter 3 can assert itself in one of two ways:

(a) A protest against the "trivial" theology of hope and submission in chapter 3 compared to the "authentic" spirituality of rage and protest in Lamentations 1 and 2.

(b) A tendency to see the hope in 3:22-24 and 31-33 as the desperate man momentarily grasping at orthodox theology before sinking back towards despair.

In the commentary that follows I shall argue that the traditional readers were correct when they saw chapter 3 as central to the interpretation of the book as a whole. However, heeding the warnings of the modern readers, I will argue that our interpretation of Lamentations 3, while it will relativize the lament and despair, must not delegitimize or undermine them. On the basis of the exegesis that follows, I propose the following way of holding the chapter together.

I. The Suffering, Despair, and Hope of the Valiant Man (3:1-24)
    1. 3:1-18 The suffering of the valiant man
    2. 3:19-21 The valiant man's transition from despair to hope

3. 3:22-24 The valiant man's affirmation of trust in YHWH's loving kindness

II. The Valiant Man Offers General Advice on Suffering (3:25-39)
1. 3:25-30 How the sufferer should posture himself before YHWH
2. 3:31-33 The reason the sufferer can hope: YHWH's loving kindness
3. 3:34-39 The Lord sees injustice and is behind the punishment of sin

III. The Valiant Man Calls Israel to Repent and Leads a Communal Lament (3:40-51)
1. 3:40-41 The valiant man calls for corporate repentance
2. 3:42-47 Corporate lament (led by the valiant man?)
3. 3:48-51 The valiant man weeps at the suffering of his city

IV. The Valiant Man's Persecution, the Beginning of His Salvation, and His Expected Full Deliverance in the Future (3:52-66)
1. 3:52-54 The valiant man was hunted by enemies and death seemed inevitable
2. 3:55-58 The valiant man called on YHWH and was rescued from immediate danger
3. 3:59-63 The valiant man declares that YHWH knows all the evils committed against him by the enemies and calls on YHWH to judge them
4. 3:64-66 The valiant man declares/prays that YHWH will punish his enemies

I propose, against a current trend, that there is a progression of thought in this poem and it will be helpful to sketch this out before we jump into the detail, lest we fail to see the forest in our attention to the individual trees. The poem opens with an extended and vivid portrait of a man who suffers at the hands of YHWH (3:1-18), just as Jerusalem had in chapter 2. There are various parallels between his suffering and the suffering of Zion in the first two poems, and, read in context, this suggests that we should see the man's suffering as in some way embodying the corporate afflictions of the people. Poem 3 tells his story as a parallel to the story of the community. His transition from despair to hope in 3:19-24 is presented as a model for the community as a whole: a call for them to remember YHWH's covenant mercies. At that point in his story he, like the community, is still in the midst of affliction, and all that has changed is his perspective.

The man then proceeds, on the basis of his changed perspective, to offer some general advice, drawn in part from Israel's wisdom traditions, to the community on how to posture themselves before YHWH when in the midst of suffering (3:25-39). The advice leads directly to his call to them to examine their ways and return to YHWH (3:40-41). At this point the community takes up his call to prayer and begins a lament (3:42-47). It may be that the communal prayer is actually a prayer led by the valiant man himself. The man then, speaking for himself rather than for the community, weeps uncontrollably and declares that he will continue to do so until YHWH delivers his suffering people (3:48-51). It seems to me that the transition from the man's own suffering in 3:1-18 to the suffering of the people in 3:40-51 reinforces the view that his sufferings are intended to be closely related to theirs.

The abrupt transition back to the valiant man's own suffering in 3:52-66 must not be removed from the flow of the poem thus far. I suggest that the man is telling his own story as model to the community of how their story can be seen in such a way that hope for the future is recovered. Just as his suffering has embodied theirs, *so the salvation that he has begun to experience can become a foretaste of the future of the community.* The man drops the audience right back into the midst of the troubles he has described in vv. 1-18 but with a critical difference. In 3:1-18 the affliction was pictured in terms of *YHWH* violently attacking the man (human enemies were not in the picture at all). After the recovery of hope the situation is reconceived in terms of the *human* enemy violently attacking the man and YHWH as the man's source of help (3:52-55). The man tells the people of how he reached what seemed to be a point of inevitable doom and then, after calling out to YHWH, he was delivered! Of course, his enemies were still out there and his salvation is not total, so he calls on YHWH to judge them (3:59-63). He ends by declaring/praying that God will indeed punish them for what they have done (3:64-66). The story of this man, so I contend, is being offered to the survivors in Jerusalem as a picture of how their own story will go.

Who is the man in chapter 3? The following suggestions have been made:

(a) *Jeremiah, the author of Lamentations* (so the classical Jewish and Christian tradition, but more recently Wiesmann).[13]
(b) *A literary, idealized Jeremiah.* Rudolph considers that a follower of Jeremiah writes in the voice of Jeremiah to show how the prophet overcame the affliction of his ministry and to present the prophet as a model for handling adversity (see also Gottwald, Löhr).[14]

---

13. Wiesmann, *Die Klagelieder,* 44-84.

14. Rudolph, *Die Klagelieder,* 196-99; Gottwald, *Studies in the Book of Lamentations,* 37-46; Löhr, "Threni III."

(c) *The anonymous author of Lamentations* (Weiser).[15]

(d) *A particular Davidic king.* Suggestions include Jehoiakin (Porteous) and Zedekiah (Sæbø).[16]

(e) *A generic Davidic king* (Dobbs-Allsopp).[17]

(f) *A suffering soldier* (Lanahan).[18]

(g) *A literary "everyman."* A literary individual sufferer whose suffering is the same as, and thus poetically represents, the suffering of all the people (Hillers, Renkema).[19]

(h) *The personified, Job-like voice of those taken into exile* (Berlin).[20]

(i) *Zion personified as a man* (John Wesley, Eissfeldt, Albrektson).[21]

(j) *A literary collective personality* who personifies the suffering people *as a whole* (Gerstenberger).[22]

The man is never named, nor is he explicitly identified in terms of a specific role like king, prophet, priest, or the like. The most important point to grasp is that the man, whoever he is, functions in the role of *a representative of the populace at large.* His suffering is a participation in their suffering, and thus his story becomes a model for them to emulate and a source of hope. The only suggested identities that would not allow the גבר/*geber* to perform this function are options (i) and (j) above because they *literally identify* the *geber* with those he represents. But both views fail to do justice to the text for that very reason. The man speaks *to* the people, not *as* the people (3:40-41). He distinguishes himself from the people and his city (3:48, 51).[23]

I tentatively suggest that, when reading in context following Poems 1 and 2, the implied readers will at least entertain the hypothesis that the valiant man is the narrator of the first two poems. This hypothesis would be reinforced by (a) the man's tearful, Jeremiah-like response to the suffering of

---

15. Weiser, *Klagelieder*, 228-35.

16. Porteous, "Jerusalem-Zion"; Sæbø, "Who is 'the Man'?"

17. Dobbs-Allsopp qualifies this by saying that only an archetypal image of the king has been used and that a more explicit identification with the king has been intentionally suppressed; *Lamentations*, 108-9. Dobbs-Allsopp sees this kinglike figure functioning as an "everyman."

18. Lanahan, "Speaking Voice."

19. Hillers, *Lamentations*, 122; Renkema, *Lamentations*, 350-51.

20. Berlin, *Lamentations*, 84-86.

21. Wesley, "Lamentations"; Eissfeldt, *Old Testament*, 502-3; Albrektson, *Studies in the Text*, 127-29.

22. Gerstenberger, *Psalms, Part 2*, 493.

23. Also, option (i) is implausible because no reader coming to chapter 3 from chapters 1 and 2 is likely to identify the *man* in the third poem with the *woman* in the first two poems.

his people in vv. 48-51 — a response that bears a close similarity to the narrator's tearful response in 2:11, (b) the calls to prayer in 2:18-19 and 3:40-41, and (c) the similar theological assessment of the suffering in 1–2 and 3. However, it could be that a third speaker enters the book at this point.

The Suffering, Despair, and Hope of the Valiant Man (3:1-24)

In 3:1-18 a strong man (גבר/*geber*)[24] makes a vivid, though implicit, protest against YHWH's violent treatment of him before narrating how he called the traditions of YHWH's love and compassion to mind and rediscovered hope in the midst of adverse circumstances (3:19-24). It is interesting that, while YHWH is clearly the foe in 3:1-18, he is not explicitly named until v. 18. F. W. Dobbs-Allsopp argues that this has the effect of decentering YHWH and focuses on the "I" and his experience of pain. When God is finally named it receives extra emphasis.[25]

The unit has many features of an individual lament.[26] However, unlike in the conventional accusation against God, this speaker does not address God himself but a human audience, transforming the accusation into a description of misery.

The descriptions of suffering all use highly metaphorical and traditional language drawn from Israel's psalmic traditions. Consequently it is not possible to identify literally what happened to the man. The diverse metaphors are heaped one upon the other, and there is no consistent logical flow from one to the next, although sometimes one can see links — "a kind of collage of horror."[27]

vv. 1-3 א/'*ālep* The man opens with the words, "I am the man who has seen affliction." It is not clear why he speaks of himself as "*the* man" who has seen affliction as opposed to "*a* man" who has seen affliction. It may suggest that the audience will already know about the man who suffered so much, and so the speaker identifies himself: that man is *me*. Dobbs-Allsopp maintains that the best parallels for "I am the man" come from the self-presentation formulas of ancient Near Eastern kings (e.g., "I am Azitiwada, the blessed one of

---

24. גבר/*geber* is not a general word for "man" but a word connoting physical strength (hence the common translation "strong man") and strength of faith in YHWH ("devout man"). The word may well have both connotations in this poem.

25. Dobbs-Allsopp, *Lamentations*, 110.

26. Westermann, *Lamentations*, 169-71.

27. Bergant, *Lamentations*, 83.

Baal," or "I am Zakkur, king of . . .").[28] This may possibly be one of several allusions to the *geber* as a king-figure, but we cannot be certain.

The word "affliction" ties his suffering to the "affliction" of Jerusalem in 1:3, 7, 9c. The cause of his "affliction" is "a rod of [YHWH's] fury (עברתו/ *'ebrātô*)." This reminds readers of how "[God's] fury" is the cause of Jerusalem's pain too (2:2). As we have seen, the motif of YHWH's anger dominates chapter 2, and this leads straight into the third poem, where an individual participates in the punishment of the city. The reference to a "rod" of anger may bring to mind images of the staff of a king (a symbol of his power, Ps 45:6; 125:3), the parent's rod to chastise children (Prov 22:15), or the shepherd's stave (Ps 23:4; Ezek 20:37; Mic 7:14). Delbert Hillers sees a possible link pastoral between the "rod" in v. 1 and the fact that in v. 2 YHWH "drove/led/ guided" him into darkness. Perhaps we might see it as "a reversal of the Twenty-Third Psalm":[29] this shepherd *afflicts* his sheep with his rod and leads them into *danger!* The implied readers may also be expected to pick up an allusion to Isa 10:5, where Assyria is the rod of God's anger used to beat his disobedient people. This suggests that the afflicting rod is the human enemies.

The man continues by saying that Adonai made him "walk into darkness and not light." This may pick up on the Day of YHWH theme that was found in the first two poems. Amos 5:18 uses this exact phrase to speak of the Day of YHWH: contrary to Israel's expectations that day is "darkness and not light."[30] In context we suggest that it is the darkness of God's judgment on Judah and Jerusalem that this man is experiencing.

There is no rest for the man as God strikes him again and again and again. The hand that strikes the *geber* is the *same* hand that earlier bound Jerusalem's sins into a yoke and laid them upon her (1:14) and which destroyed the wall of Daughter Zion (2:8), yet again linking his suffering to hers.

vv. 4-6 ב/*bêt* It may be that the wasted flesh and the broken bones of 3:4 are the result of the severe beating in 3:3, although the wasted flesh more likely indicates the results of famine. His "shattered" bones (a reversal of Ps 34:20) also provide an allusion to the "shattering" of God's city and people (1:15; 2:9, 11). Yet again we see clues that the man shares in the experience of Jerusalem. This becomes even clearer in 3:5, where God (lit.) "built up against me and encircled." The image is of the man as a city under siege surrounded by the

---

28. Dobbs-Allsopp, *Lamentations,* 108.

29. Hillers, *Lamentations,* 124. Berlin also sees the shepherd-sheep imagery in this verse and throughout 3:1-13; *Lamentations,* 86ff.

30. Joel 2:1-2 and Zeph 1:14-16 also portray the Day of YHWH as a time of darkness.

enemy building siege ramps. The "poison and adversity" may be the enemy that besieges him, or it may be an allusion to the cup of God's wrath, which is poison to him.

Employing Ps 143:3 (see also Ps 88:4-8; 74:18-20), the man speaks of being made to dwell in darkness, just like the dead (an allusion to the darkness of Sheol, with perhaps a secondary allusion to the darkness of the Day of YHWH). The man is in a hopeless and God-forsaken situation like the dead, who cannot worship God.[31]

vv. 7-9 ג/*gîmel* The theme in this unit is the constriction of the man's movement. The image of dwelling in darkness in v. 6 leads into the prisoner motif in vv. 7-8. The man is walled up and chained up so that he cannot escape (cf. Ps 88:8). The diversity of metaphors used in 3:1-18 warns readers against being too quick to take the language literally here. The aggressor is like a cruel jailor who locks the *geber* up and then refuses to respond to his desperate calls for relief. This prison is *so* secure that even the *geber*'s voice cannot escape from it. Here the man's experience of unanswered pleas for help parallels Zion's.

The idea of being walled up in a prison leads into a different image in which the man is no longer chained up. Now his paths are walled off with tightly interlocking blocks of cut stone that do not allow the man to progress down the road he was going in his life (Job 3:23; Hos 2:6). The adversary has frustrated his plans.

vv. 10-12 ד/*dālet* The frustrated "ways" of the man (3:9) are picked up in the next image when the divine adversary is compared to a wild bear and a lion (Hos 13:8) that "forced me off my *ways* and tore me to pieces" (3:11). Clearly the prison image has now been left far behind. Lions and bears were very dangerous animals that could cause serious physical harm, and in this image they lie in wait to spring out on their unsuspecting prey. The man tries to escape but fails and is ripped open. He is "desolate" (שׁמֵם/*šomēm*), just like Jerusalem and her children (1:4, 13, 16).

Yet again the metaphor shifts and we see God as an enemy archer preparing to shoot his arrows at the *geber* (Job 16:12-13). The readers have already encountered YHWH-as-enemy-archer in 2:4, where he "killed all who were precious to the eye." *Yet again* the language and imagery link the strong man's

---

31. Anderson believes the lamenting psalmists are in a ritual state of mourning and so cannot praise God. Thus they become like the dead; *A Time to Mourn*, 92-93. Berlin suggests that the destruction of the temple locks the lamenters into a permanent state of mourning like the dead; *Lamentations*, 89-90.

suffering with Jerusalem's. The metaphor is left unfinished with the Lord about to shoot.

vv. 13-15 ה/*hê* 3:13 completes the image as the arrows find their target in the strong man's internal organs (the seat of his emotions, Job 19:27; Prov 23:16).

The man is now presented as publicly humiliated — a laughingstock all day long to all (his?) people. The reference to "my people" has caused some discussion. One may more naturally expect a reference to mocking by foreign peoples much as we find in chapters 1 and 2. Indeed some Hebrew manuscripts, a MT marginal note, and the Syriac *do* read "all peoples." Only one letter separates עמי/*ʿammî* ("my people") from עמים/*ʿammîm* ("peoples"), so one can imagine how it may have dropped out in transmission. If the original text was "I was a laughingstock to all peoples," then the humiliation of the *geber* again parallels Zion's humiliation in 1:7 and 2:15-16. However, the majority of Hebrew manuscripts, the LXX and the Vulgate all read "my people." If that is the original text, then the man is socially isolated in his suffering — even his fellow sufferers shun him and mock him (cf. Jeremiah's experience, Jeremiah 39–44). Either way, God has metaphorically given him wormwood (a bitter herb) to drink and thus made his life bitter.

vv. 16-18 ו/*wāw* It is possible that the feeding images from 3:15 are picked up here with the man eating gravel and dust or eating food from the ash heap. However, the image may refer to no more than the imposed abasement of the man. This is no *self*-humbling before God — God himself grinds the man's teeth in the gravel and presses him down into the dust.

In a summary statement he says that his "self" is cast[32] so far away from peace that he cannot even recall the good things in life. Iain Provan notes that "it is not so much that peace has left him, more that he has been banished from the realm of peace."[33] His future[34] and any hope for it he may have from God are destroyed. He feels utterly hopeless. Yet the naming of YHWH for the first time in the poem may, in retrospect, be seen as the first glimmer of a recovery of hope. The *very next word* (v. 19) begins to see a change in his attitude.

vv. 19-21 ז/*zayin* 3:19-21 serve as a transition from despair to hope. Thus they serve as a summary of 3:1-18 and an introduction to 3:22-24. 3:1-18 is recalled by reference to the man's "affliction" (cf. 3:1), the "wormwood" (cf.

---

32. The same verb occurred in 2:7 when YHWH "rejected" his altar.

33. Provan, *Lamentations*, 89.

34. Or, his splendor (perhaps the glory of YHWH himself that shines upon God's people or the glory of his past) or perhaps his endurance is removed.

3:15), and the "poison" (cf. 3:5). God is called to remember them. The *geber* says that he certainly remembers them and his soul is downcast. The stanza not only looks back but also leads into vv. 22-24 with the words "This I remind my heart, therefore I wait hopefully." But *what* does he remind his heart? To find out we have to read vv. 22-24.

The prayer in 3:19 ("Remember my affliction and my wandering") not only picks up on the earlier reference to the man's "affliction" in 3:1 but also serves to connect his experience to Jerusalem's. The narrator, in 1:7, spoke of both "her affliction and her wanderings" and the use of the same two terms serves as yet another link between his experiences and hers. The man's "wandering" is the same word used of Jerusalem in 1:7, and, in context, it may have exilic overtones.

Having reached the bottom of his pit of despair, the man begins his journey back up again towards hope. Perhaps the naming of YHWH as the final word of v. 18, even in despair, provokes him to call out again, "Remember my affliction and my restlessness!"[35] So far his prayers have fallen on deaf ears (3:8), and he has despaired of hope from YHWH (3:18); indeed, he still despairs when he contemplates his situation (3:20), but he does not abandon prayer. Instead, he speaks to himself and reminds himself of something (as yet the reader knows not what) which inspires hope again. The transition from hopelessness (3:18) to hope (3:21) is sudden and surprising, reflecting not a change in his circumstances but a change in his attitude. Whatever has inspired hope is something he has (lit.) "caused to return to [his] heart."

vv. 22-24 ח/*ḥêt* What, the implied readers are asking themselves, has the man reminded himself of in order to restore hope? The answer is "the loving kindnesses of YHWH" and "his tender mercies." The two divine qualities are set up in a chiastic parallel

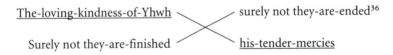

The-loving-kindness-of-Yhwh ⟍ ⟋ surely not they-are-ended[36]

Surely not they-are-finished ⟋ ⟍ his-tender-mercies

---

35. Assuming, with the Peshitta and Vulgate, that זכר/*zĕkār* is an imperative and not an infinitive construct. The issue is hard to settle with certainty. If זכר/*zĕkār* is an infinitive construct, then the subject is the soul and the words are not a prayer to God (see LXX).

36. The MT reads תמנו/*tāmĕnû*, "*we* are not ended." On this reading the fact that the speaker and his audience have survived the enemy onslaught as a kind of remnant is itself a sign of God's mercy. One Hebrew ms reads תמו/*tāmmû*, and Syriac and Targum seem to suggest "*they* are not ended." The chiasm supports the latter reading, but certainty is not possible.

In Robin Routledge's words, "[A]t the heart of *ḥesed* is loving commitment within the context of a relationship. It represents both the attitude of loyalty and faithfulness to the relationship and to the related parties, and the corresponding kind and dutiful action, often expressed as help or deliverance, that arises from it. . . . God's *ḥesed* is expressed in a faithful commitment to the relationship [with his people], both to act in accordance with it, and to preserve it despite the failure of his covenant partner."[37] The point is driven home by making the same claim about his tender mercies (רחמיו/ *raḥămāyw*). God's רחמים/*raḥămîm* are his deep feelings of love rooted in a natural bond and often rendered "tender mercies" or "compassions." It may be that the concrete acts of kindness (חסד/*ḥesed*) flow from the feelings of deep love (רחמיו/*raḥămāyw*). Paul House draws attention to the link with these terms and God's covenant with Israel in Exod 34:6-7.[38] There the reason God decides to renew the broken covenant with Israel after the golden calf incident is that he is "compassionate [רחום/*raḥûm*] and gracious" and "full of mercy [חסד/*ḥesed*] and faithfulness." The theme of God's ongoing love for Israel even after their constant sin and his judgment of them is a recurrent one in the Old Testament. Hillers writes, "Not God's love, but his anger is a passing phase."[39]

The man then exclaims, literally, "New-things for-the-mornings!" Presumably he means that the "acts of loving kindness" are, or will be, renewed each morning. The character of God, as revealed through Israel's past experience of him, is the foundation of the man's hope. Even the disaster that he and his nation have experienced from God does not mark the end of YHWH's love. So the man turns momentarily from addressing the people *about* God and speaks directly *to* God: "Great is your faithfulness!"

This recollection of God's character has brought a turn-around in the *geber*'s attitude. The soul that said "perished is . . . my hope from YHWH" in v. 18 now asserts in v. 24, "My inheritance is YHWH, therefore I will wait hopefully for him." The idea of God as one's inheritance is also found in the traditions about the Levites, who, unlike the other tribes, inherited no section of the land of Canaan. Instead, Adonai himself was their inheritance (Num 18:20; Josh 22:25, 27). Like the priests the man must look to God for his provision. Berlin also points out that to "have a portion [an inheritance] in" a king

---

37. Routledge, "*Ḥesed* as Obligation," 195-96. Routledge is bucking the recent trend towards minimizing the link between *ḥesed* and obligation within an established relationship. A link between *ḥesed* and God's covenant relationship with Israel certainly makes sense within Lamentations 3 with its allusion to Exod 34:6-7.

38. House, *Lamentations*, 414.

39. Hillers, *Lamentations*, 129.

is to acknowledge his Sovereignty (cf. 2 Sam 20:1) and thus to have YHWH as one's inheritance is perhaps to acknowledge his sovereign rule as well as to look to him for support.[40]

3:22-24 (esp. v. 24), in form-critical terms, is an "avowal of confidence" not uncommon in individual lament psalms but here worked out most beautifully.[41] One question is whether the man simply reminds himself of Israel's ancient traditions and confessions in the midst of his terrible situation *even though evidence of mercy is not to be seen*, or whether he actually sees signs of mercy in the midst of the horror. If the MT reading "for *we* are not ended" is followed in v. 22, then the survival of the man and his people is a sign of God's חסד/*ḥesed*. If, as in this commentary, we do not follow the MT, then we cannot know whether or not the man was able to see actual signs of light in the midst of his darkness (3:23 *may* suggest he does) or whether he simply recalled God's חסד/*ḥesed* and drew hope from that confession.

The Valiant Man Offers General Wise Advice on Suffering (3:25-39)

3:25-39 form a block of general guidance on suffering and how to handle it. The *geber* turns from narrating his own shift in attitude (3:1-24) towards providing general advice to his audience. The somewhat eclectic advice seems to have been inspired, in part, by Israel's wisdom traditions, although much of it is hard to place form-critically. "3:25-39 serve as an extended elaboration of what the man calls to mind (3:21) and of why he settles on hope."[42]

vv. 25-27 ט/*ṭêt* Each verse in the ט/*ṭêt* stanza not only begins with the same letter but with the same word, טוב/*ṭôb*, meaning "good." The first verse provides the link from the preceding section. The valiant man declared in v. 24 that he would wait for YHWH with expectation. That leads directly into the opening of this new section: (Literally,) "YHWH is good to the one who hopes in him, to the soul that seeks him." Because of that it follows that "it is good to wait hopefully in silence for the deliverance of YHWH." Clearly 3:24-26 envisage a situation in which salvation has *not* arrived but can be confidently expected in the future. The basis for the expectation is an understanding of *who YHWH is*. Because he is good, one can expect future deeds of goodness, even if

---

40. Berlin, *Lamentations*, 93.

41. Westermann, *Lamentations*, 173; Gerstenberger sees 3:19-36 as an "affirmation of confidence"; *Psalms, Part 2*, 492-93.

42. Dobbs-Allsopp, *Lamentations*, 120.

one does not see evidence of them now. The goodness of YHWH to his people is something deeply embedded in Israel's traditions of faith (Ps 106:1; 107:1; 118:1; 135:3; Jer 33:11, etc.) as is the call to trust him and seek him.

The recommendation of waiting *in silence* raises a difficult question — how does this advice fit into the context of the book as a whole? On its own it sounds fairly innocuous and conventionally pious (Ps 37:7; 39:2, 9; 62:1, 5; Isa 30:15), but patient silence is *not* the mode of response found in the rest of Lamentations. Lady Jerusalem was clearly not silent in the first two poems. Is the man suggesting that her response was inappropriate? The narrator in the first two poems was not silent either, and it was he who urged Jerusalem to "Arise! Cry aloud in the night . . . pour out your heart like water in front of the presence of the Lord!" (2:19). Hardly a recommendation of pious silence! *If*, as I tentatively suggest, that narrator in chapters 1–2 *is* the *geber* of chapter 3, is he now repudiating his own advice? The *geber* himself in 3:1-20 is hardly a model of silent patience, but of loud lament with more than a hint of implicit "protest." For the reader who is coming to this verse for the second time after having read the entire book, the advice seems even more peculiar. Chapters 4 and 5 do not model silent waiting, but, even more pertinently, neither does the rest of chapter 3. The man himself calls on the community to pray, and the resulting prayer has the same overtones of implicit protest found elsewhere in the book (3:40-47); then in vv. 48-51 he commits himself to incessant weeping until YHWH acts to save. How does any of this fit with the comment that "it is good to wait hopefully *in silence* for the deliverance of YHWH"? The implied reader is bound to ask how the advice should be taken.

It seems to me that there are two basic families of response to this puzzle. The majority view is to claim that we have (at least) two kinds of response to suffering in Lamentations and they are not fully compatible. It may be that the more "orthodox" response in 3:25-39 comes in the voice of a new speaker (e.g., Lee),[43] or it may be that the *geber*, in his grief, is simply inconsistent and wavers between faith and despair. Either way, on this view an irreconcilable conflict in viewpoints should be allowed to stand in the text. Exactly how readers are to respond to this conflict of viewpoints is disputed. Some suggest that the "alien" and "superficial" theology of vv. 25-39 should be understood as fundamentally undermined by the rest of the book. Heath Thomas, on the other hand, proposes that the two modes of response to evil are presented as equally viable possibilities and that the text leaves it open for the reader to decide whether to adopt the parenetic teaching as normative or not.[44] Still oth-

43. Lee, *The Singers of Lamentations*, ch. 5.
44. Thomas, "Poetry and Theology in Lamentations," 206.

ers seek to retrieve valuable insights in both modes of response and refuse to absolutize either. An alternative response to the puzzle is to suggest that the "silence" advocated by the man must, given 2:11-19 and 3:19-24, be compatible with prayer. So it is not a *literal* silence that the man is recommending but an attitude of expectant trust. Extending this strategy, it may be that the advice of 3:25-39, *once nuanced by its context*, is fully compatible with lament and urgent prayer of the kind found in 3:40-51 (even if not with the kind found in 3:1-18). This is similar to the surprising way in which God sees Job's raging protests as compatible with reverence for YHWH.

The final piece of advice is the general claim that it is good for a man (*geber*) to carry the yoke of (presumably) suffering while he is young. The reference to the "yoke" will remind readers of the "yoke," woven together from her sins, that Jerusalem has laid upon her by God (1:14). There are three ways in which this verse could be understood. First, with Johan Renkema, we could reject the translation that I just gave and render the verse as "He [YHWH] is good to a devout one [*geber*] when he must bear a yoke in his youth."[45] The claim is simply that God is good to the *geber* when he suffers. Good in what way? The text does not say, but in context one may suppose that it is in the God-grounded hope of an end to suffering. This suggestion makes theological sense within Lamentations, but it seems a more strained rendering of the Hebrew and it makes the words "in his youth" redundant.

Alternatively, perhaps the point is that it is good that a person bear the yoke of suffering. Maybe this is because one can learn from it. But this view is problematic for two reasons. First, there is nothing elsewhere in Lamentations to suggest that it is good to suffer. Indeed, this speaker himself will *contrast* the current "evil" being experienced with the "good" in v. 38. Second, just like the first view, it makes the words "in his youth" redundant.

Most likely the point is that the young are stronger and hence better able to bear the yoke. Thus, if one *has* to suffer, it is better to suffer *when one is young*. It is important to emphasize that most wisdom advice should not be absolutized into exceptionless principles. This verse cannot be taken to support the view that suffering is *always* easier for the young. We also need to appreciate that this word of comfort applies to the *geber* himself but is comforting neither to the man's older fellow sufferers nor to the very young ones.

vv. 28-30 ʾ/*yôd* The yoke was laid upon the sufferer by God himself, and for this reason he should sit alone in silence. The silence here is presumably, as in

45. Renkema, *Lamentations*, 396-98.

v. 26, the silence of the hopeful expectation of divine deliverance. It reminds readers of the image of Jerusalem sitting alone in 1:1, but here the man is advising the acceptance of that fate. It is only implicit, but the idea hinted at is that, if God is the cause of the yoke, then one can expect it to be removed at some point.

Given that God is the cause, there may be hope if one humbles oneself before him. So the sufferer is advised to put his mouth to the dust (an act of self-abasement, Mic 7:17; Ps 72:9) and to take the blows from the enemy without retaliating. The slapping of the cheek is a sign of scorn and contempt for a person, and it is this shaming behavior that the audience are advised to endure. That this is no mechanical process with built-in guarantees is indicated by the words "*perhaps* there is hope." This "perhaps" seems to jar a little in context, because all the other affirmations seem to indicate that YHWH's deliverance is certain. Claus Westermann observes that "in an avowal of confidence such a qualifier would have no place; there the expression of confidence is voiced without hesitation. One never finds an avowal of confidence hedged this way in the Psalms, for example."[46] How could the confident speaker of 3:22-24 and of 3:31-33 say "*perhaps* there is hope"?[47] It may reflect a wavering of faith that is understandable given the circumstances. "[T]he authors paint a picture of wavering anticipation which, in the climate of otherwise total hopelessness which held sway after the fall of the land and the city, has to be expected, at least from the human perspective . . . the text contains no suggestion of certainty in faith (Heb 11₁). What is evident is the fidelity of a faith under challenge (Mark 9₂₄)."[48] It also manifests a recognition that God is sovereign and cannot be treated like a blessing-dispensing machine. The prophets also sometimes spoke in terms of the *possibility* of God's salvation after judgment (Amos 5:15; Zeph 2:3).

vv. 31-33 כ/*kāp* This stanza contains perhaps the most profound theological insight of the whole book, and its location is perhaps no coincidence. *Right at the literal center of the book of Lamentations is an appreciation of the being of YHWH as the ground of hope.* It opens with the word "for," indicating that what follows is the *reason* that the sufferer should adopt the counter-intuitive posture of silent hope, self-abasement, and submission to enemy attack. Why do such difficult things? Because, although YHWH has rejected

46. Westermann, *Lamentations*, 177.

47. The Syriac and Peshitta also sense this tension and understand the verse to mean "*because* there is hope." Martin Luther dropped the word "perhaps" from his German translation of the text, finding it nonconducive to his theology.

48. Renkema, *Lamentations*, 403.

them, he will not reject them *forever*.[49] Why? Because of *who he is*. While God has indeed afflicted them, he will have mercy according to the abundance of his covenant kindness (חֶסֶד/*ḥesed*). "You see," says the speaker, "while God does afflict and bring grief to humanity, he does not do so 'from his heart'" (i.e., the center of his emotions and decisions). This is theology proper — an appreciation of who God is in his very being. God gets *no pleasure* from inflicting pain on people — his judgments are not the way he *wants* to relate to humanity but are his response to human sin. Punishment is an "alien" work of God given reluctantly and after numerous warnings. In his innermost self God is full of loving kindness and mercy, and that is how he *wants* to relate to humans. Consequently, affliction is temporary and is followed by mercy. Here then is an understanding of who YHWH is, an understanding grounded in his self-revelation to Moses (Exod 34:6-7) and his acts of mercy shown over and over again through the history of Israel (e.g., Gen 32:11; Ps 25:6; 89:1, 49; 106:7; 107:43; Isa 63:7). This theology forms the basis for hope in the midst of crisis. But, of course, such a theology of hope is *in*duced, not *de*duced, from God's dealings with Israel in the past and allows for the "perhaps" of v. 29. In context this is *a strong hope but not a water-tight hope*.

Excursus: Problems with the Exegesis of 3:34-39

Lamentations 3:25-39 contains some of the most difficult material in the whole of Lamentations. Things are fairly straightforward as far as v. 33, but from v. 34 to v. 39 a host of problems emerge as the reader tries to make sense of the text.

Issue 1: Which is the verb governing the infinitive constructs in 3:34-36?
3:34-36 are problematic in that each verse begins with an infinitive construct and infinitive constructs do not occur without a verb to govern them. But which verb? There are two options here. Either

(a) "see" in 36b
(b) "bring grief"/"afflict" in 33

If we take it to be (a), then we will translate the vv. 34-36 something like Adele Berlin does:[50]

---

49. Dobbs-Allsopp sees this claim as "contradicted directly in 2:7a ('the Lord has rejected his altar')" (*Lamentations*, 121), but Dobbs-Allsopp is mistaken — 3:31 does not deny that God rejects but only that God rejects *forever*.

50. Berlin, *Lamentations*, 79; cf. Waltke and O'Connor, *Biblical Hebrew Syntax*, 36.2.3b.

The crushing underfoot of
    all the prisoners of the land,
the perverting of a man's justice
    before the presence of the Most High,
the subverting of a person in his lawsuit —
    does not the LORD see it?

If, on the other hand, we take it to be (b), then we may translate it with Hillers as follows:[51]

Because he does not deliberately torment men,
    or afflict them
By crushing under foot
    all the prisoners of the earth,
By denying a man justice
    before the Most High,
By twisting a man's case
    without the Lord seeing.[52]

So on this view vv. 34-36 expand on the afflictions which the Lord may bring for a time but which are not "from his heart" (3:33).

Issue 2: Who is the oppressive one in 3:34-36?

Who is it that is crushing prisoners and denying them justice? One's answer will, to some extent, depend on how one resolves issue 1. Two alternatives again present themselves:

(a) The crusher could be God himself (these are afflictions that YHWH does not inflict "from his heart" or "forever").

(b) The crusher could be evil people (these are things done by evil people that YHWH does not approve of, does not see, or does see [see issue 3]).

Issue 3: How do we interpret 3:36b?

3:36b reads, אֲדֹנָי לֹא רָאָה. How are we to take this expression? Yet again two options present themselves:

(a) A statement? If so, a further issue must be addressed — do we interpret רָאָה as:
    (i) "to see" ("The Lord does not *see*") or
    (ii) "to approve of" ("the Lord does not *approve*")?

(b) A rhetorical question? "Does the Lord not see it?" with an implied, "Of course, he does!"

---

51. Cf. Waltke and O'Connor, *Biblical Hebrew Syntax*, 36.2.3e.
52. Hillers takes אֲדֹנָי לֹא רָאָה in 3:36 be a circumstantial clause.

Issue 4: How do we interpret 3:37b?
A parallel problem to issue 3 is encountered in 3:37b. In a similar way this can also be construed as either:

(a) A statement? "The Lord did not command [it]."
(b) A rhetorical question? "Did the Lord not command it?" with an implied, "Of course, he did!"
(c) Consider House's translation: "Who spoke this and it came to pass/ if the Lord did not command (it)?"[53]

(b) and (c) could be understood as suggesting the same proposition, namely that *the Lord* spoke and it came to pass: *he* commanded. Alternatively, (c) could be taken to mean that *the enemy* spoke and it came to pass *but only because* the Lord commanded that he should.

Issue 5: Who is speaking in 3:34-36?
Depending on how one handles the above issues, one may end up taking 3:34-36 in a way that stands in tension with its context. That is to say, vv. 34-36 may be taken as very critical of YHWH's action in the midst of a section that essentially defends YHWH. If one goes this route, then one has to ask if the words in 3:34-36 represent the words of the same speaker as the rest of 25-39 or the words of an opponent. It could be that in 3:34-36 an opponent speaks up to challenge the speaker and then in 3:37-39 the speaker replies. Alternatively, perhaps the speaker quotes his opponent's real or expected response in order to dismiss it in 37-39. On the other hand, if one understands the message of 3:34-36 as in line with the rest of 3:25-39, then one will perceive the same voice throughout the verses. So again we have two options:

(a) An opponent speaks (or is quoted) in vv. 34-36.
(b) The same person speaks throughout vv. 25-39.

Issue 6: How do we interpret 3:38?
3:38 reads מפי עליון לא תצא הרעות והטוב. This can also be taken in one of two ways. Either:

(a) As a statement. Consider Renkema, "From the mouth of the Most High come not evil words, but the good!"[54]
(b) As a rhetorical question. So with the NIV, for instance, "Is it not from the mouth of the Most High that both calamities and good things come?"

The issue is whether the speaker is claiming that this "evil" is *not* from YHWH (view a) or whether he is claiming precisely the opposite (view b).

---

53. House, *Lamentations*, 401.
54. Renkema, *Lamentations*, 421.

To begin to disentangle these problems I suggest that we begin with issue 1 and the problem of which verb governs the infinitive constructs, but allow ourselves to move back and forth between problems as appropriate. Now ל + the infinitive construct should not precede its governing verb, and this lends initial weight to option (b) because that allows the governing verbs to come before the three infinitives. This view requires us to see 3:34-36 as actions which YHWH performs (2a). In support of this view we may note that 3:34 begins with the words "by crushing under *his* feet. . . ." In context it is most natural to take the pronoun to refer to *God's* feet because he was the subject in 3:33 and no others have been introduced. 3:36b, on this view, becomes somewhat awkward. It could be taken as a circumstantial clause (cf. Hillers's translation quoted above). Alternatively, it could be taken as a complete sentence: "The Lord does not see/approve."

However, despite initial appearances, the arguments for this view (1b & 2a) are not as compelling as they seem. While it may be conceded that ל + the infinitive construct should follow the governing verb, the acrostic structure of the poem requires each verse to begin with ל, and this could explain the unconventional grammar. Indeed, if ראה/*rā'â* in 3:36b is the governing verb, it could be argued that the text is rhetorically effective *precisely because* it keeps the audience hanging on until v. 36b before they can make sense of vv. 34-36a.

There are also problems with this view. For a start, it requires us to see YHWH as "denying a man justice *before the Most High*" and, if 3:36b is a circumstantial clause, "twisting a man's case *without the Lord seeing.*" This is an odd way to speak if YHWH is the subject of the verses (2a). It would make more sense to follow view (b) on issue 2 and to see enemies, not YHWH, as the oppressors in 3:34-36. However, I grant that this objection is not overpowering.[55]

Second, no other strophe in the book is grammatically incomplete without the preceding strophe. Readers would certainly expect by the time they get to the end of 3:33 that the sentence is complete and that a new sentence will begin in the next strophe. Even though the opening ל + infinitive pattern in the ל strophe will strike them as unconventional, once they get to 3:36b and find a verb to govern the infinitives they will not need to look back to the previous strophe to find such a verb.

Third, and most important, this view cannot do justice to 3:36b. If we take 3:36b as a straight sentence, then the text ends up contradicting itself. This is because after explaining the afflictions that God reluctantly brings for a while it would add, "The Lord does not see." But how would God not notice his own actions? The alternative is to take 3:36b as a circumstantial clause, but this is awkward for several reasons. For a start, there are no linguistic markers to indicate that it is such. It is more natural to

55. Hillers's reply to it is to point out that in 2:20, 22 and 3:66 similar phenomena occur. For instance, 3:66 reads, "May you [the Lord] pursue them in anger and wipe them out from under *the LORD's heaven.*" However, none of these examples form an exact parallel to our text, for in 3:36b YHWH would be spoken of in the third person, not addressed in the second person as in 2:20, 22 and 3:66 (not "You do x in the presence of the YHWH" but "YHWH does x in the presence of the YHWH").

take it as the governing verb. On top of that, if we take 3:36b as a circumstantial clause, then 3:36 and 3:35 stand in parallel, as in Hillers's translation:

> By denying a man justice
>> before the Most High,
> By twisting a man's case
>> without the Lord seeing.

But this seems to create an odd contradiction. On the one hand, the denial of justice takes place in the very presence of the Most High, but in the parallel clause it takes place "without the Lord seeing." Presumably the expression "before the Most High" would suggest that the Most High is aware of what is happening, so how is it that he does not see? Indeed, to suppose that *God* is the one who does the afflicting in 3:34-36, as he is on this view, makes it very hard to take 3:36b as a circumstantial clause. How, after all, are we supposed to make sense of the claim that "God does not afflict the sons of man from his heart . . . by twisting a man's case *without the Lord seeing*"? Does God not notice what he is doing? Also, 3:36b and 3:37b stand in parallel in Hebrew:

> לעות אדם בריבו
> אדני לא ראה

> מי זה אמר ותהי
> אדני לא צוה

However, if we take 3:36b as a circumstantial clause, we obliterate the patterning of the text. Here is Hillert's translation of the two verses:

> By twisting a man's case
>> *without the Lord seeing.*
> Who was it who "spoke and it was done"?
>> *It was the Lord who gave the command.*

All these considerations militate strongly against taking 3:36b as a circumstantial clause. It is much more plausible to take it as the clause governing the infinitives in 3:34–3:36a (i.e., to opt for 1a and 2b).

So we can take 3:34-36 as a grammatically self-contained unit. The question now is whether to understand the unit as one that is critical of YHWH or not (issue 5). This question pivots on how we interpret 3:36b (issue 3). Three possible translation strategies present themselves. I paraphrase them as follows:

(i) Issue 3(a)(i): "The Lord does not *see* the crushing underfoot of all the prisoners of the land."

(ii) Issue 3(a)(ii): "The Lord does not *approve of* the crushing underfoot of all the prisoners of the land."

(iii) Issue 3(b):   "Does the Lord not *see* the crushing underfoot of all the prisoners of the land?"

Now (i) above would be a critical comment on YHWH for not paying attention to the
extreme suffering of his people and would presumably be the words of an opponent
of the main speaker (5a). (ii) and (iii) would both construe 3:34-36 in ways favorable
to YHWH (5b). In (ii) sufferers are assured that YHWH does not look with approval
on the deeds of oppressors. In (iii) sufferers are assured that YHWH does indeed see
the terrible oppression they experience.

Now grammatically the most natural way of taking the text is as a statement (3a),
and hence the appeal of (i) or (ii). If 3:36b was a rhetorical question, one would expect
an interrogative particle. 3:36b could just as easily have read הלא אדני ראה, which
would be an unambiguous rhetorical question. It does not. So *prima facie* we have a
statement, not a rhetorical question. The most natural understanding of the text is that
it asserts that YHWH does not see the oppression of his people (translation i). In its favor, and against (ii), we may note that I am unaware of any other passages in which
ראה means "approve of." We may add to this that the issue of YHWH's seeing (and his
not seeing) the suffering of his people is already an issue in Lamentations. The problem is that the complaint that God does not see the suffering would be unexpected *in
the current context,* which has been so much about giving hope to suffering people. Has
the speaker backtracked? Given that 3:37-39 seem to defend YHWH, we cannot give
much credence to the idea that the speaker is wavering back and forth. If 3:34-36 really
do criticize YHWH, then we must assume that the voice is that of another (5a).

But, before we settle on the opposing voice option for 3:34-36 we need to look at
some problems with it. First, it is not clear how the comment that YHWH has not
seen the oppression of his people is supposed to be a critique of the main speaker's
claims. The main speaker has asserted that, although God does afflict people, such afflicting is not "from his heart" and is temporary. An appropriate criticism would be to
reject one of the speaker's claims: to assert, for instance, that God afflicts people *and
enjoys it,* or that God has rejected his covenant people *forever* this time. It is also not
clear how 3:37-39 would provide the most relevant response to the objection that God
does not see his people's suffering.

Second, as we pointed out earlier, 3:36b and 3:37b seem to stand in parallel. This
would suggest that both verses have the same speaker. Now 3:37-38 cannot be separated in terms of content, so if 36 and 37 express the same voice, then the speaker in
3:36 is unlikely to be criticizing YHWH because 3:37-38 must be read as favorable to
YHWH. This would suggest that 3:34-36 are also favorable to YHWH.

To really test the meaning of 3:34-36 we need to move on to consider the problems in 3:37 (issue 4) and 3:38 (issue 6), because how we settle those will have implications for 3:34-36. I think that we can roll issues 4 and 6 into one discussion with three
possible options.[56] We could paraphrase the three possible senses of 3:37-38 as follows:

56. 4(a) combined with 6(b) results in a contradiction, so is not a live option. It would

(i) Who did this? Not YHWH (4a). From him comes not evil (like this situation) but good (6a).

(ii) Who did this? YHWH (4b). However, from YHWH comes not evil but good (6a) (implied: so this situation must really be good not evil)

(iii) Who did this? YHWH (4b). From YHWH come both bad events and good ones.

In Hebrew 3:37-38 are as follows

מי זה אמר ותהי
אדני לא צוה

מפי עליון לא תצא
הרעות והטוב

Option (i) is defended by Renkema, but it really makes little sense. In Lamentations *all* the voices (including the speaker in 3:37-38) agree that the suffering endured by Israel has come ultimately from YHWH. To suppose that the speaker has moved from admitting that YHWH is the cause of the affliction in 3:31-33 to now denying that he has anything to do with it (3:37-38) stretches plausibility beyond breaking-point. On top of that we may reflect on the fact that there is a strong likelihood that the Ps 33:9 and Lam 3:37 texts are related to each other. Speaking of God's work in creation, Ps 33:9 says, "For he [God] spoke and it came to be; he commanded and it stood firm." Psalm 33 also shares other key vocabulary with Lamentations 3, such as God's "faithfulness" (33:4), "justice" (33:5), "loving kindness" (33:5). In addition, it also stresses the need to wait in hope for YHWH (33:20-22). The interconnections strongly suggest that we should not read Lam 3:37 as a statement to the effect "The Lord did not command it." For these reasons we can dismiss option (i).

Option (ii) is possible. It could translate the verses as follows:

Who is this that spoke and it came to pass?
Did the Lord not command it?

From the mouth of the Most High goes forth
not the evil but the good.

However, it seems unlikely because the situation that the Lord has commanded (3:37) would surely be described as evil (i.e., calamity not moral evil) by all the speakers in Lamentations.

This leaves option (iii). On this view, the speaker asserts that YHWH is the root cause of the suffering experienced because *all* things, both calamity and pros-

---

amount to asserting that God did not command this situation (4a) and then asserting that the good *and the bad* (like this situation) come from the mouth of the Lord. We can dismiss that possibility as incoherent. That leaves the options above.

perity, come ultimately from his hand. This view makes sense in the context of Lamentations as a whole and in the immediate context (see later). But what is interesting is that this view requires us to take a clause that is grammatically in the form of a statement (אדני לא צוה) as a rhetorical question ("Did not YHWH command it?" or, perhaps better, "YHWH did not command it?").

But opting for (iii) has implications for 3:37 and 3:36. 3:38 is an expansion of 3:37. If 3:38 means, "Do not both evil and good go forth from the mouth of the Most High?" (6b), then 3:37 *must* mean, "Who is this that spoke and it came to pass? Did the Lord not command it?" (4b). Otherwise we end up with a contradiction between 3:37 and 3:38. But then we have yet another clause that is in the grammatical form of a statement but which has to be construed as a rhetorical question. This in turn drives us back to 3:36. The parallel between 3:36b and 3:37b leads us to suppose that, if 3:37b is a rhetorical question, then so is 3:36b (3b). In which case 3:34-36 are not a criticism of YHWH at all but a list of oppressive actions which the speaker assures people that the Lord sees.

But there is more that has to be said. For while the passage finally makes best sense when construed in the way I suggest above, the readers, both implied readers and real readers, have to work hard to wrestle this meaning out of the text. Whatever we suppose the author's intentions to have been, one inevitable effect of the way he has expressed himself is to slow readers down so that they explore various ways of construing the text. Readers must wrestle to make sense of the advice, just as they must wrestle to make sense of their situations.

vv. 34-36 ל/*lāmed* The speaker seems to reassure his audience that YHWH is aware of the injustice that they are suffering. The man focuses on the victims of legal injustice in each of the three lines, but each sentence is left unfinished until the very end of the stanza where the words "does the Lord not see?" completes each of the previous three sentences. The rhetorical question invites the reply, "Of course, he sees these things." The poet cleverly expresses his rhetorical question in the words אדני לא ראה/*'ădonāy lo' rā'â*, which is literally, "the Lord does not see." On first reading it is not obviously a question at all but a statement of complaint that God has not seen the suffering of his people — a theme that has recurred throughout Lamentations. However, when the reader ponders the text in context, it cannot mean this and the "complaint" is reconfigured as a rhetorical question ("the Lord does not see?") affirming God's knowledge of their situation. But the ambiguous syntax compels readers to ponder difficult theological issues as different linguistic possibilities are contemplated and to play an active role in making sense of both the syntax and their own situation.

The three situations which God sees are the mistreatment of prisoners

113

(3:34), the (lit.) "bending-of a-valiant-man's justice in-the-presence-of-the-Most-High" (3:35), and (lit.) the "making-crooked a-man in-his-lawsuit" (3:36). The violation of basic rights is behind the idea of bending a man's justice (Exod 23:2, 6; Deut 16:19; 24:17; 27:19) — something which the wicked do. To do this *in the presence of God* indicates both brazen wickedness and foolishness! How could God not see such behavior? Presumably it is the enemy who mistreat the inhabitants of Judah in this way. Here the paradox already explored in chapter 1 manifests itself again — God uses the unrighteous and culpable acts of humans to bring about his righteous, albeit unwilling, punishment. That focus on God's use of human evil comes in the next stanza.

vv. 37-39 מ/*mêm* In the מ stanza the man highlights the point that *God himself* is the source of all things and hence the present calamity also. This is the other side of the human freedom–divine sovereignty interface to that considered in the ל stanza with its focus on the evil *human* acts that lie behind much suffering. That God is aware of, and disapproves of, injustice and abuse is clear from 3:34-36, but the valiant man does not wish his audience to infer from this that God is no longer sovereign in such situations. Through the use of rhetorical questions the man gets his audience to recognize that, as in Genesis 1, it was *God* who spoke and it came to pass; it was *the Lord* who commanded;[57] and that from out of the mouth of *the Most High* come both calamity and good (cf. Amos 3:6; Isa 45:7; Ezek 20:25; Job 2:10). For Israel there is but one God, the creator of heaven and earth, and hence all events, both good *and bad*, must ultimately be ordained in some sense by him. Hence the unflinching, albeit uncomfortable, claim throughout Lamentations that YHWH is the ultimate cause of the suffering. House writes, "The fact that God sent judgment means he can restore their fortunes."[58]

The wisdom section ends with the probing question that boils down to this: given that humans sin, why should someone complain if they don't like the consequences of their actions? Renkema argues that יתאונן/*yit'ônēn*, the *hithpolel* of אנן/*'ānan* ("to murmur/to grumble"), suggests a rebellious complaint in which the guilty one shifts the blame and complains about others (Num 11:1).[59] This is possible, though uncertain. There are some tricky issues in the interpretation of 3:39. First, why is the man described as a "*living* man"? Most suggest that it refers to one who has survived the calamity: "it is better

57. The wording in 3:37 ("Who is this that spoke and it came to pass? Did the Lord not command it?") is very close to Ps 33:9, which reads "For he spoke and it came to pass; he commanded and it stood still."

58. House, *Lamentations,* 419.

59. Renkema, *Lamentations,* 423.

to be alive, even with suffering, than to be dead. . . . God is showing mercy by keeping a person alive."[60] The survivor is like Baruch in Jeremiah 45 — he still suffers with his fellow citizens, but his life is granted as a gift, and where there is life there is hope (only the dead are without hope). Second, there is debate whether חטאו/*ḥăṭā'āw* should be translated as "his sin" or as "his punishment." If the former, then it could mean either "What *should* the living man complain about? Each about his sins!"[61] or that the man should not complain about his suffering on account of the fact that he has sinned and hence deserved it. If חטאו/*ḥăṭā'āw* means "his punishment," then the man should not complain on account of his punishment for sin. However that dispute is resolved, the upshot is much the same: the man should not complain about his circumstances if he has been allowed to survive. Perhaps he is told to complain about his own sins instead or perhaps to recognize that his sins are the cause of his circumstances.

The Valiant Man Calls Israel to Repent and Leads a Community Lament (3:40-51)

vv. 40-42 נ/*nûn* The call to self-examination and repentance in 3:40-41 follows directly from the recognition of the sin of the sufferer in v. 39. The response to suffering advocated here is not that of cursing God but that of considering whether the suffering may have resulted from sin. "Silence and trust alone . . . are not enough, conversion must be part of their response also."[62] It is not clear whether the words here are those of the *geber* as he addresses the community and then leads them in prayer or of the community itself responding to the advice of vv. 25-39. I shall presume that the words are those of the *geber* (a presumption supported by the transition from the plural form to the singular form in 3:46-48).

The smooth transition, via 3:19-39, from the suffering of the man in 3:1-18 to the suffering of the community in 3:40-51 reinforces our earlier claim that his suffering and their suffering are closely linked. Having told the story of his own recovery of hope in the midst of despair (3:19-24), and having drawn out some general advice from his own experience and the religious traditions of Israel (3:25-39), he now addresses the suffering of his people.

He first calls the community to intense self-examination (the words

---

60. Berlin, *Lamentations*, 95.
61. Budde, "Die Klagelieder," 96.
62. Renkema, *Lamentations*, 427.

"investigate" and "examine" are common in Wisdom literature) and to a repentant turning back to YHWH. While YHWH is the ultimate cause of their suffering, he has caused it only in response to the persistent unrighteous behavior of his people. Hence, the road to recovery must be the road of repentance. He then calls the community to honest and sincere prayer (lifting up the hands to God was a common posture for prayer, e.g., Ps 28:2), presumably prayer of repentance and prayer for deliverance. The prayer is to involve the lifting up of their hearts to YHWH, suggesting a sincere offering of their deepest selves to him in mind, emotion, and will.

In 3:41 the man begins to lead the community in prayer. He opens with a blunt confession: "We transgressed and were rebellious" (cf. 1:18a). There is again no sense in Lamentations that the people of Judah are *innocent* victims, even though they are victims. The vocabulary of transgression (פשע/*pāša'*, 1:5, 14, 22) and rebellion (מרה/*mārâ*, 1:18, 20) suggests serious violation of the covenant relationship.

The prayer continues, "You have not forgiven." Some have suggested that at this point the man falls back into hopelessness and that we have here his *complaint* that, *even though* Judah has repented, YHWH has refused to forgive. Consequently, all the "wise" teaching of 3:22-39 about God's loving kindness and tender mercies crumbles into dust.[63] However, the text does not need to be read in this way. Judah has not yet repented — the man has only got as far as calling them to self-examination and prayer. He then opens his prayer with a confession of sin (an important step on the road to repentance) and notes that YHWH is still angry and is still punishing Judah, and so has clearly not forgiven them yet. Forgiveness was conceived of very concretely — for God to forgive would be for the situation to change, and clearly that has not yet happened. The text does not say, "we *repented* but you have not forgiven" — it merely says, "we *transgressed* . . . you have not forgiven." This is not a complaint that God has ignored Judah's repentance. However, it *is* a heartfelt lament, and it *does* have an overtone of complaint. This complaint, unlike that in 3:1-18, is directed *towards God* with the goal of persuading him to forgive. As such it is markedly different from the man's earlier lament.

vv. 43-47 ס/*sāmek*–פ/*pê*   What does it mean to say that YHWH has "not forgiven"? 3:43-47 expands on its concrete manifestation. The first line is a little ambiguous. Either God has covered *himself* in a garment of anger or he has covered *the people* in anger and pursued them. If the former, then the imagery

---

63. Westermann, *Lamentations*, 182-83; Berlin, *Lamentations*, 95-96; Dobbs-Allsopp, *Lamentations*, 123; O'Connor, *Lamentations and the Tears of the World*, 53.

is drawn from the theophany in which God manifests himself wrapped in clouds and lightning. This would *parallel* 3:44 ("you have covered yourself in a cloud"). If the anger covers the people, then this verse *contrasts* 3:44: God covers *the people* in anger and covers *himself* in clouds. Either way, the upshot is much the same — God is angry (cf. 1:12; 2:1, 3, 6, 11, 22) and so pursues (cf. 1:3, 6) his people like hunted animals. YHWH has killed (cf. 2:4, 21) the people without mercy (cf. 2:2, 17, 21).

God has made himself impervious to prayer by wrapping himself in cloud so that prayers cannot reach him. Here the theophanic imagery is clear, but now the clouds represent not God's awesome presence with his people but his total inaccessibility: "The cloud-covered God is invisible, hidden, and beyond reach."[64] This does suggest that the people have indeed called to YHWH for help in their suffering (not necessarily in repentance), but no change in their situation has followed — he has not forgiven. The ineffectual prayer of the people here parallels the *geber's* own experience of ineffectual prayer in v. 8 ("He shut out my prayer"). But this is not a cry of utter despair, because these very words of complaint *are themselves part of a prayer* — a prayer that the man expects will, at some point, be answered. Yes, God has shut out the prayers of the people but that does not mean that they should give up praying to him because at the most fundamental level of his being God is merciful and he will not block himself off from prayer forever.

The people that God elected to be his treasured possession chosen from all the nations of the earth have been made like filth and rubbish in the presence of those very nations (cf. 1:7-8; 2:15-16). Israel's current experience feels like a divine *un*election. And yet, as such, the reader knows that things are not the way that God *wanted* them to be, and this also creates a space for hope. Nevertheless, at this point such hope is only seen in the silent spaces between the complaints.

The nations observe Judah's new status as garbage, and his enemies open their mouths in mockery against him (cf. 2:16). Judah's fate is a "pit" that induces "panic" (פחד ופחת/*paḥad wāpaḥat*) — the kind of pit dug as a trap for a hunted animal — and that resulted in "decimation and destruction" (השאת והשבר/*haššē't wĕhaššāber*).

vv. 48 פ/*pê*–51 ע/*ayin*   The man now turns to his own response to this destruction: relentless weeping. "It is as if the corporate attempt to rehearse the disaster before God has proved too much for him."[65] He weeps because of the

---

64. O'Connor, *Lamentations and the Tears of the World*, 54.
65. Provan, *Lamentations*, 102.

ruin of the daughter of his people, and he will continue to weep until YHWH takes notice. 3:50 with its focus on YHWH seeing stands between two verses, both of which begin with the word עֵינִי/ʿênî, "my eyes." The man's eyes see and weep, but YHWH does not see (as indicated by the fact that he has not acted to save). So Jerusalem's prayers that YHWH "see" her plight (1:9, 11, 20) have not yet been answered. However, the "until" indicates a hope that the divine refusal to pay attention to the pain of his people is *not* the end of the story. The current "absence" of God is only temporary. This reflects the impact of the vision of YHWH found in 3:31-33. The man knows that YHWH does not want to inflict punishment on his people, and so "with his incessant prayer of tears he endeavors to raise this painful tension in YHWH's heart to such a pitch that it becomes unbearable and he looks down and acts to save his people."[66]

There is a close connection between 3:48-49 and Jer 14:17, which reads, "Let my eyes run down with tears night and day, and let them not cease, for the virgin daughter of my people is destroyed with a great wound, with a very grievous blow." This link casts the speaker in a Jeremiah-like role, and it seems likely that the implied readers would be expected to make that connection. The man remains as traumatized by Zion's fate as he was in 2:11-13.[67]

It is not clear in 3:51 whether "the daughters of my city" refers to the young women in the city or, less likely in my view, to the other towns throughout the land that look to Jerusalem as their "mother." Either way, their fate causes the speaker deep anguish. Either his eyes hurt from weeping at their fate or his eyes afflict by revealing to him their fate.

We have argued above that this lament and weeping is not uninformed by the positive vision of YHWH in 3:22-33 nor devoid of hope. I suggest that the juxtaposition of lament and weeping with the teaching in 3:25-39 invites the readers to ponder exactly how the two sections relate to each other. Do 3:40-51 present a conscious *abandonment* of the advice in vv. 25-39, a legitimate *alternative* response to the suffering that can exist alongside that of vv. 25-39, or *a concrete manifestation* of what the penitent, hopeful, "silent" posture recommended can look like in practice. Could it be that waiting in hope on YHWH is compatible with intense weeping, loud prayer, and lament?

---

66. Renkema, *Lamentations*, 442.

67. This section of the poem stands in close relationship with the narrator's words in 2:11-13. Both focus on the speaker's intense grief and weeping on account of "the destruction of the daughter of my people" (the exact same expression occurs in both 2:11 and 3:48). This indicates that the speaker here is the narrator of chapters 1 and 2.

The Valiant Man's Salvation: Past and Future (3:52-66)

The shift from the lament over the suffering of Jerusalem to this final section of the poem, with its echoes of the psalm of praise genre,[68] is unexpected and somewhat jarring. It seems at first blush that the situation in Jerusalem has been left far behind and we have here an individual narrating his personal trials at the hands of his enemies and his prayer for YHWH's deliverance. However, if we are to consider Lamentations 3 as a *single* poem rather than as a disconnected set of fragments from different poems, then we need to ask how this final section connects with what precedes it. I propose that the *geber* is still the speaker and that he is still speaking to his fellow sufferers in Jerusalem. Here, as throughout the poem, his trials are to be taken as a microcosm of their own trials. Hence, from the fact that the focus moves back from Jerusalem's pain to his own pain, *it does not follow that Jerusalem's pain is no longer in view.* His story is intimately connected to hers, and it is precisely this fact which is the rationale behind the final section. I propose that the man tells his story as an encouragement to his fellow sufferers in Jerusalem.

This final section of the poem (3:52-66), in which the man speaks of his afflictions, corresponds to the first section (3:1-18), allowing the poem to end, as it began, with the man telling his story. However, the differences between the end and the beginning are very telling, and it is clear that, while the man narrates his persecutions, things have moved on both in terms of his attitude and in terms of God's response. The change in the man's attitude found in 3:19-24 has affected the way in which he perceived his situation. It is interesting that now, in this final section, he no longer speaks of YHWH as his enemy but rather as the one who can deliver him from his human enemies. The recovery of hope has not led him to deny that YHWH is the ultimate cause of his distress, but it has led to a shift in emphasis. The focus now is on the *immediate* cause of his sorrow (his human enemies) and on God as his savior.

vv. 52-54 **צ**/*ṣādê*   This stanza depicts the man's persecution at the hands of his enemies. Like a bird pursued by hunters, he flees from them (Ps 11:1; 124:7; 140:5; Jer 16:16; cf. Lam 1:6, 13; 3:47). Why did they hunt him? For no reason he can think of. Their malicious behavior appears to him to be arbitrary and unjustifiable: "There is neither political, nor social, nor personal history that might explain their hostility."[69] His enemies then captured him, threw him

---

68. Westermann sees the motifs as more than echoes — he thinks 3:52-58 is a reused fragment of an actual psalm of praise; *Lamentations*, 184-85.

69. Bergant, *Lamentations*, 102.

into a cistern, placed a stone over the top, and left him to die.[70] Readers may be reminded of Joseph being thrown into a cistern by his brothers (Genesis 37) or how Jeremiah was similarly thrown into a well by his enemies (Jer 38:4-28). Indeed, the man does not say merely that they "threw" him into the cistern, but that they *"destroyed* [or 'silenced'] my life in the cistern." The pit was often used in Israelite literature as a metaphor for the place of death (Ps 28:1; 30:3; 88:5; 143:7; Prov 1:12), so this man's fate is laden with symbolic overtones. Indeed, it may be that the entire description is not to be taken literally at all but as a metaphor of his impending doom. At any rate, his death was certainly the intention of his enemies. The rain would cause the water level in the cistern to rise until it was higher than his head and all hope of salvation seemed lost. Perhaps the deathly waters of Sheol are represented here (Jonah 2:5-6; 2 Sam 22:5-6; Ps 69:1-2, 14-15). Like the city, his situation was about as hopeless as one could imagine — the grave seemed his inevitable fate, so he cries out, "I am cut off!" (i.e., dead; cf. Ps 88:6; Isa 53:8).

Excursus: The Perfect Tenses in 3:52-66

The Issue

It is necessary to reflect on an issue that has generated considerable disagreement among commentators on Lamentations: the meaning of the perfect tenses in 3:52-66.

View 1: The traditional view, dating back at least as far as the LXX, is to treat them as straightforward *past tenses.* This is the way in which most modern English Bible translations take the words.

> *I called* your name, YHWH,
> from the deepest pit;
> *You heard* my voice, "Do not cover your ear
> to my relief, to my cry of anguish!"
> *You drew near* in the day I called to you,
> *You said,* "Do not fear."

View 2: By far the more popular alternative, however, is to see the perfect verbs as precative perfects expressing a desire or request. This view can be found in influential recent commentaries such as those by Gordis, Provan, Hillers, Berlin, and Dobbs-Allsop.[71]

---

70. The hunting imagery combined with the pit may remind the readers of how Israel could say, "A terrifying pit was ours" (3:47; cf. 1:6). This is a clue that his cistern mirrors their pit and guides the readers not to disconnect his suffering from Israel's suffering.

71. A minority alternative is to translate the perfect verbs in the *present tense* (so Renkema, *Lamentations,* 450). This is possible (Joüon 112f.; GKC 106n; Waltke and O'Connor,

I called [*call*] your name, YHWH,
  from the deepest pit;
Hear my voice; Do not cover your ear
  to my relief, to my cry of anguish!
Draw near in the day I call to you,
  Say, "Do not fear."

The issue is this: is the man reporting *a past deliverance* from the pit (view 1), or is he still in the pit awaiting *future* deliverance and simply *asking* YHWH to deliver him (view 2)?

Now the issues are complex, but all sides seem to agree that the simple past tense view should be the default position for the translation of the verbs and that it is only problems with that view which lead readers to understand them in other ways. So we will need to consider the objections to the traditional view and ask whether they drive readers towards non–past tense understandings. I shall argue that they do not.

It is necessary to say a little more about the traditional view. It is clear that towards the end of 52-66 the man is praying for deliverance from present oppression. So if the perfective verbs are really to be taken as *past tense* perfects, we need to see 3:52-66 as looking back to a past deliverance *and also* looking forward to a future deliverance. As Provan says, "The crucial question of interpretation in Lam. iii 52-66 is this: are two situations of distress described in this passage, or only one?"[72] So what are the problems with the traditional view? The best presentation of them is that of Iain Provan.[73]

Provan's Case against the Traditional View

Provan's main objection is that there is no obvious point at which the speaker ceases to speak of salvation in the past and begins to consider his present plight. Traditionally the transition was seen between v. 58 and v 59. Provan has two objections to this. First, "it is not a natural reading of the text to break it at this point, differentiating between 'You have taken up my cause' in v. 58 and 'You have seen the wrong done to me' in v. 59."[74] Second, in the thought world of ancient Israelites, according to Provan, there is no distinction between God seeing and God acting. If God has seen, *then God has acted to deliver* (cf. 3:50). So if the man believes that God "has seen" his *current* plight (3:59), it should follow that God has delivered him from it. But clearly that is not the case, or else he would not call on God to "look," using the imperative, in 3:63.

Provan also raises a subsidiary problem for the traditional view: 3:56 reads, "You heard (verb in perfect) my voice. Do not cover (verb in imperfect, jussive in

---

31.3) and would have the man still in the pit but waiting in hope for future salvation. I think this alternative preferable to Provan's, but also less plausible than the traditional view.

72. Provan, "Past, Present and Future," 168.
73. Provan, "Past, Present and Future," 164-75.
74. Provan, "Past, Present and Future," 169.

meaning) your ear to my relief, to my cry of anguish!" Now the second sentence is embedded in what, according to traditionalists, is a section about a past deliverance from the pit. Yet it is a plea *in the present tense.*

A second, lesser difficulty Provan could have mentioned is 3:57, which reads, "You drew near (perfect form) in the day *I call* (imperfect) to you." For traditionalists one would expect the text to read, "You drew near (perfect) in the day *I called* (perfect) to you." If one takes the imperfect verb to mean "in the day *I will call* to you" or, more plausibly, "in the day *I call* to you," then the perfect verb ("you drew near") cannot be in the past tense.

In light of these problems Provan concludes that "only a future reference for the perfect verbs of *vv.* 56-61 really does them justice."[75] Provan proposes that taking the perfect verbs as *requests* removes all of the above difficulties with the passage.

What are we to make of this critique? It is helpful to clarify that for the traditional view, as for all of the views, the enemies in 3:52-66 *must be the same enemies throughout.* They are introduced in 3:52 as "my enemies" and thereafter are simply "they." I suggest we see a transition in 3:58-59 as follows. In 3:52-58 the crisis in the pit is dealt with. The situation is described, and death seems inevitable (3:52-54); the man called on YHWH (3:55), who heard (3:56), drew near to reassure the man (3:57), and freed his life (3:58), bringing the *immediate* danger to an end. The crisis in the pit does not appear again after 3:58, which is consistent with the traditional view, according to which the man is currently no longer in the pit. In 3:59-66 the man draws YHWH's attention to the *ongoing* plots, murmurings, reproach, and mocking of these same enemies. (If the waters of the pit are still rising above his head, as nontraditionalists think, he strangely seems to have his mind on other things such as his enemy's mockery day in and day out.) The man calls on YHWH to act by judging them for their past and present treatment of him. It makes sense for the man to see YHWH's past action of rescuing him from the pit as evidence that the Lord has taken up his soul's case (3:58). God is acting as his lawyer. But this is not to say that the case is *over* and there is no contradiction (contra Provan) with the request in the next verse that God "judge" his case (3:59).

Provan claims that it would be nonsense to imagine the poet claiming that God had "seen" the wrong done to him (3:59) if the situation of oppression was ongoing (as it clearly was). However, while there is an intimate link between God's seeing and his acting, it does not follow that the two are identical. To take one paradigmatic example: God could say that he had seen (רְאָה/*r'h*) the suffering of his people in Egypt while their suffering was still ongoing (Exod 2:25; 3:7, 9). God's seeing means that deliverance is at hand, but it need not mean that deliverance has yet occurred.

Provan also worries that there is an awkward tension on the traditional view between the man's confidence that God had "seen" his suffering (3:59) and the call for God to "Look!" (3:63). But again, this is far from persuasive. Most importantly, if we listen to the actual prayers of ordinary believers, we will be familiar with a back-and-

75. Provan, "Past, Present and Future," 172.

forth between confidence that God will do x and requests that God do x. Moreover, the two verbs are not the same in Hebrew. The root נבט/*nbṭ* used in 3:63 indicates "a more penetrating visual observation"[76] than the root ראה/*r'h* used in 3:59-60. In 1:11 Lady Jerusalem calls on YHWH to "look" (ראה/*r'h*) and to "observe" (נבט/*nbṭ*). Renkema suggests that YHWH must *not only* look *but also* observe.[77] In which case it is possible to imagine that the poet knows that God is aware of his situation, but in his distress he calls for him to look even closer and thus be moved to complete the deliverance he has begun to experience. This final imperative to look leads straight into the calls for retribution and makes perfect sense.

What of the cry, "do not *cover* your ear to my relief, to my cry of anguish" in 3:56? If, as traditionalists claim, the passage is dealing with a past crisis, why is the verb in the imperfect (jussive in meaning)? Most traditionalists take the prayer as a report of the words spoken by the man from the pit.

> You heard my voice,
> "Do not cover your ear to my relief, to my cry of anguish!"

This is certainly possible, as Provan admits.[78] However, it is a little surprising. Provan points out that there are no other examples in the Old Testament where God is said to have heard something and then the words that he heard are reported. So this remains a problem for the traditional view, although it does not seem to me a strong enough reason to overturn the view.

Regarding the problem of the imperfect in 3:57a, we may simply note that the imperfect can refer to *past* time with certain particles such as אז/*'āz* and טרם/*ṭerem*.[79] I tentatively suggest that the expression "in the day" functions in this clause in a way similar to אז/*'āz* and טרם/*ṭerem*. So we could with justification translate the clause as, "You drew near in the day that *I called* to you."

Problems with the Precative View

There are problems with Provan's alternative. First, we must recall that the existence of a precative perfect in Hebrew is controverted, and even those who acknowledge its existence admit that it is very rare. The upshot of this in terms of hermeneutical method is that no perfect should be taken to be a precative *unless there is a strong reason to do so*. If the poet did intend the perfects as precative, he was certainly running a high risk of readers misunderstanding. That this is the case is clear from the fact that the very early readers who translated the LXX took the perfects to be past tense, and this was not because they did not know their Hebrew!

Second, it should give us pause for thought that, given the dire crisis faced by

---

76. Renkema, *Lamentations*, 463.
77. Renkema, *Lamentations*, 150.
78. Provan, *Lamentations*, 105; "Past, Present and Future" 171.
79. Merwe, Naudé, and Kroeze, *A Biblical Hebrew Reference Grammar*, 147; Waltke & O'Connor, *Biblical Hebrew Syntax*, 513-14.

the speaker in this section, it would have been much more rhetorically effective for the poet to use the strong imperative form of the verbs (as in 3:59, 63) rather than the weaker precative perfect if it was requests he wanted to express.

Third, Provan, Berlin, and others in this tradition translate the perfects, the imperatives, and the imperfects in 3:52-66 in exactly the same way — as imperatives. But one wonders why the Hebrew author bothered to use three different modes of the verb if he did not intend his readers to detect any differences between them.

Fourth, if we read the entirety of 3:52-66 as a simple request to YHWH for help, then we are in danger of evacuating the section of the confidence in YHWH that is expressed by taking the perfects as past tense (or even present tense or prophetic perfects). But such confidence makes sense in the light of the man's earlier recollection of YHWH's love and mercy (3:22-39). To empty this section of the confidence of faith is to imagine the man forgetting what he earlier remembered.

In conclusion, it seems to me that the most plausible interpretation is the simple past tense interpretation.

vv. 55-58 ק/*qôp*-ר/*rêš* This stanza marks the great transition from immanent death towards salvation. The man addresses God in prayer and recalls how he called on YHWH's name from the deepest pit. His crisis situation had closed down all options but prayer, and to that he turned. He cried out, "Do not cover your ear to my [cry for] relief, to my cry of anguish!" Given his previous experience of unanswered prayer (3:8) and Jerusalem's similar experience (3:44), it is hardly surprising that he speaks to God in this way. And then we read that, "You heard my voice!" This is the first and only time in Lamentations that God is said to actually hear prayers. God drew near to the man in his pit and reassured him — "Do not fear!" Again, these are the first and only direct words from YHWH to any of the sufferers in Lamentations. The words "Do not fear" may have been a common formula spoken by priests or prophets in the cultic liturgy, and this man "hears" them again in his mind as he prays and perceives that God is speaking them to him right then and there.

3:58 is the climax of the salvation story in 3:55-58: the man prayed, God heard, drew near, spoke words of comfort, and then, in v. 58, took up his soul's case and redeemed his life! God *acted* to rescue the man from his crisis situation: he took him out of the pit and the immanent threat to his life that it represented. By acting as his redeemer, God is taking on the responsibility of blood kin towards the man (Lev 25:35). And if God listened to him, then he may listen to Jerusalem's suffering people; if God drew near to him, then he may draw near to them; if God spoke words of comfort to him, then he may speak words of comfort to them; if God took up his case and redeemed him, then he may redeem Jerusalem.

vv. 59-63 ר/*rêš*-שׂ/*šîn* While the man has been delivered from the immediate danger of the pit, that is not the end of the matter, for his enemies are still at large. We could say that YHWH has *begun* to deliver him by redeeming his life from the pit but that the full deliverance from his foes is *not yet a reality.* So he pleads with God: YHWH has seen what they have done to him (their vengeance and their plots), so the man calls on him to "judge my case."[80]

The reader will notice links with the wisdom teaching in 3:34-36. There we read of those who deny a man's "justice" (מִשְׁפַּט/*mišpāṭ*) and who "pervert a man's lawsuit" (רִיב/*rîb*). The speaker rhetorically asks, "does the Lord not see?" (רָאה/*rā'â*). In vv. 58-60 the man picks up this teaching and applies it to his own concrete situation. He says that God has taken up his soul's lawsuit (רִיב/*rîb*), effectively becoming his lawyer; twice he says that God has "seen" (רָאה/*rā'â*) the evil done to him, and he calls on God to judge his "case" (מִשְׁפַּט/*mišpāṭ*). The fact that God has saved him from the pit indicates that God *has seen* the crimes committed against him and God *has heard* his cries for help, so while the plight is not fully over, the man now faces it with a growing confidence that God will complete what he has started. He is powerless to act in the face of the oppressors, but he looks to God to ensure justice is done.

The penultimate stanza drives home the ongoing evil plotted against the man by the enemies who threw him into the pit. The focus is upon their words: they reproach the man, they plot, they rise up whispering against him incessantly (cf. Jer 51:1), and, whatever they are doing, whether sitting or standing, they mock him (cf. 3:30). This public dishonoring of the man through mockery draws his ongoing suffering into line with that of Jerusalem in 1:7d; 2:15-16. In 3:59-60 God "saw" their evil *deeds,* and here God has "heard" their evil *words.* The sense of continuing anguish the man feels at this ongoing persecution is indicated both by the number of words he devotes to the description of their plotting and by the fact that, although he is now assured that God has indeed seen and heard, he cannot help interrupting his sentence in v. 63 midflow with the cry to God to "Look!"

vv. 64-66 ת/*tāw* The final stanza contains the prayer of an oppressed man for justice — a cry closely parallel to Zion's prayer in 1:21c-22. The four imperfect verbs may be understood as implicit imperatives making this a request ("Cause to return," "give," "pursue," "destroy"), or they may be expressions of confidence about what God will indeed do ("you will cause to return," "you will give," "you will pursue," "you will destroy"). I suggest that it makes sense

---

80. Assuming that the imperative of the MT is correct.

to see them as expressions of confidence concerning how God will punish the enemies *and also* as implicit requests that God indeed act in this way.[81]

The *geber* first declares/asks that YHWH punish them according to their deeds. The fact that they have been instruments for YHWH's punishment of Judah in no way excuses their wicked behavior in the eyes of the pray-er. God's justice requires that he treat the "rod of his anger" (Isa 10:5) as morally responsible. Second, we need to appreciate that the man proclaims/prays that God will punish them *as their deeds deserve* — not less and not more. Third, we need to understand that, until the enemies are out of the picture, they will be the wound in the man's side. Thus this is the prayer of a persecuted man who requests deliverance. Fourth, it is important to appreciate that the man does not take justice into his own hands (in his case this was not even an option) but surrenders the right of retribution to God.[82] Finally, as Renkema notes, "One should read 3_{31-33} side by side with 3_{64-66}: YHWH does not reject forever and grieving others is not according to his nature. The formulation of 3_{33} is general and applies to all human persons — ['sons of man'] — including Israel's enemies."[83] In light of the teaching in 3:31-33, we should not suppose that the vengeance declared/requested rules out all future hope for his enemies, even if such matters are not his concern in the prayer.

The *geber*'s second request is that God curse them with dullness of heart. It is not entirely certain what he has in mind, because the word translated "dullness" occurs only here in the Old Testament. Perhaps he wishes God to *harden* their hearts as he hardened Pharaoh's as a prelude to judgment. Alternatively, the prayer may be for them to have "*anguish* of heart."[84]

Finally, the man asks God to "pursue" them in anger, just as he "pursued" Israel (3:43). Indeed, they have "pursued" Israel too (1:3, 6), and God is asked to return the "favor" by turning the hunters into the hunted. God's pursuit of them will end in their being obliterated from the face of the earth![85] Then the man will at last be free. This final deliverance for the man would also, according to our reading of the poem, be full deliverance for Jerusalem, as her fate is bound up with his. It is interesting that the poem began with the man's complaint against God, and he would not even name God until 3:18. However, with the changed attitude and situation the poem's final word is "YHWH."

---

81. Rightly Renkema, *Lamentations*, 464.

82. On which see Firth, *Surrendering Retribution in the Psalms.*

83. Renkema, *Lamentations*, 468.

84. So Hillers, *Lamentations*, 119; Renkema, *Lamentations*, 467-68.

85. While this sounds like a prayer for *utter annihilation,* we need to take into account the rhetoric of wrath that is employed and not press it too literally (cf. Jer 48:42, 47).

Excursus: Does Lamentations 3 Undermine Lament?

Lamentations 3 opens with a complaint against God, but then the man calls to mind the traditions of God's loving kindness (3:22-24) and advises a submissive, silent, and hopeful attitude to facing suffering. It seems that the complaint of 3:1-18 is presented only in order to reject it. Does Lamentations 3 thus undermine the spiritual appropriateness of lament?

First, we should note that when 3:1-18 was composed the author had already made the transition from despair to renewed hope in YHWH, yet the integrity of the bleakness he has previously felt is preserved. In other words, he does not allow his later recovery of light to shine back into his portrayal of the darkness he was in. Such a move would have undermined the felt depths of that darkness. The man, after his recovery of hope, does not ask forgiveness for his earlier negative assessment of God, nor does he rebuke his fellow sufferers for feeling the same way. His was an understandable response, the integrity of which is preserved for later generations. The poem presents this bleak period in the man's relationship with YHWH as a part of a longer journey and not as a final destination, but that should not be seen to undermine it. While the accusation in 3:1-18 is indeed relativized, it is not delegitimized.

Second, even the recovery of hope allows for continuing lament, albeit lament in a different mode. Concerning his own situation, the man experiences a breakthrough in his redemption from the cistern but still complains to God about the behavior of his enemies and prays for their destruction (although he no longer complains about *God's* behavior towards him). Concerning the fate of the nation, he still weeps incessantly until YHWH looks down, sees, and delivers. These modified lament responses also do not indicate the end of the journey with God but merely a further phase of it. The poems look beyond their present to a future in which *šālôm* is restored, but until that point is reached lament in one mode or another has its place.

The coexistence of hope and praise with lament in 3:22-66 is indicative of the ambiguities of walking with God in this world. The Christian may express the tension in terms of the now and the not-yet. When does the new age of salvation begin? On the one hand, now, because Christ has been raised and the Spirit has been given, enabling believers to participate in the new life of Christ. On the other hand, not-yet because sin and death are still so evident in human experience. Present Christian existence is a tension between the now and the not-yet of redemption. Consequently, like the man, the "Hallelujah!" of praise marks the Christian life, but so too does the "Alas!" of lament with its focus on our *present* sufferings, and the "Maranatha!" of hope, with its focus on our deliverance *yet-to-come*.

LAMENTATIONS 4: SIEGE AND SALVATION

v. 1 א/*'ālep*

> Alas! [The] gold has dulled!
> > The pure gold has changed!
> The holy stones are poured out,
> > at the corner of every street.

v. 2 ב/*'bêt*

> The precious sons of Zion,
> > Worth their weight in fine gold,
> Alas! They are considered earthen pots,
> > the work of a potter's hands.

v. 3 ג/*gîmel*

> Even wild animals offer the breast,
> > they nurse their cubs.
> [But] the Daughter of my people has become cruel,
> > like the ostriches in the wilderness.

v. 4 ד/*dālet*

> The tongue of the suckling child sticks
> > to the roof of his mouth because of thirst.
> Children request bread;
> > there is nobody breaking it for them.

v. 5 ה/*hê*

> Those who ate delicacies
> > are desolate in the streets.
> Those raised in scarlet [clothing]
> > embrace ash heaps.

v. 6 ו/*wāw*

> Indeed, greater was the transgression-punishment of the daughter of
> my people
> > than the sin-punishment of Sodom,
> which was overthrown in a moment,
> > and no [human] hands were turned against[1] it.

---

1. The meaning of the verb חלו/*ḥālû* here is disputed. If it derives from חלה/*ḥālâ* ("to become weak/sick"; cf. LXX, Syr), it says that "no hands were *wearied* in her." This is rather ambig-

v. 7 ז/*zayin*

> Her Nazirites were brighter than snow,
> > they were whiter than milk.
> Their bodies were ruddier than corals,
> > their hair² was *lapis lazuli.*

v. 8 ח/*ḥêt*

> Their appearance is darker than soot,
> > they are not recognized in the streets.
> Skin shrivels on their bone,
> > it has become as dry as wood.

v. 9 ט/*ṭêt*

> Better off were those pierced by the sword
> > than those pierced by hunger —
> those who bled from being stabbed
> > by the lack of produce from the field.

v. 10 י/*yôd*

> The hands of compassionate women
> > have cooked their children.
> They became their food
> > during the destruction of [the] daughter of my people.

v. 11 כ/*kāp*

> YHWH completed his fury;
> > He poured out the burning of his anger,

---

uous and may mean that no sadness was felt by others at her downfall (hands wearing from wringing them) or perhaps that, as there was no extended famine, none of the inhabitants had time to weaken and fade. If it derives from חול/*ḥûl* ("to dance/to writhe/to twist"), it may mean that no hands were *wrung* over the fate of Sodom or perhaps none of the inhabitants had time for their hands to "tremble." Alternatively, חול/*ḥûl* can have the connotation "to turn against" (2 Sam 3:29; Jer 23:19; 30:23; Hos 11:6, McDaniel, "Philological Studies in Lamentations," 45-48) and may mean "attack." If that is the case, the clause means that no human hands attacked Sodom (God punished without human mediation). My translation follows this latter route because it has a slight edge contextually.

2. Lit. "their cut," so many take it as a reference to "their form." This is indeed possible. However, Hillers makes a reasonable case to translate the text as "their *beards* were [like] dark [blue] stone" on the grounds that in the ancient Near East it was common for facial hair on sculptures to be represented by inlaid blue stone; *Lamentations,* 140-41. This also fits with a reference to Nazirites, who did not shave.

And he kindled a fire in Zion
and it devoured her foundations.

v. 12 ל/lāmed

The kings of the earth did not believe,
nor did any of the inhabitants of the world,
that an adversary or an enemy could enter
through the gates of Jerusalem.

v. 13 מ/mêm

[This was] because of [the] sins of her prophets
[and the] iniquities of her priests,
who shed in the midst of her
[the] blood of [the] righteous.

v. 14 נ/nûn

They stagger, blind, through the streets.
They were defiled by the blood
so they [i.e., others] were not able
to touch their garments.[3]

v. 15 ס/sāmek

"Depart! Unclean!" they called to them.
"Depart! Depart! Do not touch!"
So they fled, they even wandered.
[But] they said, among the nations,
"They should not continue to sojourn [with us]."

v. 16 פ/pê

The presence of YHWH divided them,
He does not continue to show regard for them.
The presence of the priests they did not honor;
To the elders they did not show favor.

3. Alternatively, it may be that "they" are the priests and prophets. Perhaps they touched with their clothing what they were not allowed to touch — unclean things. Thus Renkema (534-37): "Things forbidden to them, they touch with their clothing"; *Lamentations*. The subject is taken as "others" by Berlin, House, O'Connor. LXX reads, "her watchmen staggered in the streets, they were defiled with blood in their weakness, they touched their raiment." Here those who stagger are not the priests but are contaminated by accidentally touching the priests. For a survey of the many different suggested emendations and interpretations of this very difficult text, see Albrektson, *Studies in the Text;* and Hillers, *Lamentations*, 142.

v. 17 **ע**/*ʿayin*

> Our eyes continue to be spent
> > [looking] for our helper — pointless!
> In our watchtower we watched
> > for a nation that will not save us.

v. 18 **צ**/*ṣādê*

> They stalked our steps
> > so that we could not walk in our town squares.
> Our end drew near,
> > our time was up,
> > > yes, our end had come.

v. 19 **ק**/*qôp*

> Our pursuers were swifter
> > than eagles of [the] heavens.
> Over the mountains they chased us;
> > In the desert they lay in wait for us.

v. 20 **ר**/*rêš*

> [The] breath of our nostrils, YHWH's anointed,
> > was captured in their pits —
> [He of] whom we said, "In his shade,
> > we will live among the nations."

v. 21 **ש**/*šîn*

> Rejoice and be glad, Daughter Edom;
> > You who dwell in the land of Uz!
> Also to you [the] cup will pass,
> > You shall become drunk and strip yourself naked.

v. 22 **ת**/*tāw*

> He will finish your transgression-punishment, Daughter Zion,
> > He will no longer keep you exiled.
> He will attend to your transgression-punishment, Daughter Edom,
> > He will uncover your sins.

Introduction

From the reflections on the strongman's suffering in Poem 3 we are drawn back again to consider the terrible suffering of the people left behind in Jerusalem. Some think that chapter 4 is the most hopeless in the whole book. However, this reading does not give due attention to 4:21-22, which are, in fact, the most hopeful and confident in Lamentations. In my view, chapter 3 has provided cause for Zion to hope that the *geber's* journey from the pit to salvation can be hers. Chapter 4 brings the readers back into the midst of Zion's ongoing crisis and makes very clear that Zion has not yet begun to see the *geber's* story mirrored in her own. The implied audience, coming to the poem via chapter 3, will be asking whether this crisis in which Zion finds herself is the end of her story. The climax of the poem is an "oracle" asserting that it is not and that, like the strongman, she too will be delivered. The deep darkness of 4:1-20 should not be allowed to obscure the bright light of 4:21-22. But, in the same way, the word of hope at the climax of the poem must not be allowed to render the terrible plight of the inhabitants of the city less dreadful or shocking. Lamentations 4 is dominated by the theme of degradation: all that was precious and beautiful has become worthless and ugly. Normal social structures have collapsed, and the world has been turned upside down. Lamentations 4 takes the darkness *very* seriously, even if it does not allow it the last word.

There are three speakers in chapter 4: the narrator (4:1-16),[4] the people of Jerusalem or their leaders (4:17-20), and an authoritative voice promising salvation, perhaps, but not necessarily, a prophet or priest (4:21-22). It is possible that the final words of promise are actually the narrator's. If that is so, then there are only two voices in the poem. The narrator describes the pathetic plight of people under siege. He is more detached in his descriptions, although he indicates his unity with the sufferers by his references to "my people" (4:3, 6, 10). This lessened emotional engagement, given the highly shocking subject matter, perhaps gives the impression of emotional exhaustion on the part of the narrator.[5]

---

4. But taking issue with Gerstenberger, who sees the narrator's voice as YHWH's voice or that of YHWH's authorized officiant; *Psalms, Part 2,* 498. Renkema sees Jerusalem as speaking in 4:1-6, 10-11, and 4:7-9 as the direct voice of the poets; *Lamentations,* 488. However, this seems unlikely, as the voice speaks about "the precious children of Zion" (4:2), not "my children," and in v. 11 clearly speaks of Zion as one distinct from the speaker. Miller argues that in 4:1-16 the first person speech is that of Zion (4:3, 6, 10) and the third person speech is the narrator (4:1-2, 4-5, 7-9); "Poetry and Personae," 186. This is possible, but it is not necessary to multiply speakers. A single speaker in 4:1-16 makes sense of the data we have and is to be preferred.

5. O'Connor, *Lamentations and the Tears of the World,* 58; Dobbs-Allsopp, *Lamentations,* 129. Berlin disagrees; *Lamentations,* 103, n. 1.

The poem does not conform to any pure genre but does have clear resemblances with chapters 1 and 2 with its mix of lament and dirge elements. Claus Westermann thinks that 4:1-10, 14-16 is a description of misery from a direct complaint of the community. 4:11-13 corresponds to an accusation against God and an attribution of guilt, while 4:21-22 is the final element of a communal lament.[6] Westermann argues that the current poem has been reorganized around the acrostic pattern, messing up some of the pure genre structures. Also, some expected elements (like the accusation against the enemies) have been cut while alien elements (e.g., the description in vv. 17-20) have been introduced. Such speculation on the prehistory of the poem is not of direct relevance for us as we seek to understand the poem in its final form. We should note, however, that the contrast between the glorious past and the woeful present so characteristic of the dirge is more prominent in Lamentations 4 than elsewhere in the book.

In light of the above and the following exegesis, the structure of the chapter can be analyzed as follows.

I. Narrator: Degradation within the City (4:1-16)
  1. The neglected children and the starving inhabitants (4:1-10)
    A. Zion's starving children and "cruel" mothers (4:1-4)
      B. Zion's wealthy citizens made desolate (4:5)
        C. Zion's lingering punishment is even worse than Sodom's swift punishment (4:6)
      B1. Zion's Nazirites wither (4:7-8)
        C1. Better to die quickly by the sword than slowly by famine (4:9)
    A1. Zion's mothers eat their children (4:10)
  2. YHWH punishes the city and the sinful "holy" men (4:11-16)
    A. YHWH punishes the city (4:11-12)
      (i) YHWH burned Zion to the ground (4:11)
      (ii) The kings of the earth were stunned at Zion's fall (4:12)
    B. YHWH punishes the "holy" men (4:13-16)
      (i) The cause of this fall was the "murder" of the righteous by priests and prophets (4:13)
      (ii) The priests and prophets became unclean from the shed blood and were shunned by their own people, the Gentiles, and YHWH (4:14-16)
II. Community: Hunted and Caught (4:17-20)

6. Westermann, *Lamentations*, 198-200.

    A. Looking in vain for help from an ally (4:17)

    B. Hunted by the swift pursuers

       (i)   Hiding from hunters in the city (4:18)

       (ii) Pursued by the hunters across mountains (4:19)

       (iii) Our king captured in their pits (4:20)

III. "Prophetic" Voice: An "Oracle" of Judgment and Salvation (4:21-22)

    A. The cup of judgment shall pass to Edom (4:21)

      B. Zion's exile is ended (4:22a)

    A1. Edom's sins will be punished (4:22b)

What is missing in Lamentations 4 is any direct prayer to God. For that we must await the next chapter, which is an extended prayer for salvation. Lamentations 4 should not be read in isolation.

The Neglected Children and the Starving Inhabitants (4:1-10)

Lamentations 4:1-10 is very dark. "The cause of the degradation is the famine of the siege, and its effects are described in a realistic sequence in which starvation weakens the population: first the children, who are starving (vv. 3-4); then the adults, whose health deteriorates precipitously (vv. 5-8); then the ultimate trope for starvation: cannibalism (v. 10)."[7]

    Adele Berlin points out the effective use of color. Before the siege the colors are bright and shining — gold and scarlet, dazzling white, red, sapphire (vv, 1, 2, 5, 7) — but the famine washes the color out of everything and all that is left is black (v. 8).[8]

v. 1 א/*ālep*–v. 2 ב/*bêt* The opening word of chapter 4 ("Alas," איכה/*'êkâ*) serves to tie the poem in with chapters 1 and 2, both of which open in the same way. The mournful cry of despair introduces the awful descriptions that follow *and the way in which they should be interpreted* (i.e., with shock and despair).

    The emphasis in 4:1-2 is on how that which is precious and valuable is treated as though it were worthless. At first sight 4:1 seems to describe the valuable gold and holy stones, most likely from the temple, that are simply scattered in the streets and left to fade and grow dim. Zion's glorious temple is rendered valueless, or in the words of 2:1, "[YHWH has] cast [down] from

---

7. Berlin, *Lamentations*, 103.

8. Berlin, *Lamentations*, 103-4.

heaven to earth the splendor of Israel."[9] The fact that pure gold does not tarnish accentuates the shocking and "impossible" devaluation of such precious material. But as the reader absorbs 4:2, he or she realizes that the tarnished gold and the scattered holy stones are in fact the *sons* of Zion. It is those children, worth their own weight in gold, that are treated as worthless pottery that when broken is simply discarded. *They* grow dim, and *they* lie scattered on street corners (cf. 2:12, 19). In this way the destruction and devaluation of the temple and of the children are drawn into parallel.

v. 3 ג/gîmel–v. 4 ד/dālet The way that the precious children are treated as valueless is expanded in 4:3-4. If even wild animals that inhabit desolate places (Isa 13:22; Mic 1:8) suckle their young, then how much more should humans (4:3)? Yet the suckling children in Zion[10] have no breast milk to drink, and nobody shares any bread with them (4:4; cf. 2:11c-12). The famine (caused by the siege?) has overridden the normal biological impulses that motivate care for one's young and has dehumanized the survivors. "Suffering's corrosive cruelty has reduced her to behaving in a manner not even found among scavengers."[11] Nobody shares any bread with the children when they ask for it. Was this because there was none or because adults were keeping what little there was for themselves? The context may indicate the latter. The "daughter of my people" has become like the ostrich, a ritually unclean bird (Lev 11:16; Deut 14:15) that abandons its own eggs in certain situations (cf. Job 39:13-17).[12]

v. 5 ה/hê The focus moves from starving children to the fate of prominent adults.[13] Those who once ate rare and expensive foods (Gen 49:20) and were dressed in the finest crimson-dyed clothing now share in the same desolate calamity as the children. In a reversal of fortunes they are now "desolate in the streets," living and scavenging among the incinerated rubbish like the desti-

9. Many commentators shy away from seeing any allusion to the temple gold and "holy stones" (either the stones from which the temple was built or the twelve stones on the high priest's breastplate), but given the focus in Lamentations on the temple and the reference to "holy (קדש/qōdeš) stones" there seems no good reason to avoid a temple allusion, even if the case for one is not watertight; see Renkema, *Lamentations*, 491-96.

10. Children were breast-fed for considerably longer than they are in modern Western societies (1 Sam 1:21-24).

11. Dobbs-Allsopp, *Lamentations*, 131.

12. Ancient Israelites interpreted this behavior as a lack of maternal care (for more information on the behavior, see Provan, *Lamentations*, 112). Modern biologists may well see it differently.

13. Alternatively the verse may refer to Zion's wealthy *children*.

135

tute (1 Sam 2:8; Ps 113:7; Job 24:10; cf. the *geber's* fate in 3:15). This is a famine so severe that even those one may expect to be most insulated against its effects join its victims. Starvation is no respecter of persons in this "democracy of deprivation."[14]

v. 6 ו/wāw   The story of Sodom's terrible sin and its speedy annihilation was well known in ancient Israel (Gen 18-19; Deut 29:23; 32:32; Amos 4:11; Isa 1:9-10; 3:9; 13:9; Jer 23:14; 49:18; 50:40; Ezek 16:46-58; Zeph 2:9). Here it is not totally clear whether the poet is contrasting the severity of Sodom and Israel's sin (Israel's transgression far outstrips *even Sodom's* sin), or the severity of their punishment (Sodom's *speedy* destruction was far less severe than Israel's *lingering* death), or perhaps both. The word עֲוֺן/ʻāwôn normally means "transgression" and חַטָּאת/ḥaṭṭāʼt normally means "sin," but both can be used to refer to the *punishment* for transgression and sin (1 Sam 28:10; Zech 14:19; Lam 3:39; 5:7). In the context of Lamentations 4, with its eye on the dreadful and prolonged suffering of Jerusalem's populace, a focus on punishment seems likely. However, this should not lead us to think that Israel's sinfulness is not also in view. The choice of words allows the text to function both ways, and I have translated the words as "transgression-punishment and "sin-punishment" to highlight the link between the effect and its cause.

The verb חָלוּ/ḥālû near the end of 4:6 is difficult. Certainty evades us, but I am inclined to take it to mean that no human hands were turned against Jerusalem to attack it. Thus the contrast is between Sodom's fate (quick and *not mediated via human enemies*) and Jerusalem's fate (lingering and *mediated via human opponents*). The contrast is shocking because Sodom was so notorious for both its great sin and God's fierce punishment of it. Yet, the poet laments, Jerusalem's covenant faithlessness constitutes a sin even greater than Sodom's, and her punishment makes that of Sodom pale into insignificance.

v. 7 ז/zayin–v. 8 ח/ḥêt   Famine will ravage the health of a human body, transforming friends and acquaintances into barely recognizable "monsters." Such is the fate of Jerusalem's Nazirites. There is some disagreement over who these "Nazirites" are. A minority see them as the religious group spoken of in Num 6:1-21. Nazirites were nonpriestly men who dedicated themselves to a life of holiness to YHWH. They abstained from alcohol, never cut their hair, and did not contaminate themselves by touching dead bodies. It is perfectly possibly that it is this "holy" group of men who, along with the rest of the city,

---

14. O'Connor, *Lamentations and the Tears of the World*, 61.

are withering away (cf. Amos 2:11-12). Alternatively, it is possible to translate "Nazirites" as "princes" or "nobles" (Gen 49:26 and Deut 33:16 use the word to refer to one who wears a crown [רזנ/*nēzer*]).

4:7 extols the physical beauty of the Nazarites: pure and healthy white skin (or clothing), a ruddy complexion, a beard (or form) as stunning as the transparent blue stone *lapis lazuli* (cf. Songs 5:10-15). The famine has changed all that. The skin purer than snow and whiter than milk (4:7) is now blacker than soot (4:8).[15] The (lit.) bone(s) that were ruddier than coral (4:7) now have shriveled skin like dry trees on them (4:8). The people who could be compared with precious jewels are now compared to worthless wood. Before they would have been known by all the citizens, but now they wander the streets unrecognized and unrecognizable (cf. Job 2:12).

v. 9 ט/*ṭêt*–v. 10 י/*yôd* The graphic descriptions of the famine reach a dreadful but inevitable conclusion in 4:9 and a horrific climax in 4:10. Returning to the theme highlighted in the contrast between Sodom's swift destruction and Jerusalem's lingering suffering in 4:6, the poet sums up: it is better to be pierced by the sword and to die quickly than to be pierced by hunger and to die a slow, painful, and dehumanizing death. That is the poet's conclusion.[16] And the horrific climax? That the children we heard about in 4:3-4 are not merely neglected and starving, though that is shocking enough, but are actually being cooked and eaten by their own mothers (a scenario depicted as a covenant curse in Lev 26:29 and Deut 28:52-57; cf. 2 Kgs 6:29; Lam 2:20)! In the normal course of things, a mother's strongest instinct is to protect and nurture her children at all costs. The women here are not monsters; they are described as "compassionate" (a related word to the word for "womb"; cf. God's compassion in 3:22). Yet the experience during "the destruction of the daughter of my people" (cf. 2:11; 3:48) was so severe that caring mothers do what would normally be utterly unthinkable. The poet suggests the tensions felt by the women by speaking, not of how the *women* boiled the children, but how their *hands* did. The sick irony is that the children were the means by which the women would survive into the future (by caring for them as they got older and by surviving them), and yet in order to survive the mothers must eat their own means of survival. One may assume that the mothers only ate the children who were already dead, but even so one could hardly imagine

---

15. Perhaps blackened from hunger and illness, or perhaps from searching the ash heaps for food like those in 4:5.

16. And it suggests that the implied claim in 3:39 (that if one has survived one should count one's blessings) is not always true.

a more shocking and sickening image to serve as a climax to the description of the famine in vv. 1-10.[17]

YHWH Punishes the City and the Sinful "Holy" Men (4:11-16)

v. 11 כ/*kāp* The poet now turns from Jerusalem's suffering to their source: Jerusalem's own God. YHWH has given full vent to (lit., "completed") his fury (2:4).[18] There were no half measures here, and God's wrath works itself out until it achieves its purposes! This fury is then described as the "pouring out" (cf. 2:4, 19; 4:11) of burning anger (cf. 1:12; 2:1, 3, 6, 21, 22; 3:43, 66). In a possible allusion to Sodom's destruction (cf. 4:6), we read that God's burning anger kindled a fire in the city that utterly consumed not merely the walls, houses, palaces, and the temple but *the very foundations* on which the city (and particularly the temple) was built. There is nothing left to rebuild upon. The effect of the hyperbole is to emphasize *total and utter destruction*. The temple-city that YHWH founded and loves he has now razed to the ground.

v. 12 ל/*lāmed* Many Israelites believed that Jerusalem was invulnerable to enemy attack because YHWH would protect it (e.g., 2 Sam 7:11-16; Ps 48:1-6; 78:68; 132:8, 13-14; Jer 26:11). Gentiles would not have seen things in that way. Nevertheless, Jerusalem had stood for centuries and had survived previous attacks. Even though this verse is hyperbolic and reveals more of an Israelite astonishment at the fall of Jerusalem than of a Gentile one, "it is not far-fetched to think that kings marveled that this long surviving city had now fallen."[19] The destruction of YHWH's city is a fact so utterly impossible to absorb that not only God's people but *even Gentiles*, from kings to farmers, are presented as standing in amazement!

v. 13 מ/*mêm* So why did YHWH do this astonishing deed? 4:13 says that it was because of the sins of Zion's prophets (cf. 2:14) and the iniquities of her priests. The audience will understand that the poet is not suggesting that *only* the prophets and priests are to blame. In chapter 1 it is Lady Zion, repre-

---

17. It is not clear whether this description of cannibalism is to be taken as a literal account of what actually happened or as a literary symbol, inherited from the tradition (e.g., Lev 26:29), of extreme famine (for a nonhistorical approach see Hillers, "History and Poetry in Lamentations," 157-61).

18. Berlin sees a contrast with 3:22, which says, "his compassions are not completed" (i.e., not used up); *Lamentations*, 109.

19. House, *Lamentations*, 443. See also Renkema, *Lamentations*, 525.

senting *the whole city,* who is blamed, and this is confirmed by the communal confession in 3:39-42. However, a failure of leadership seems to be perceived as central to the degeneration of the people (2:14). This verse focuses on how the prophets and priests shed the blood of the righteous in Jerusalem (a crime for which no sacrifices could atone). Perhaps this is not intended literally and is merely an indirect reference to idolatry, which was associated with bloodshed (Ezek 22:1-5; Ps 106:36-39). Alternatively, it may mean that the failure to provide leadership led to the catastrophe, making them guilty of the blood shed by the enemy. However, it is quite possible that stories like that in Jeremiah 26 are in mind. Jeremiah is initially sentenced to death by the priests and prophets for his subversive message (Jer 26:1-11). While, in the end, he is spared, we read that the prophet Uriah was killed for what he preached (Jer 26:20-23). Jeremiah's ongoing conflicts with the prophets and priests in Jerusalem leading up to the Babylonian exile testify to their resistance to "the righteous," even if they would not have seen it that way. By shedding blood, those who were intended to be the most pure have become impure and have polluted the land (Gen 4:10-12; Num 35:33; Ps 106:38-39; Ezek 22:1-5)

v. 14 נ/*nûn*–v. 15 ס/*sāmek* Who are the "they" that wander blind in the streets, defiled by blood? The righteous?[20] The people?[21] The priests and prophets covered in the blood of their victims? In the context of 4:13-16 it makes most sense to take the prophets and priests as the subjects. Perhaps blindness is a metaphor for distress (Deut 28:29; Isa 59:10; Zeph 1:17) or more likely for the lack of divine guidance: the seers cannot see (cf. Lam 2:14; Isa 56:10).

By shedding innocent blood the prophets and priests have become unclean. The cultic holy men are pictured as being rejected by their own people for being ritually and morally "dirty" (Lev 21:11; Num 16:26)! Yet another reversal! Nobody would touch them for fear of being ritually contaminated by the impure "holy" men. We should note that there would be a special disgrace for a priest to defile his holy, cultic garments with the blood of the righteous. They (the priest? the people?) urgently call out to them (the people? the priests?), "Depart! Unclean! Depart! Depart!" just as lepers do (Lev

---

20. This is unlikely because (a) how do *dead* people wander the streets? (b) why would the *victims* be considered defiled?

21. I judge this unlikely because (a) 4:13 was about the priests and prophets and 4:14 continues with "they" and *no new subject is introduced;* (b) in 4:13 the priests and prophets shed blood and in 4:14 "they" are covered in blood and polluted. Given (a) this most likely suggests the holy men covered in the blood of their victims.

13:45).[22] And just as the leper cannot come into contact with God's holy space, so now the holy priests and prophets themselves are cut off from God! As fugitives they flee from their own people and become homeless wanderers (cf. Cain in Gen 4:11-12). But even the nations will not allow them to remain as resident aliens, perhaps because they are *so profoundly* defiled that even the unclean Gentiles cannot tolerate them in their midst.

Given that the rest of Lamentations portrays the continuing presence of prophets and priests in the ruined city (e.g., 1:4, 19; 2:9, 14), this unit either refers only to a *subgroup* of prophets and priests or it is a *quasi-fictional description* designed as a critique of the religious leadership. The latter is more likely, as the description of priests wandering the city soaked in the blood of their victims is unlikely to be literal.

v. 16 ‎פ‎/*pê* YHWH himself is the cause of the scattering of the priests and prophets described in 4:14-15. Exile is the climax of the divine curses against God's sinful people, and in this imaginative portrait the sinful leaders experience *not only* expulsion from the Holy Land but even from the surrounding nations. "The presence of YHWH" scatters them; he no longer honors them (lit., "observes/regards them"; cf. Zion's plea in 1:11c for YHWH to "observe"). As a consequence, the leaders of the nations do not show respect for "the presence [lit., 'the faces'] of the priests" nor show favor to the elders. Elders were due special respect, but the values of the world have been turned horribly upside down on the Day of YHWH's judgment. The shift from priests and prophets in 4:13 to priests and elders in 4:16 is most likely because the reference is to the leadership of Judah in general: priests, prophets, and elders.

Community: Hunted and Caught (4:17-20)

The poem shifts in 4:17-20 as the suffering community (note the use of "we," "us," and "our"), or its representative, speaks of the vain wait for salvation (4:17) and the panic of being hunted by the enemy (4:18-20).

v. 17 ‎ע‎/*'ayin* During the siege the people longed for another nation to come and deliver them. Most likely they had hoped that Egypt would come to

---

22. In the Hebrew it says that "they called to/about them," so it is not totally clear whether the people call out about the priests or the priests call out to the people. The parallel with the leper may make the latter alternative more likely, although it may be best to allow the text to remain ambiguous.

be "our helper" (עֶזְרָתֵנוּ/ʿezrātēnû) (cf. the expectation that Egypt would aid prior to the original Babylonian attack, Jer 34:21; 37:5-11). They looked and looked and wore out their eyes with looking, but it was pointless (הֶבֶל/hebel). The military deliverer did not come. As in the past, Egypt had again proven to be "a broken reed" that could not be relied upon (Isa 36:6). As Isaiah said, "Egypt's help (יַעְזֹרוּ/ya'zorû) is worthless (הֶבֶל/hebel) and empty" (Isa 30:7a).

v. 18 צ/ṣādê–v. 19 ק/qôp The human opponents of Jerusalem appear for the first time in this poem. The imagery is of a hunt with only one possible outcome — capture. The people had to hide away, for they were being hunted down (cf. 3:52), and to venture into the public squares where they could be seen would be to court disaster. Presumably this refers to when the walls were breached and the foe entered the city.[23] One can evade the enemy for only so long, and time was up: the population's end drew near, the wall was breached, and the end came. They run! Their pursuers (cf. 1:3, 6) are inhumanly swift like eagles; there can be no escape. They are determined and continue the chase up onto the mountains; they cannot be shaken off. They are also crafty and patient as they lie in wait, ready to ambush the people in the wilderness. The description is likely grounded in the actual experience of the final flight from Jerusalem of Zedekiah and others after the wall was breached (e.g., 2 Kings 25). However, it is generalized and poetic, allowing for wider applications.

v. 20 ר/rêš The climax of 4:17-20, indeed of 4:1-20, is the point at which the ambush laid by the pursuers is sprung and the king of Judah is caught in their traps. Westermann sees 4:17-20 as a mini-lament for the loss of the king, with the words "was captured in their snares" corresponding to the theme of the announcement of death in a dirge.[24] Most commentators think that the particular king in question is Zedekiah, who fled from Jerusalem towards the desert when the wall was broken through. He was captured by the Babylonians, his sons were put to death in front of him, his eyes were put out, and he was taken off into captivity in Babylon (2 Kgs 25:4-7; Jer 39:1-10; 52:1-11). Lamentations 4:17-20 fits this scenario well. The king is not just any citizen, he is "YHWH's anointed" and rules over the people on behalf of God (Ps 89:19-27). He is "the breath of our nostrils," which is to say that the lives of the people depend upon him.[25] The people had thought that their God-

---

23. Elsewhere in Lamentations the public squares were not empty but full of suffering people.

24. Westermann, *Lamentations*, 204.

25. Canaanite and Egyptian leaders were described in this way also (see Hillers, *Lamentations*, 151-52).

appointed king would, like a tree on a hot day, offer them protective shade as they lived in their promised land located in the midst of the nations (2 Sam 7:10-11). Their confidence in the Davidic ruler would be based in part on their God's own promise to David that one of his descendants would always sit on the throne (2 Samuel 7). The loss of the king puts the divine promise under threat and was a devastating blow to Judah's self-understanding. "For Judah the Davidic king was visible theology. The prolonged continuity of Davidic monarchy was a sign that, in spite of the many failures and disobedience of their kings, YHWH still remained mercifully close by. Their present experience, however, appeared to be evidence that God's patience had reached its end."[26] Lamentations has already described the loss of much of the populace, of the impregnable Holy City, and of the very House of YHWH. It now seems to put the nail in the coffin by speaking of a rupture in the Davidic dynasty. Such a thing had never happened in the centuries-long history of the royal line! Is this the end?

"Prophetic" Voice: An "Oracle" of Judgment and Salvation (4:21-22)

4:21-22 comes right out of the blue! The tone of chapter 4 has been to focus on the absolutely dire situation in Jerusalem, and by 4:20 the audience is left with the distinct feeling that the end has come. Suddenly, from left field, comes what has the feel of a prophetic oracle[27] proclaiming divine judgment on Edom for its treatment of Judah and an end to Judah's exile. The shift from no-hope to confident-hope is so dramatic and so unexpected that one is left disorientated.[28] What precipitated it? Nothing in chapter 4 has provided any grounds for hope. Could it be that the experience of the strong man in Lamentations 3 provides the inspiration for hope? While I do not think that the king in 4:20 is the man in chapter 3, the reference to the "pit" in which the

---

26. Renkema, *Lamentations*, 557.

27. Westermann refers to the verses as a "petition" and a "wish" (*Lamentations*, 205) and Dobbs-Allsopp thinks that contextually they should be understood as "wishes instead of declarative sentences" (*Lamentations*, 138). However, the language cannot be described as either a "wish" or a "petition" — it expresses either a *confident expectation* or a promise of what will happen.

28. Westermann's tentative speculation that it was originally preceded by a petition now removed and replaced by 4:17-20 does nothing to account for the inexplicable shift in the current text. Indeed, one wonders why the final redactor would remove the prayer if there ever was one; *Lamentations*, 199.

king was captured will remind readers of the "cistern" from which the man in chapter 3 was delivered. By calling Lamentations 3 to mind one is calling to mind the paradigm of hope for the nation. Will the king experience deliverance like the man? 4:21-22 suggests that he will.

v. 21 שׂ/*šîn*–v. 22 תּ/*tāw*   For the first and only time in Lamentations an opponent nation is named — Edom. Relations between Edom and Israel in the exilic period were as fractious as those between their ancestors, the brothers Esau and Jacob. Edom was a traditional enemy in the prophetic literature (Isa 34:5-17; 63:1-6; Ezek 25:12-14; 35:3-15; Joel 3:19; Obadiah; Mal 1:2-5), and during the exilic period feelings of anger against Edom were especially high. It is speculated that Edom, instead of assisting its "brother" Judah against Babylon, rejoiced at the attack and used it as an opportunity to plunder the land in Babylon's wake (Obad 11; Ps 137:8; Ezekiel 35; Joel 3:19-21).[29]

The "oracle" first calls on Daughter Edom from the Land of Uz (Gen 36:28; 1 Chr 1:42-43) to "Rejoice and be glad!" But the call is a mocking one: rejoice *while you still can.* The cup of God's wrath that Daughter Judah has drunk from will pass to Edom, so Zion and Edom will effectively swap places. The imagery of the cup of divine anger is common in the Old Testament (Ps 75:8; Isa 51:17, 22; Jer 25:15-29; 49:12; 51:7; Ezek 23:31-34; Hab 2:15-16). The alcoholic content of the cup could be diluted, indicating less severe punishment. Daughter Edom will be passed this cup, will become drunk with punishment, and will strip herself naked. Her body will be shamefully exposed for all to see, as was Zion's in Lam 1:8-10. The parallel between 4:21d ("you shall . . . strip yourself bare") and 22d ("He will expose your sins") indicates that the public stripping is a metaphor for God's exposure of her sins.

As for Judah, we see that her iniquity-punishment is finished and her exile is over! The very last word in Lamentations that fits the acrostic pattern that runs through chapters 1 to 4 is תּם/*tam* ("he completed"). In this way the poetic form itself portrays deliverance as the end of Zion's story. The perfect tense ("he completed") is best taken as a so-called prophetic perfect indicating a certain future ("he will complete").

Edom and Zion swap places in these verses. Zion has drunk from God's cup of wrath, but now Edom will. Zion has been stripped bare, but now Edom will be. Zion's punishment (עֲוֹנֵךְ/*ʿăwōnēk*) is completed, but Edom's

---

29. See esp. Lindsay, "Edomite Westward Expansion." Lindsay argues that the evidence supports the view that Edom tried with increasing intensity from the ninth to the sixth centuries to expand westward and that its siding with Babylon was the breakthrough it needed in overthrowing the Judahite state and establishing settlements in the Negev.

iniquity (עֲוֹנֵךְ/ʿăwōnēk) will be attended to by God. There is also a wordplay on Edom's *uncovering* (גִּלָּה/gillâ) and Zion's end of *exile* (הֶגְלוֹתֵךְ/haglôtēk) as both words have the same root: גלה/glh.

4:21-22 represents the assurance of an answer to Lady Zion's prayer in 1:21-22 that God would punish her enemies for their sins with the same punishments that she had received for her own sins (cf. 3:61-66). It also represents the assurance of an answer to Zion's prayers that YHWH would see her pain and deliver her. The promise is that Zion's prayers will be answered.[30]

LAMENTATIONS 5: RESTORE US

v. 1   Remember, YHWH, what has happened to us!
  Look and see our reproach!

v. 2   Our inheritance has been turned over to strangers,
  our homes to hostile foreigners.

v. 3   We have become orphans without a father,
  Our mothers are like widows.

v. 4   Our water we drink for silver,
  Our wood they will bring for a price.

v. 5   On[1] our necks we were pursued,[2]
  We are weary, we have no rest.

v. 6   [To] Egypt we gave [the] hand,
  [To] Assyria to be satisfied [with] bread.

---

30. A fascinating Evangelical reinterpretation of this verse is found in a sermon from Charles Spurgeon preached on 16 November 1862. For Spurgeon, Zion is the individual sinner who deserves nothing. Nevertheless, God has laid "her" iniquity on Christ, thus bringing it to an end. This text is a promise of life to such anguished, sinful souls (he takes his audience through the text of Lamentations to expose different aspects of her anguish). It is also a promise of coming wrath for those individual sinners not elect unto salvation (Edom).

1. Gottlieb suggests reading עַל/ʿal ("upon") as עֹל/ʿōl ("yoke") (*A Study on the Text*, 69), thus "yoke of our neck." I retain the MT reading. Alternatively, in this context it may be better translated as "*by* our necks" if the whole line is rendered as "By our necks we were driven hard."

2. Gottlieb (*A Study on the Text*, 69) and Albrektson (*Studies in the Text*, 198) suggest "driven hard" may be a better rendering of the verb in this context.

v. 7 Our fathers sinned, they are no more,
    We have borne their iniquities.

v. 8 Slaves rule over us,
    There is no one tearing us from their hand.

v. 9 At risk to our lives we bring in our bread,
    because of [the] sword of the wilderness.

v. 10 Our skin is hot like an oven,
    because of the raging heat of hunger.

v. 11 Women are raped in Zion,
    Maidens in [the] cities of Judah.

v. 12 Princes are hung up by their hand[s];
    The presence of [the] elders is not honored.

v. 13 Young men take up [the] millstone;
    And boys stagger under the [loads of] wood.

v. 14 Elders have ceased from the gate,
    Young men from their music.

v. 15 Our heart has ceased from rejoicing,
    Our dancing was turned to mourning.

v. 16 [The] crown on our head has fallen,
    Woe now to us for we have sinned.

v. 17 Because of this our heart became faint;
    Because of these our eyes became darkened.

v. 18 Because of Mount Zion which is desolate;
    Jackals roam on it.

v. 19 You, YHWH, sit [enthroned] forever;
    Your throne [endures] from generation to generation.

v. 20 Why do you continually forget us,
    [and] forsake us for so many days?

145

v. 21 Restore us, YHWH, to yourself and we will be restored,[3]
      Renew our days as in times past.

v. 22 Even though you have utterly rejected us,
      [and] have been exceptionally angry with us.

Lamentations 5 is the shortest poem in the book, being half the length of chapter 4 and only a third the length of chapters 1–3. Twelve of the twenty-two lines are composed of two halves of equal length, and this marks the poem off from earlier chapters, which made the *qinah* meter more prominent. Chapter 5 is also the only poem in the book that is not an acrostic, although its 22 verses seem to mimic the 22 parts of each of the first four poems.

In terms of form, almost all scholars see the poem as more or less a communal lament. It contains a complaint in the face of disaster, a request that God rescue them, a self-reproach for the arising of the situation. Jill Middlemas, while seeing no hope communicated through the *content* of the poem (it will become clear that I take a more positive approach towards the content), does see hope embodied in the poetic *form* because communal lament was motivated by the hope that God might act to redeem.

> By the *form*, although not the message, of the final chapter, the structure of Lamentations turns ever so slightly towards a belief in future hope. . . . The formfulness of their grief . . . suggests that despite their pessimism, they believed fundamentally that in the setting of worship, their present could be transformed.[4]

There is only one voice that speaks — that of the community or its representative(s) — and God is directly addressed throughout the entire poem. Some Greek and Latin manuscripts even contain a superscription labeling the poem as *a prayer* of Jeremiah.

The poem has an opening plea (5:1) and two main sections: a complaint (5:2-18) and an appeal (5:19-22). The complaint serves to strengthen the plea and the appeal.

   I. Opening Plea — "Remember! Look! See!" (5:1)
  II. Complaint over Sufferings (5:2-18)

---

3. The Qere is cohortative. Hence Berlin's "Take us back, LORD, to yourself; *O let us come back* (italics mine)"; *Lamentations*, 115.

4. Middlemas, *The Troubles of Templeless Judah*, 222, 226.

1. Economic impoverishment under foreign rule (2-10)
2. Social humiliation for different groups (11-14)
3. The sorrow of the community (15-18)
III. Appeal for Help (5:19-22)
1. Declaration of YHWH's reign: a basis for hope (19)
2. Accusing question (20)
3. Closing prayer for restoration (21-22)

In the context of the book of Lamentations as a whole, the prayer of chapter 5 serves as a climax. It is a response of the afflicted people to their ongoing suffering described in each of the previous chapters. In particular, it can be seen as a response to the promise of salvation at the end of chapter 4: a promise of restoration followed by a final prayer for restoration.

v. 1 Opening Plea   The opening petition serves as an introduction to the entire poem, the only one of the poems in Lamentations to open with a prayer. It will remind the audience of Lady Jerusalem's anguished prayers in 1:9c, 11c, 20; 2:20. This is not a polite request but an urgent plea for YHWH to "remember" (cf. 2:1; 3:19), to "look" (1:20; 3:63), and to "see" (1:9c, 20; both verbs combined in 1:11, 12; 2:20) the reproach that the people still suffer. Clearly the speakers do not mean that God is *literally* unaware of what is happening to them. They mean that he has been behaving *like* someone who is unaware of, or is ignoring, their pain, and they call on him to stop acting in this way.[5] "To ask God to remember a distressful situation is to ask God to remedy it."[6] The "reproach" or social "disgrace" that they suffer is an often overlooked dimension of suffering. 5:2-18 fill out in detail the nature of this humiliation.

vv. 2-18 Complaint over Sufferings   In 5:2-18 complaint is piled upon complaint, and the rhetorical impact of the whole must not be lost sight of in our attention to the parts. This complaint is framed by petitions (5:1, 21-22), making clear that its purpose is that of attracting YHWH's attention to their plight. No other communal lament in the Old Testament places as much emphasis on complaint as this one.[7] The situation depicted is that of the sufferings of those living in the land of Judah under foreign occupation. The siege of Jerusalem is past, but the Babylonian conquest has ongoing consequences.

---

5. Psalms 74 and 89, like Lam 5:1, both combine "reproach" with the imperatives "look" and "see" and forms of "remember."

6. Bergant, *Lamentations*, 126.

7. Middlemas, *The Troubles of Templeless Judah*, 203.

- 5:2-10 describes the economic hardship the people face under the rule of the foreign invaders. The description is written in first person plural speech.
- 5:11-14 describes the humiliation of different social groups in the ruined city. The description is in the third person.
- 5:15-18 serves to summarize the community's sorrow and, as 5:2-10, is written in the first person plural.

v. 2 The inheritance lost to outsiders refers to the inalienable landholdings of families that are passed from father to son down the generations (Lev 25:25-28; Numbers 27; 36; 1 Kgs 21:3). "Being deprived of one's 'ancestral land' is more than a financial loss; it is a deeply felt religious or cultural loss as well, and it signifies the breakdown of society and the breakdown of God's laws."[8] The loss of family landholdings serves as a metaphor for the bigger idea that the *land* of Canaan as a whole is the inheritance of the people of Israel (Num 26:53; Deut 4:21, 38; 25:19; 26:1) but now it has been "thrown down" or "turned over" (implied: by God) to the outsiders. This loss of the land spells economic hardship but is also a clear sign of the God-forsakenness of the people. Not only their land but also their houses (and perhaps also their households) are now forfeit, turned over to hostile foreigners.

v. 3 The loss of a father or husband, whether he be dead or not, made an ancient Israelite family very vulnerable, and the speakers are depicting a breakdown of their social structures caused by the loss of adult males. If this is taken literally, then we are to envisage the loss of many men in battle or exile. This is certainly plausible if some hyperbole is involved, although some feel that the percentage of men taken in this way was too low for the community to speak in terms of such a universal loss. Many of the speakers of this lament would have been adult males, and it seems odd for them to describe themselves as orphans. Consequently, commentators often detect a figurative level or meaning in the verse in which the community feels "fatherless" with the loss of the king[9] (4:20), community leaders in general, or, more likely, with the absence of YHWH.[10] At any rate, the people are certainly depicting themselves as socially vulnerable targets for exploitation.

---

8. Berlin, *Lamentations*, 117.

9. So Budde, "Die Klagelieder," 105. But then, who are "our mothers"?

10. So Renkema, *Lamentations*, 593-98. The mothers are the cities of Judah who are *like* widows now that YHWH has abandoned them.

v. 4 The people are forced by the invading foreigners to pay high prices for their basic needs: water for drinking and wood for building and for burning. Yet this water and this wood are from their own land and, by rights, belong to them anyway. But the Judeans no longer control their own basic resources, and that situation is exploited by those who now do.

v. 5 The first line is difficult to translate but may picture the people being driven to do harsh, back-breaking work like oxen with yokes upon their necks. The speakers are treated like slaves in their own land and are worked into the ground by their unsympathetic taskmasters. Alternatively, and perhaps more likely, the phrase may simply be an idiom for persecution that is persistent and in which danger is imminent. The hunter is right at their necks! Either way the speakers are exhausted (from forced labor or from being pursued) and are not able to rest (cf. 1:3). Iain Provan notes that in the biblical literature Canaan is said to be a place of "rest" for the people (e.g., Deut 12:10), but here they are in that promised land yet having no rest.[11]

v. 6 The loss of control of their resources has created a situation in which the survivors often go hungry. How will food be found? Many see this verse as a reference to the spreading out of hands in past alliances (Ezek 17:18; 1 Chr 29:24) with the likes of Egypt and Assyria; alliances that did not help them during the attack by their foes (cf. 1:2, 12, 19; 4:17-20); and alliances that are no use now in their ongoing need for food.[12] Provan sees Judeans remaining in the land being reduced to spreading out their hands to request food from outsiders (he is agnostic about whether any formal alliances were involved).[13] That their ancient enemies (Egypt and Assyria) are those they look to for help is indeed ironic. Johan Renkema, on the other hand, thinks that the verse describes Judeans who chose voluntary exile in Egypt, the "land of bread" (Jer 42:14-15; 44:1), and elsewhere[14] to find food. We cannot tie the meaning of the verse down with certainty, but what is clear is that the speakers are seeking food from nations that were historically enemies or unreliable allies.

---

11. Provan, *Lamentations*, 127.

12. Kraus, *Klagelieder*, 88; Rudolph, *Die Klagelieder*, 261; Hillers, *Lamentations*, 157, 163.

13. Provan, *Lamentations*, 128.

14. The reference to Assyria could not be literal in this period as, by 586, it was long gone. Perhaps we have a traditional linking of Egypt and Assyria (Jer 2:18; Hos 7:11; 12:1; Zech 10:10-11) to indicate foreign territory. Alternatively, it may be a generic reference to Mesopotamia (Ezra 6:22) and, following Provan, symbolically indicating places of exile (Isa 27:13; Hos 9:3; 11:5, 11; Zech 10:10-11).

v. 7   In Jer 31:29 and Ezek 18:2, the exiles grumble that "The fathers have eaten sour grapes; and the children's teeth are set on edge." This is clearly a complaint that they are being punished for the sins of others, and neither prophet is much impressed by the attempt to shirk responsibility.[15] Lamentations 5:7 is similar *except that* the speakers here clearly associate themselves with the fathers ("*our* fathers") and make no attempt to deny their own sin (5:16; cf. 1:18-22; 2:20-22; 3:40-42; Jer 3:25, "we have sinned . . . we and our fathers").[16] The point here is that in a community the sins of one have consequences for others. This communal impact of sin is especially clear in the case of community leaders — indeed, different generations can suffer the impact of the sins of the fathers (Exod 20:5). So it that the fathers sinned and the wider community, while not guiltless, suffers with them.[17]

Renkema sees the fathers as contemporary spiritual leaders: prophets and priests (cf. 2:14; 4:13). These "fathers" are no longer among the people (4:15), but the impact of their sin continues to be felt among those in Judea. More likely, the fathers are community leaders from previous generations who are now deceased (cf. 5:3).[18]

v. 8   Who are the slaves/servants that rule over the Judeans now? Actual slaves who had risen to power? Babylonian soldiers? Babylonian officials? Babylonian-appointed governors? Nations such as Edom that Judah once ruled? We simply cannot be sure, and perhaps the vague language allows for multiple referents. The point is to emphasize the breakdown of the social order and the shocking reversal that has taken place.[19] The king is gone (4:20), Judah is ruled over by those who should not be ruling over them (Prov 30:21-23), and there is no escape from their dominion.

v. 9   The situation may be that the Judeans had hidden food supplies in the desert (Jer 41:8; Judg 6:11). However, enemies were aware of this and lay in

---

15. Dobbs-Allsopp (*Lamentations*, 145-46) and O'Connor ("Lamentations," 1069) see Lam 5:7 as a protest against innocent suffering. I do not.

16. Berlin sees ambiguity in the word עָוֹן / *'āwôn*. Does it mean "punishment for iniquity" or "iniquity"? In other words, do the people participate in the punishment for the iniquity of the fathers *or the iniquity itself* (*Lamentations*, 120)? This ambiguity may further support the claim in the main text that the speakers are not claiming to be innocent: the suffering is the result of a long history of sin that continues to the present day.

17. Note, suffers *with*, not *instead of*, them.

18. Some see a reference to sinful past alliances with foreign nations (which are *possibly* in view in 5:6). This is not clear.

19. Provan, *Lamentations*, 129.

wait in the wilderness to kill those who sought to bring the food back. Renkema sees a cynical allusion to 4:9, in which death by the sword is preferable to starvation.[20] Alternatively, the "sword of the wilderness" may be a metaphor for the ravages of drought and famine (Deut 28:22).[21] Either way, the point is that the act of securing the food needed for basic survival is itself life-endangering.

v. 10 With the lack of water (5:4) and food (5:6, 9) the people physically deteriorate (cf. 4:7-8). Their skin is degraded from malnourishment. The famine metaphorically burns it like a furnace, making it possibly blackened or perhaps coarse.

v. 11 In the ancient world rape was often used as a deliberate strategy of humiliation to signal to opponents that they could not protect their own women. Even after the siege and the fall of Jerusalem, the situation remains one of ongoing violence in which the women of Judah (both married and unmarried women) are raped in Zion and in the other cities (cf. 1:8-10). There is nowhere safe. Judah's enemies want to make clear who is in control. The Hebrew word that here means "raped" (עָנָה/ʿānâ; cf. Gen 34:2; 2 Sam 13:14) often means "to humiliate" or "to afflict." The *humiliation* of the women who are raped and also of the men who cannot protect them is the focus.

v. 12 The Judean leaders who remain behind — princes (1:6; 2:9) and elders (1:19; 2:10; 4:16) — are treated with disdain. To be hung up by the hands may refer to being hung on a wooden stake after being stoned to death (Josh 10:26; 2 Sam 4:12) or perhaps to a non-Israelite form of execution such as impaling on a stake or crucifixion.[22] The elders who, as representatives of families, were held in high esteem within Israelite society are dishonored. This represented a snub to Israel's social order, with its high valuation of families, and to the law of Moses which affirmed those values.

v. 13 The millstone had to be lifted up each time a new sprinkling of cereal was placed on the large, flat stone below it. The young men here take up work

---

20. Renkema, *Lamentations*, 605.

21. Berlin, *Lamentations*, 121. Yet others see it as a metaphorical reference to bedouin or bandits.

22. Alternatively, the hands may be those of the enemy. So Hillers: "Their hands hanged our princes." Note that hanging by the neck was not a means of execution in the ancient world, so this could refer to a displaying of corpses after execution or perhaps to some kind of publicly humiliating torture of the living; so Provan, *Lamentations*, 131.

that normally belongs to the servant women. Perhaps they are being forced by their captors to perform what was perceived to be a demeaning type of labor for a man. Alternatively, Adele Berlin suggests the men are being forced to "pull" the millstone that grinds the grain, taking on the back-breaking work normally performed by animals.[23] Similarly, the boys are forced to carry piles of wood, and, perhaps partly due to their hunger, the weight is too much for them.

v. 14 In normal times the area around the city gate was the center of public life: decisions were made, business was conducted, and legal disputes were sorted out by the elders (Gen 19:1; Deut 21:19; Josh 20:4; Ruth 4:1-2; 1 Kgs 21:10; Prov 1:21; 31:23, 31). But the elders no longer gather at the city gates, which have been taken by the enemy (4:12). Normality is ruptured — a point made clear by the cessation of music from the young men. The music has stopped because judgment has come and joy has departed (Isa 16:10; Jer 7:34; 16:9; 25:10; 48:33; Ezek 26:13).

v. 15 The result of all these woes is that "our heart has ceased from rejoicing." The joyful dancing is transformed into mourning (cf. Jer 7:34; 16:9). Berlin sees this as a reference to the cessation of temple worship. "Joy is not a state of mind but a ritual performance in the presence of God, while mourning signals the absence of God."[24] The ritual joy and dancing ceases with the loss of the temple, and ritual mourning replaces it (cf. 1:4; 2:6).

v. 16 The crown symbolizing the honor and glory of the people has fallen from their heads in disgrace. The fallen crown may be a reference to the loss of the Davidic king (4:20) or perhaps to Jerusalem itself, its walls,[25] or its temple.[26] The imagery is open enough to encompass all these referents. This causes the people to cry out in despair, "Woe now to us for we have sinned!" This acknowledgement of the sin that led to disaster is consistent with the attitude throughout Lamentations (1:5, 8, 14, 18, 22; 2:14; 3:42; 4:6, 13, 22; 5:7).

vv. 17-18 5:17-18 form the climax of the lament. "This" and "these things" in 5:17 refer both backwards to 5:2-16 and forwards to 5:18.[27] That which makes

---

23. Berlin, *Lamentations*, 123.

24. Berlin, *Lamentations*, 124.

25. Dobbs-Allsopp, *Lamentations*, 147. He notes that Palestinian city walls are often referred to as crowns worn by the cities.

26. Renkema, *Lamentations*, 617.

27. House sees "this" as a reference to the sin in 5:16 and "these things" as a reference to the woes in 5:2-16.

the heart faint (1:22; Isa 1:5; Jer 8:18) and the eyes darkened in 5:17 is first of all the series of woes recounted in vv. 2-16. However, 5:18 reveals the climactic reason for the grief: the desolation and abandonment of Mount Zion, which is now the home of jackals (cf. Isa 13:19-22). The temple mount, once the dwelling place of YHWH on earth, is now a ruin inhabited and profaned by unclean animals. This is a situation that has left the speakers themselves in ruins.

Renkema suggests the eyes are darkened by tears (cf. 1:16; 2:11; 3:49; 4:17),[28] while Provan proposes, on the basis of Ps 69:23 and Eccl 12:3, that it is because "the events described have sapped the people's vitality."[29]

vv. 19-22 Appeal for Help   In 5:1-18 the speakers have been drawing YHWH's attention to their reproach (5:1). Now they turn to make their appeal.

v. 19   They begin with an expression of praise to the sovereign Lord. The shift from the plight of the people and the city to a focus on God's ongoing reign is striking. The destruction of the dwelling place of a deity would signal to many in the ancient Near East the defeat of that deity. The speakers have just spoken of the desolation of Mount Zion with its temple, and this could suggest the defeat of YHWH by the gods of Babylon. Yet the speakers immediately declare,

> You, YHWH, sit [enthroned] forever;
> Your throne [endures] from generation to generation.

There is never any question in Lamentations that the destruction of God's city and God's temple might be the result of his inability to defend them. On the contrary, his throne is in heaven and he himself is the one who has destroyed Mount Zion. YHWH's absolute sovereignty is not in doubt. *For that very reason,* even in the midst of such hopelessness, God's ongoing reign is the basis for hope and for prayer (Ps 102:12-13). While this is not a full-fledged avowal of confidence, it is a step towards one.

vv. 20-22   The speakers now make their complaint in the form of a biting question. The focus is on the *duration* of YHWH's "abandonment" of them.

> Why do you continually forget us,
> [and] forsake us for so many days?

28. Renkema, *Lamentations,* 619.
29. Provan, *Lamentations,* 132.

As elsewhere in Lamentations, the issue is not that the people think that they do not deserve to be punished. Their complaint is over the devastating *severity* of the punishment and, in this verse, its seemingly *unending duration*. Why have you afflicted us this harshly and *for this long?* Implicit in the question is the suggestion that the time has come to restore them. What is often missed by commentators is that this very question presupposes a belief in YHWH's *ongoing* covenant relationship with his people. The book of Lamentations then closes with an explicit request for deliverance.

> Restore us, YHWH, to yourself and we will be restored,
>> Renew our days as in times past.
> Even though you have deeply rejected us,
>> [and] have been exceptionally angry with us.

The extremity of God's anger at Israel and the severity of his ongoing rejection of them cannot be doubted. But the people pray that, *in spite of* the unprecedented magnitude of the breakdown in the relationship between YHWH and Israel, he would restore them. They ask for a restoration of their former glory as in days gone by (cf. 1:7), but fundamentally it is the relationship with YHWH that they wish to be repaired. It is God himself who must effect this reconciliation, for he is the offended party ("Restore us, YHWH, to yourself"). The people have repented, but it is now up to YHWH to forgive. If the sovereign God does restore them, then they *will* be restored. Their future is in *his* hands. The book of Lamentations then ends with this plea hanging in the air. God is still silent. It would be incorrect, in my view, to maintain as Kathleen O'Connor does that this final prayer can be entitled "What God Should Do *But Probably Will Not*."[30] The ending of Lamentations is not one of giving up on God, nor of the triumph of despair. Equally, it is not one of resolution. The book ends with a plea for restoration in the face of ongoing divine anger, and any divine response to this prayer is agonizingly still future. But, as Jamie Grant comments, "the bare fact of a cry to God is indicative of hope that prayer will be answered by the One who is able to 'do stuff.'"[31]

Excursus: The Meaning of כִּי אִם/*kî 'im* in 5:22.

The final verse of Lamentations has generated considerable discussion because it has implications for how Lamentations *as a whole* is interpreted. What is the meaning of the opening words in v. 22, כִּי אִם/*kî 'im* (lit., "for if")?

30. O'Connor, *Lamentations and the Tears of the World*, 77.
31. Grant, "Psalm 44," 10.

1. A Doubting Conclusion?

The expression might mean "unless." On this reading, the book of Lamentations ends on a note of doubt: "Restore us, YHWH . . . *unless* you have completely rejected us."[32] The key problem is that this use of כי אם/*kî 'im* occurs elsewhere only when preceded by a negative statement: "not A *unless* (כי אם/*kî 'im*) B" (e.g., Gen 32:26[27]; Lev 22:6; Ruth 3:18; Isa 55:10). While "unless" cannot be ruled out here, there is no exact parallel elsewhere to an "A *unless* (כי אם/*kî 'im*) B" structure, and so it should be treated with caution.[33] A second problem, rarely noted, is that it is clear in Lamentations that YHWH *has* "deeply rejected" Israel and *has been* "exceptionally angry" with them. The anger of God and his rejection of Israel is the *reason* they are praying for restoration in the first place. So it would be very odd for the community to pray, "Restore us . . . *unless* you have deeply rejected us."

2. An Open Conclusion?

Tod Linafelt renders the verse, "*For if* truly you have rejected us, bitterly raged against us. . . ." He sees כי אם/*kî 'im* as introducing a

> conditional statement that is left trailing off, leaving a protasis without an apodosis, or an "if" without a "then." The book is left opening out into the emptiness of God's nonresponse. By leaving a conditional statement dangling, the final verse leaves open the future of the ones lamenting. It is hardly a hopeful ending, for the missing but implied apodosis is surely negative, yet it does nevertheless defer the apodosis. And by arresting the movement from an "if" to a "then" the incomplete clause allows the reader, for a moment, to imagine the possibility of a different "then," and therefore a different future.[34]

This is a fascinating and appealing approach but, as Berlin notes, "this interpretation may resonate with the modern reader, but it is likely too modern for the ancient author."[35]

---

32. BDB; Westermann, *Lamentations*, 217-19; Rudolph, *Die Klagelieder*, 257-58; Albrektson, *Studies in the Text*, 206-7; Middlemas, *The Troubles of Templeless Judah*, 204. Some have a doubting conclusion by translating "Restore us, YHWH . . . *or have you* completely rejected us?" (cf. Löhr, *Der Klagelieder des Jeremia*, 31-32; Westermann, *Lamentations*, 218-19; Renkema, *Lamentations*, 631-32; RSV). There is no syntactic basis, however, for translating כי אם/*kî 'im* as a question.

33. A point noted by many scholars, e.g., Gordis, "Conclusion of the Book," 290; Linafelt, "The Refusal of a Conclusion," 341; Hillers, *Lamentations*, 60.

34. Linafelt, *Surviving Lamentations*, 60-61 (see also Linafelt, "The Refusal of a Conclusion"). It would be possible to translate the verse "*for if* you have completely rejected us [*then*] you have been exceptionally angry with us," but this is not likely as the second colon restates the first colon rather than its consequence (Hillers, *Lamentations*, 160; Linafelt, *Surviving Lamentations*, 60; Provan, *Lamentations*, 133).

35. Berlin, *Lamentations*, 126.

3. A Protesting Conclusion?

Some think it means "instead."[36] On this reading Lamentations ends on a note of complaint: "Restore us, YHWH . . . [but] *instead* you have completely rejected us." While אם כי/*kî 'im* can mean "except" or "instead," the problem with this interpretation is that it does not fit the context comfortably. No sooner have the speakers gotten out the request that God restore them than they complain, "instead [of restoring us] you completely reject us." But this feels out of place because YHWH will only have had a matter of moments to answer the prayer! One could imagine a prayer that went, "We asked you to restore us . . . [but] *instead* you completely rejected us," but that is not what we have. So this interpretation ought to be treated with caution.

4. A Hopeful Conclusion?

(a) Possibly the אם/*'im* should be dropped as unoriginal (the LXX and the Syriac do not translate it, and a few medieval Hebrew manuscripts lack it). In this case the verse simply says, "Restore us, YHWH . . . *for* [until now] you have 'completely' rejected us." It provides the reason for the prayer for restoration. However, it is most unlikely that the אם/*'im* is not original to the text.[37]

(b) Keil sees אם כי/*kî 'im* as introducing a hypothetical situation which is known to be impossible.[38] "Restore us, YHWH . . . *unless* you have completely rejected us" (implied: and we know that this cannot be so). Keil here translates the כי אם/*kî 'im* in the same way as the "doubters" in 1 above, but he understands its import differently. This is possible, but reading 5:22 in light of the rest of Lamentations it is not obvious that the speakers do consider a total and final abandonment by God to be *obviously impossible*. It is plausible to imagine them doubting that they have a future. In addition, as we have seen, translating אם כי/*kî 'im* as "unless" here is problematic (see 1).

(c) Some translate אם כי/*kî 'im* as "even though," in which case the final note of the book is the prayer for salvation: "Restore us, YHWH . . . *even though* [until now] you have 'completely' rejected us."[39] 5:22 is, on this view, a subordinate clause and 5:21 is the main clause that ends the book.

Interestingly, in Jewish tradition the custom is to repeat 5:21 after 5:22 in public recitations of Lamentations so as to end on a positive note. This suggests that 5:22 was understood to be negative.[40] The question for us then is whether Lamentations ends on a negative note (as a doubt, deferred hopelessness, or a protest) or on a prayer for restoration (view 4). Many, such as Provan, think that "it is clear. . . that the poem

---

36. Hillers, *Lamentations*, 160-61; Berlin, *Lamentations*, 125-26; GKC, 163b.

37. After all, what scribe would take a perfectly intelligible text and then make it ambiguous?

38. Keil, *Jeremiah, Lamentations*, 454. See too Rudolph, *Die Klagelieder*, 258.

39. Gordis, *The Song of Songs and Lamentations*, 198; Gordis, "Conclusion of the Book"; House, *Lamentations*, 470-71.

40. But see Gordis, "Conclusion of the Book," 290, for an alternative understanding of the implications of this synagogue tradition.

does not have a confident ending."[41] While there is no problem in principle with Lamentations ending on a negative note — indeed for many readers that would be a welcome ending — all of the negative interpretations listed above are, as we have seen, problematic. The least problematic interpretation, it seems to me, is that of Robert Gordis (view 4c), even though it is currently out of favor. Gordis notes that in some contexts, one in Lamentations itself, אִם כִּי/*kî 'im* probably does mean "even though" (Jer 51:14; Isa 10:22; Amos 5:22; Lam 3:32-33), that it makes sense in the current context, and that Ps 89:50-51 provides a parallel to the syntactic structure in Lam 5:21-22.

So why have people objected to this interpretation? First, Gordis takes the verbs in 5:22 as pluperfects ("even though you *had* despised us greatly and *were* very angry with us"), and this, as Claus Westermann notes, is unlikely on the grounds that the wrath is *not yet past* for the speakers.[42] However, Gordis's rendering of אִם כִּי/*kî 'im* as "even though" is not dependent on the use of pluperfects. 5:21-22 ask for God to restore Israel, even though their *current situation* remains one of deep and utter rejection. Second, some, like O'Connor, complain that Gordis and others distort the Hebrew text because they are keen to achieve a happy ending.[43] However, even if this were the case, pointing it out is not a substitute for responding to Gordis's positive arguments. Indeed, the sword cuts both ways as the desire to *avoid* a "happy" ending seems to be an important motive for many of those who embrace a negative interpretation. The matter cannot be decided one way or the other on such a basis. Third, Westermann objects that there is no parallel in Psalms of Lament in which a subordinate clause states the attendant circumstances to the petition of a main clause.[44] While there is no parallel *in the Psalms of Lament*, the structure is not, as Gordis shows, without parallel.[45] On balance, it seems to me that Lamentations ends with a prayer for salvation in the midst of ongoing suffering.

---

41. Provan, *Lamentations*, 134. See also, Dobbs-Allsopp, *Lamentations*, 149; O'Connor, *Lamentations and the Tears of the World*, 78-79.

42. Westermann, *Lamentations*, 218 followed by Renkema, *Lamentations*, 630-31.

43. O'Connor, *Lamentations and the Tears of the World*, 78.

44. Westermann, *Lamentations*, 218.

45. Gordis, "Conclusion of the Book," 292.

Theological Horizons of Lamentations

Jewish and Christian Liturgical Use of Lamentations and Hermeneutics

A helpful way into reflections on contemporary theological interpretation of Lamentations is to observe how the text has functioned liturgically in Jewish and Christian worship. I hope to show in the remainder of this commentary that both traditions have much to contribute to the ongoing reception of the text.

On the annual fast day of *tiš'â bě'āb*, the 9th day of the month of Ab (in July or August), Jews commemorate the two saddest events in Jewish history, the destruction of the first temple by the Babylonians and the destruction of the second temple by the Romans. Both events, separated by 656 years, took place in the month of Ab. But this solemn day of fasting also became a focus for other catastrophes experienced by the Jewish people, from the failure of the Bar Kokhba rebellion and the subsequent razing of Jerusalem by Rome, through the Crusades, the expulsion of the Jews from England in 1290 and from Spain in 1492, to the Holocaust.

Eating and drinking, washing, wearing leather shoes, applying creams and oils, and physical affection are prohibited for the day, as is study of the Torah. All this is to facilitate the sense of mourning and solemnity. On the 9th of Ab the synagogue changes from a joyous house of God to a house of mourning. Traditionally, words of greeting are discouraged, the lights are dimmed, the ark and Torah scrolls are draped in black, and the congregation sits on low benches or on the floor. It is during the evening service that the book of Lamentations is read. Interestingly, the recitation ends by repeating 5:21 after 5:22 to allow the book to end on a more positive note. This indicates that the fast, while mournful, is pregnant with implicit hope. There is one

Jewish tradition that the Messiah will be born on the 9th of Ab. Most in Orthodox Judaism believe that until the arrival of the Messiah this day will continue to be observed as a fast, but once the Messiah comes it will become a great celebration. The implicit hope comes to the surface on the next day when the words of Isaiah 40, beginning "Comfort, comfort my people," are read. Hope of an end to exile then comes to dominate. This association of Lamentations and Deutero-Isaiah is theologically suggestive and has strong biblical warrant, as we shall see later.[1]

So on *tišʿâ bʾĕāb* the text of Lamentations is clearly linked to the destruction of Jerusalem by the Babylonians but is also brought into association with countless sufferings experienced by the Jewish people over the centuries. All of Jewish history is thus swept up in the tears of "Jeremiah," and Jews from generation to generation can weep with him. This liturgical usage allows the text to transcend its original context.

In Christianity, readings from the book are used in the service of *Tenebrae* (Latin for "shadows") during the Thursday through Saturday of Holy Week.[2] Over time the services were moved from the morning to the night before and are now observed on Wednesday through Friday. The service is celebrated in the Western church (Roman Catholic and certain strands within various Protestant denominations) and probably got its name from the way in which the lights in the building are gradually extinguished, a ritual probably dating back to the fifth century. On Easter Saturday the church was left in darkness save for a single candle by the lectern. The service was considered as a kind of funeral service and a lament for Christ, the three days corresponding to his three days in the tomb. The tone is "dark," as the regular prayers of the *Te Deum*, the *Gloria Patri*, and the blessings are omitted. For our purposes, it is critical to observe that among the readings we find extended sections of the book of Lamentations.

Each office consists in three *vigiliae;* each *vigilia* consists in three psalms with responsories and three readings with responsories. The Lamentations are read/sung in three readings at each of the first *vigilia*. The Lamentations therefore consist of three sets of three readings, for Thursday/Wednesday, Friday/Thursday, and Saturday/Friday. Each reading is ended with the call from Hos 14:1: "Jerusalem, return onto the Lord thy God." Numerous European

---

1. See Stern, "Lamentations in Jewish Liturgy."

2. For details, see Cameron-Mowat, "Lamentations in Christian Worship"; and for a much expanded version of the reflections here, see Parry, "Wrestling with Lamentations in Christian Worship." On some musical receptions of Lamentations, some in the context of worship, see Schopf, "Musical Responses to Lamentations."

composers put the Lamentations readings to music, with some of the most haunting and famous coming from the sixteenth to eighteenth centuries.

Here the text transcends its historical roots. What is most fascinating to me is the way in which the church brought the book of Lamentations into such a close association with the death of Jesus. The connection with the original context of the book is not nearly as clear as with the Jewish liturgical usage. Somehow the destruction and loss of Jerusalem was implicitly seen as a type of the crucifixion of the Messiah. That ancient Christian linkage between this biblical text and Christ is one that has not really been explored by commentators, and yet it is one that, as we shall explain later, is far from arbitrary and is rich in theological implications.

Lamentations in the Context of Jeremiah

For Jews and Christians, Lamentations does not stand alone but is received by the communities as part of a larger canon of Scripture. Reading Lamentations theologically requires an awareness of how it intertextually resonates within those canonical contexts.

Lamentations was probably written by people who were familiar with the book of Jeremiah, and it is even possible that Jeremiah was one of the literary voices in the book. What is even clearer is that it was not very long before Jeremiah was believed to be the author of the book. Jewish and Christian readers for centuries read Lamentations in the shadow of Jeremiah. Even those of us no longer convinced that Jeremiah was the actual author of the book can acknowledge the legitimacy of interpreting Lamentations against the backdrop of Jeremiah.[3] Obviously, this strategy means that we will take the sufferings in Lamentations to be the sufferings brought about by the Babylonian assault on Judah and the subsequent exile. But how exactly does this reading strategy impact the way we understand the *theology* of Lamentations?

First, it will fill out considerably our thinking on Judah's sin. Lamentations recognizes this sin, but its focus is on the suffering. This has led some readers to suggest that Lamentations' view of Judah's sin is flat and not altogether wholehearted. Readers who come into Lamentations from Jeremiah will *not* be inclined to see things in this way. They will enter chapter 1 with a strong and clear view of the enormity of the sin of Jerusalem, something the whole book of Jeremiah testifies to and develops. Jeremiah also fills out the

---

3. For a general introduction to the theological message of Jeremiah, see McConville, *Judgment and Promise.*

critique of the leadership that Lamentations refers to but only briefly (e.g., Jer 8:8-12; 22-23, 27-28). While readers will recognize a clear shift in focus from the sin to suffering in Lamentations, they will *not* be inclined to see the acknowledgements of sin as mere lip service, but as reminders of Judah's deep and sustained depravity depicted in Jeremiah.

Second, it accentuates the context of covenant relationship that Lamentations must be understood against and reminds readers to understand the calamity described in Lamentations as the fiery climax of a *long* story of God's patient endurance with Judah and his constant calls to repentance and salvation over many years (e.g., Jer 25:1-11). Lamentations describes God's judgment, but Jeremiah explains something of the extended journey towards it. This puts the divine wrath in Lamentations into a broader narrative-theological context.

Third, while as in Lamentations God's wrath is portrayed as terrifying and fierce, it is clear that God loves Judah, is reluctant to punish her, and takes no pleasure in so doing. Indeed, there are hints in Jeremiah that God himself is afflicted by Judah's afflictions (e.g., Jer 4:19-21; 8:18–9:2; 14:17-18, where the dividing line between Jeremiah's sorrow and God's sorrow blurs). This provides a context for interpreting God's destructive anger in Lamentations. It also inclines readers to take the insight in Lam 3:33 — that God does not afflict from his heart — seriously.

Fourth, it will incline readers to take the indicators of hope in Lamentations seriously. Jeremiah's calling was "to pluck up and to break down, to destroy and to overthrow," but it was also "to build and to plant" (Jer 1:10). His message was overwhelmingly one of judgment (a judgment the characters in Lamentations speak from the midst of), but it also included oracles of real hope grounded in God's covenant love (e.g., Jeremiah 30–33).

Lamentations in the Context of Isaiah 40–55

Moving from a text *used by* Lamentations, let us now consider a later text that *makes use of* Lamentations. Here we can pick up on the association between Lamentations and Second Isaiah noted in Jewish worship. Jewish rabbis were well aware of the association. The Jewish Midrash on Lamentations, *Lamentations Rabbah*, says that "all the severe prophecies that Jeremiah prophesied against Israel were anticipated and healed by Isaiah."[4] As mentioned earlier,

4. *Lam. Rab.* XXXVI:ii. Clearly the rabbis saw Isaiah 40–55 as an *earlier* text than Jeremiah and Lamentations.

this link is not arbitrary, for, as I will argue, Isaiah 40–55 explicitly refers to the book of Lamentations.[5] This is especially significant for Christian readers because Isaiah 40–55 has exerted more influence on the theology of New Testament literature than perhaps any other part of the Old Testament. Isaiah thus becomes a canonical bridge between Christian theology and Lamentations. If we see how the prophet appropriated the book of Lamentations and then how the New Testament writers interpreted the prophet, we can begin to imagine canonical ways of connecting Christian reflection with Lamentations in a controlled way.

The prophet of Isaiah 40–55 is usually thought to have prophesied towards the end of Israel's exilic period. He clearly anticipates the end of the period of suffering so acutely given voice in Lamentations. As part of his message he seems to have quite consciously taken up the text of Lamentations and announces YHWH's response to Zion's pain.[6] Texts from all five chapters of the lament are taken up and reused in the prophecy, and the overall effect is one of *radical reversal* for Jerusalem. Consider the following:

In Lamentations 1, Lady Jerusalem is overwhelmingly cast as one who suffers without anyone to comfort her (√נחם/*nḥm*) (1:2, 9, 16, 17, 21). The lack of a comforter is the constant refrain of that pitiful opening chapter. Second Isaiah opens with the words, "Comfort, comfort (נחמו/*naḥămû*) my people,

---

5. Apart from the commentaries, see esp. Willey, *Remember the Former Things;* Sommer, *A Prophet Reads Scripture;* Linafelt, *Surviving Lamentations,* ch. 3; Tiemeyer, "Lamentations in Isaiah 40–55." Numerous other scholars have recognized the connections, even though they have not developed them at length. For instance, Gottwald, *Studies in the Book of Lamentations,* 44-46; Porteous, "Jerusalem-Zion," 238; Turner, "Daughter Zion"; Berlin, *Lamentations;* House, *Lamentations.* It is also helpful to see that, contrary to the majority view, in Isaiah 40–55 we do *not* have a reappropriation of the Judahite text of Lamentations to fit the context of the exilic community in Babylon. There are good reasons to maintain that much, possibly all (so Goulder, "Deutero-Isaiah of Jerusalem"), of Isa 40–55 was written in Judah and *not Babylon.* Consequently, significant parts of Isaiah 40–55 (including many of those that allude to Lamentations) address the very same Judahite audience that suffered in Lamentations. See esp. Tiemeyer, "Geography and Textual Allusions."

6. It is also possible that Zechariah makes some use of Lamentations in a way akin to Second Isaiah. Love *(The Evasive Text)* argues that we find allusions to Lam 2:6 (when YHWH causes the "appointed times" to be forgotten) in Zech 8:19 (when the fasts will become happy "appointed times"); Lam 2:3, 17 (in which God cut off the horn of Israel and exalted the horn of the enemy) in Zech 1:18-21 (in which the horns of the nations that scattered Judah will be thrown down); Lam 2:8 (in which YHWH stretches out a measuring line to destroy Jerusalem) in Zech 1:16 (in which God stretches out a measuring line to rebuild it). To this one could add that Zech 1:17 (in which YHWH "will again comfort Zion") alludes to the no-comfort motif in Lamentations 1. The pattern of usage reflects a doom-turned-to-salvation very similar to that in Isaiah 40–55.

says your God. Speak tenderly to Jerusalem, and cry to her that her warfare is ended, and that her iniquity is pardoned, that she has received from the Lord's hand double for all her sins" (Isa 40:1-2). The comfort theme then recurs as a major motif throughout Isaiah 40–55, with YHWH himself coming to take on the role of the comforter (Isa 40:1; 49:13; 51:3, 12, 19; 52:9; 54:11).

The fate of those in Jerusalem was bitter. Special attention is given to the children who are not cared for by their parents (Lam 4:3), who have no water or bread (4:4), and who are even eaten by their own mothers (4:10). Isaiah 40–55 is also concerned with the fate of Jerusalem's children. The children of Zion (here a metaphor for the citizens of Jerusalem) who went into captivity (Lam 1:5) will return (Isa 49:18, 25). And the children who were slaughtered (Lam 1:20; 2:21) and who died in the famine (2:11-12, 20, 22) will be alive again and say, "This place is too crowded for me; make room for me to dwell in" (Isa 49:20).[7] Clearly this is only a poetic resurrection, but it seeks to provide a rhetorical response to the rhetoric of Lamentations. Zion will be amazed at all the children she has and will wonder where they came from (Isa 49:21).

In Lam 4:17, the besieged citizens maintain watch in the hope that another nation would come to their rescue. They looked in vain. But now, says the prophet, the watchmen lift their voices and sing for joy because they see YHWH himself returning to Zion (Isa 52:8).

After the defeat of the city Judah was led into exile (Lam 1:3) and roads mourn for lack of pilgrim travelers (Lam 1:4), but the prophet foresees a return of the exiles with the roads to Zion filled with celebrating pilgrims (Isa 51:11; 49:18). Pursuers "overtook" (√נשׂג/*nśg*, hiphil) Zion and imposed "suffering" and "groaning" (√אנח/*'nḥ*, niphal) on her (Lam 1:3-4), but now gladness "overtakes" (√נשׂג/*nśg*, hiphil) her and "suffering" and "groaning" (√אנח/*'nḥ*, niphal) flee away (Isa 51:11).

The central pain at the heart of Lamentations is the pain caused by YHWH's abandonment of Jerusalem. Lamentations draws close to an end with the words: "Why do you *forget* (שׁכח/*škḥ*) us forever, why do you *forsake* (עזב/*'zb*) us for so many days?" (Lam 5:20). This concern is picked up in Isa 49:14, where the question becomes a statement in the mouth of Zion, "But Zion says, 'The Lord has *forsaken* me (עזבני/*'ăzābanî*); my Lord has *forgotten* me (שׁכחני/*šěkēḥānî*).'" What does YHWH say to this complaint? He asks rhetorically, "Can a woman forget her nursing child, that she would have no compassion on the son of her womb?" Then, perhaps recalling the extreme situations in Lamentations itself when mothers do indeed forsake their chil-

---

7. For a defence of the claim that the poet imagines the dead children as alive again in Isa 49:20, see Linafelt, *Surviving Lamentations*, 76-77.

dren (Lam 2:20; 4:1-4, 10), YHWH continues, "Even these may forget, *yet I will not forget you*." Tod Linafelt writes, "the poet chooses here the one metaphor for YHWH that can begin to answer the rhetoric of Lamentations: YHWH as a mother who also laments and hopes for the return of her children."[8] The rest of Isaiah 49 reinforces the theme of YHWH remembering Zion. So in place of being "forgotten" (שׁכח/*škḥ*) and "abandoned" (עזב/*ʿzb*) (Lam 5:20), YHWH says that he did "abandon" Israel (עזבתיך/*ʿăzabtîk*), *but only for a moment,* and now in great pity he will gather them (Isa 54:7). Zion will now "forget" (שׁכח/*škḥ*) the shame of her youth and her widowhood (Isa 54:4). Lamentations complains of divine "anger" (קצף/*qṣp*) and "rejection" (מאס/*mʾs*) (Lam 5:22). YHWH says that while Zion was indeed "rejected" (עזובה/*ʿăzûbâ*) and that in a flood of "anger" (קצף/*qeṣep*) he did hide his face from her (Isa 54:6, 8), it was *only for a moment,* and now in everlasting love he will have compassion on her (Isa 54:8).

The prayer in Lamentations is that YHWH would forgive his people and that the pagan enemies who inflicted such cruelty on her would experience the same fate as just retribution: "Let them be as I am" (Lam 1:21-22; cf. 3:58-66). Lamentations 4 offers hope that the cup of wrath Jerusalem had drunk would be passed over to Edom, who would be stripped bare as Jerusalem had been (Lam 4:21-22). Isaiah 51:17-23 sees the imminent fulfillment of this as the cup of wrath passes from Israel to the tormenters. The humiliation experienced by Jerusalem would now be experienced by Babylon (Isaiah 47). Babylon would sit silently on the ground in the dust (Isa 47:1, 5; cf. Lam 2:10) as Zion had done. Babylon would be stripped of her clothing (Isa 47:2-3), leaving her nakedness uncovered and her shame for all to see (Isa 47:3), as was Jerusalem's (Lam. 1:8). And worst of all, she will become as a widow and lose her children (Isa 47:8-9), just as Lady Jerusalem had (Lam 1:1, 16-18). The description of Babylon's fate in Isaiah 47 seems to draw explicitly on the fate of Zion in Lamentations in order to show the fulfillment of Jerusalem's prayer in Lam 1:21-22.

And just as the enemies of Zion are punished for their cruelty to God's people, so the humiliation of Jerusalem is reversed. Zion had fallen to the ground with her skirts unclean (Lam 1:9), but now she is told to shake off the dust (cf. Lam 2:10), rise up from the ground (Isa 52:2), and "put on beautiful garments" (Isa 52:1). The yoke of sin that was placed upon her neck (Lam 1:14) must now be loosed (Isa 52:2). The "widow" (Lam 1:1) will be married to YHWH again (Isa 54:4-8), and the mother bereft of children will receive her children back. The devastated city of Jerusalem (Lam 2:5-9) will be rebuilt

---

8. Linafelt, *Surviving Lamentations*, 75.

with precious stones (Isa 54:11-12). The nations that once entered her sanctuary profaning it (Lam 1:10) will do so no more (Isa 52:1). The complaint in Lam 5:1-2 that the land of the people had been taken by foreigners so that they even had to buy water from their own wells to drink is also answered: the people possess their land again (Isa 54:3) and are invited to come and drink from the waters, to buy food, and drink without money (Isa 55:1-2).

So far we have considered the reversal of fate for both Jerusalem and her tormenters which Second Isaiah portrays. What I have not mentioned yet are the connections between the man in Lamentations 3 and the Servant of YHWH in Isaiah. It is the work of this Servant that is key in the restoration of Zion and the return from exile portrayed in Isaiah 40–55. One enters a minefield when discussing the Servant figure in Second Isaiah, and I can do no more here than to simply state my position. I think that the Servant figure is clearly the nation of Israel in chapters 40–48. However, Israel's ongoing sin means that it is unable to fulfill its mission to the nations (Isa 42:16-25; 43:24; 46:8-13; 48). Thus, in chapters 49–53 an individual takes on the identity and mission of the nation in order to deliver Israel (49:1-13) and free her up to function as the Servant to the nations.[9] So the Servant in chapters 49–53 is a Servant who embodies the mission of Servant-Israel with the goal of rescuing Israel. It seems that this deliverance is achieved in Isaiah 53, where the Servant shares in the exilic sufferings of the exiles even though he does not deserve them. His wounds brought peace and healing for Israel (Isa 53:5). The Servant dies embodying the exilic death of the nation (Isa 53:9) and is *then* glorified (52:12; 53:10b-12). Arguably, the salvation of Zion and Israel in chapters 54–55 *follows on from* the work of the Servant in Isa 52:13–53:12. Now there are numerous Zion-Servant parallels in Second Isaiah, and the effect of this is to draw their stories into parallel. Patricia Tully Willey sums up: "In each, the story line moves from abuse, shame, despair, and recrimination to promise, vindication, fulfillment, and exaltation."[10] While the Servant is not Zion, he participates in her humiliation, apparently in order to deliver her from it.

But the portrait of the Servant figure in Isaiah 40–55 has been influenced by the man in Lamentations 3.[11] To list the most obvious connections,

9. In 49:3 the Servant is clearly *identified with* Israel, but in 49:5-6 he is clearly *distinguished from* Israel. There are numerous explanations for this, but the most plausible is that an individual assumes the role of the nation. He now does for Israel what Israel was to do for the nations: he is a "covenant for the people" (cf 42:6) and releases the prisoners (49:9; cf. 42:7).

10. Willey, *Remember the Former Things*, 222. Numerous Zion-Servant parallels are listed on the same page. See also Sawyer, "Daughter Zion and the Servant of the Lord"; Wilshire, "The Servant-City."

11. Willey, *Remember the Former Things*, ch. 5.

let us start with the links between Lamentations 3 and Isaiah 50. The man advises the devout as follows: "Let him give his cheek to the one who strikes, and let him be filled with insults" (Lam 3:30). The Servant says, "I gave my back to those who strike, and my cheeks to those who pull out my beard" (Isa 50:6).[12] The man goes "into darkness without any light" (Lam 3:2), as does the Servant (Isa 50:10). Both struggle with the issue of faith in the midst of opposition. Willey lists numerous other verbal and thematic links between the man in Lamentations 3 and the Servant in Isaiah 50. In Isaiah 53 the Servant suffers in silence (v. 7; cf. Lam 3:28), is rejected by others (v. 3; cf. Lam 3:46, 53, 60-63), is stricken (v. 4; cf. Lam. 3:30), "afflicted," and "crushed"[13] (vv. 4-5; cf. Lam 3:33-34), suffers the perversion of justice (v. 8; cf. Lam 3:35), is "cut off" (v. 8; cf. Lam 3:54) and "buried" (v. 9; cf. Lam 3:53, 55).

It is of considerable interest then to note then that the man in Lamentations 3, like the Servant in Isaiah, parallels Lady Zion in numerous ways. He seems to be a representative sufferer who experiences the same kinds of suffering that Zion does. Also of interest is that the speakers in both Lamentations and Isaiah 53 look back in time to the destruction of Zion/the *geber*/the Servant and look to the future for the hoped-for restoration. This locates all the voices in the exilic present. Now the book of Isaiah develops the *geber* of Lamentations 3 in certain directions, but in retrospect one may possibly see clues in Lamentations 3 for those developments. For instance, I have argued that the man's suffering parallels Jerusalem's suffering, the beginnings of his salvation provide hope for Israel, and his expectation of complete deliverance parallels Israel's hope for future deliverance. Isaiah's Servant develops those ideas further, and the New Testament further still. It sees the glorious promises of Isaiah 40–55 as being fulfilled in the person of Jesus, the Servant of YHWH, whose death and resurrection fulfils Isaiah 53. The new exodus salvation of return from exile is now experienced in the resurrection and, in proleptic ways, in the church (although its fullness is still future).

So where does all this take us hermeneutically? First, I suggest that it confirms a longstanding Christian instinct that the man in Lamentations 3 is significant for the interpretation of the book as a whole. The man has been seen as a partial type of Christ, and the links we have observed from the *geber* to the Servant to Christ provide a nonarbitrary chain that justifies such a reading strategy. Later we shall query the over-emphasis on the man to the

---

12. Willey, *Remember the Former Things,* observes that Isaiah has expanded the one phrase of Lamentations into two parallel ones (216).

13. A rare combination of words.

neglect of Lady Jerusalem in the interpretation of Lamentations. However, the longstanding tradition of seeing chapter 3 as central to the book has theological (as well as literary) merit.

Second, Jews or Christians should not merely read Lamentations as if Isaiah 40–55 had not been written. When reflecting theologically on particular texts in Lamentations, they will be interested in how Isaiah 40–55 engages those same texts. This point is reinforced by the canonical placing of Lamentations *after* Isaiah. We recall the comment in *Lamentations Rabbah* that "all the severe prophecies that Jeremiah prophesied against Israel were *anticipated* and healed by Isaiah."[14] Reading Lamentations in the light of Isaiah is perfectly legitimate for Jewish and Christian readers. I shall argue later that there is a nonnegotiable "moment" in the reading of the text when one does need to hear its voice without the prophetic response, but such a hearing cannot be the end of the hermeneutical engagement with the text. The coming of YHWH to comfort does have implications for how we hear the pain of Lady Jerusalem, for *we now know what she did not.*

Third, New Testament development of the themes in Second Isaiah also opens up fruitful avenues for fresh hearing of the text. In Christ and the Spirit YHWH comes to comfort Jerusalem. But now we see God, not simply as the one who punishes Jerusalem, but also as the one who suffers the pains of Jerusalem, alongside Jerusalem. I will develop this insight later.

Finally, it is important to make clear that Second Isaiah uses the text of Lamentations selectively for his own contextual purposes, and we must not feel unduly limited in our use of the text by this. So it has to be emphasized that, while Isaiah should guide and shape Christian reading of Lamentations, it should not be seen to close down other insights.

Lamentations in the Context of the New Testament

If we are to read Lamentations in canonical context, we need to do so in an informed and controlled way. Seeing how Isaiah 40–55 engages with the book suggests a fruitful way of connecting with some broader biblical-theological currents to create an interpretative framework within which Lamentations will open up some of its treasures for Christian theological reflection. This framework is not proposed as the only way of mapping the canon, but it is offered as a textually-grounded and useful one that resonates well with Second Isaiah's use of Lamentations.

14. *Lam. Rab.* XXXVI:ii.

My framework requires us to appreciate the connections between humanity, Israel, Christ, and the church. I believe that the connections that I draw out here were made by many of the New Testament writers and were grounded in Old Testament texts. I do not claim that all biblical writers made them, nor that any biblical writer sets them out in the way I will do.

In a nutshell, following scholars such as N. T. Wright, I think that the story of humanity is recapitulated in the story of Israel and that the story of Israel is reenacted in the story of Christ.[15] Let's begin with the basic connections between the story of Israel and the story of humanity. It looks very much as though the story of humanity as told in Genesis has been narrated in ways which consciously reflect the story of Israel. Adam's story has been told in the light of Israel's story, with the effect that Israel's story is presented as a retelling of Adam's. Adam is created outside the garden and is placed in it by YHWH to look after it (Gen 2:8). He is arguably presented as being in covenant relationship with YHWH, living in the covenant blessings yet under a divine command and warning (Gen 2:16-17).[16] The violation of that command leads to curse and expulsion from the garden (Gen 3:22-24). That expulsion is taken a step further in the story of Cain (Gen 4:11-14). In Genesis 1–11, the human situation spirals violently downward until the flood and beyond. The canonical shaping of the book of Genesis presents the story of the calling of Abram as YHWH's strategy for dealing with the human predicament.[17] Abram is presented in Genesis as a new Adam, and by implication his descendants are a new humanity.[18] The Adam-Israel associations are found in various Old Testament traditions. The story of Israel is seen to parallel the story of Adam: Like Adam, Israel was created outside of the promised land and then placed within the land by YHWH. The land of Canaan is presented in some Old Testament books in distinctly Edenic terms (Num 13:20-27; Deut 8:7-9; 11:9, 11-15; 26:15; Joel 2:3; Isa 11:6; 51:3; Ezek 36:35, etc.), and the links between Eden and the Jerusalem temple are also strong.[19] Israel, like Adam, lives in covenant relation with YHWH, enjoying the divine blessings of the covenant (Gen 1:28; cf. 12:2; 17:2, 6, 8; 22:16ff.; 26:3ff.; 28:3, etc.)[20] and the call to re-

15. See Wright, "Adam, Israel and the Messiah." The theme is central to Wright's work.

16. Dumbrell, *Covenant and Creation*, ch. 1.

17. Clines, *The Theme of the Pentateuch.*

18. See Wright, "Adam, Israel and the Messiah"; and esp. Beale, *The Temple and the Church's Mission,* chs. 2–3.

19. See Wenham, "Sanctuary Symbolism"; Beale, *The Temple and the Church's Mission.*

20. The theme of "blessing" in Genesis 1–11 is closely linked to the theme of blessing in Genesis 12–50 (see Wenham, *Story as Torah,* ch. 3), and it is a major link between Israel and Adam.

productive fruitfulness,[21] yet is also subject to divine commands (Gen 2:17; cf. Exod 20ff.). And, just as Adam violated the covenant command and was expelled from Eden (Gen 3:23-24), so too Israel violated the commands and was sent out of the land in exile. It seems to me that, in some Old Testament traditions at least, there are some clear Israel-Adam, Eden-Canaan, and expulsion-exile links. The story of humanity (Adam) is recapitulated in the new humanity of Israel.

Interestingly, this linking of Adamic expulsion and Israel's exile is made in the opening of the rabbinic Targum of Lamentations:

> Jeremiah the Prophet and High Priest told how it was decreed that Jerusalem and her people should be punished with banishment and that they should be mourned with *'ekah*. Just as when Adam and Eve were punished and expelled from the Garden of Eden and the Master of the Universe mourned them with *'ekah*.

The rabbis linked Lam 1:1 with Gen 3:9 through Hos 6:7: "But like man (כאדם/*kĕ'ādām*) they have transgressed the covenant. . . ."[22]

Various streams of eschatological hope arose within Israel in the midst of her oppression. The prophets said that after a time of exile God would restore Israel to the land. He would enable Israel's obedience to the commandments by circumcising their hearts and putting his Spirit in them (Deut 30:6; Jer 31:31-34; Ezek 36:25-27; Joel 2:28-29). The restoration of Israel would be accompanied by the destruction of their oppressors (e.g., Isaiah 34) but subsequently by the salvation of the survivors from those very same nations (e.g., Isa 19:18-25; 45:20-25). The nations would stream to Zion to join Israel in the worship of YHWH, and creation would be renewed (Isa 2:1-4; 11:10-12; 60:1-16; Ps 138:4-5, etc.). So it will be that Israel will fulfill its God-given mandate to be the vehicle through which God would restore the whole of humanity. The return from exile will trigger events that lead to the restoration of the nations. Now these eschatological hopes are configured differently in different Old Testament traditions and in different streams of Second Temple Judaism, but the basic plotline above provides a broad summary and synthesis of some of key elements that one finds.

The actual return from exile under Persian oversight fell short of the glorious visions of prophets such as Deutero-Isaiah, and this led to expecta-

---

21. Along with the blessing theme, the reproductive fruitfulness theme is another strong link between Adam and Eve's original commission and Israel's covenant blessings. See Wenham, *Story as Torah*.

22. Brady, *The Rabbinic Targum of Lamentations*, 18.

tions for further and deeper fulfillment. Israel was still under Gentile rule (Persian, Greek, Ptolemaic, Seleucid, and Roman), and some Jews found it hard to believe that the exile had really come to its proper end.[23] Thus the promises of return, of the outpouring of the Spirit, of the restoration of Israel and the pilgrimage of the nations must await a fuller, future fulfillment. It is in this context that early Christian theology makes sense.

Christ, as the Messiah of Israel, functioned as the representative of the nation. In one sense Jesus *is* Israel. Wright has argued controversially that the cross of Christ was conceived of as the climax of the curse of the law — namely exile (Gal 3:13).[24] I think that the logic of at least some important early Christian theology would confirm this. First, I suggest that seeing Christ's cross, as the early Christians did, in terms of the Suffering Servant in Isaiah 53[25] would probably have involved seeing it in terms of participating in Israel's exilic sufferings (see our earlier discussion on the Servant's suffering). Second, the exile and return were spoken of in Ezekiel as the death and resurrection of the nation (Ezekiel 37), and, according to the prophetic expectations sketched above, the return of Israel would be followed by the outpouring of the Spirit, the reunification of Israel and Judah, and the pilgrimage of the nations. Those motifs find their counterpart in the resurrection,[26] the day of Pentecost (Acts 2), the conversion of the Samaritans (descendants of the northern kingdom) and their connection to the Jerusalem church (Acts 8), and the conversion of the Gentiles to faith in Christ (Acts 10ff.).[27] Those signs would indicate that the exile of Israel had, at least proleptically in Christ's resurrection, come to an end. That would lend weight to Wright's claim that the cross of Christ *is* the exile of Israel at the hands of the pagan nations writ small.

The connections between Christ and Israel would also illuminate the connections between Christ and the whole of humanity also found in the thought of the earliest Christians. Christ is Israel *and is thus* a new humanity

23. That many Jews at the time of Jesus thought of themselves as still in exile in the land is controversial but has been defended by Wright, *The New Testament and the People of God;* Evans, "Jesus and the Continuing Exile of Israel." It is certainly the case that the full, postexilic restoration spoken of by Israel's prophets was still thought of by many as awaiting future fulfillment.

24. See Wright, "Curse and Covenant."

25. See, e.g., Acts 8:26-35; 1 Pet 2:22-25. See Janowski and Stuhlmacher, *The Suffering Servant.*

26. On resurrection as the restoration of Israel, see esp. Gowan, *Theology of the Prophetic Books;* Anderson, "But God Raised Him."

27. See esp. Pao, *Acts and the Isaianic New Exodus.*

and a second Adam (Rom 5:12-21; 1 Cor 15:45-49). Christ's death is Israel's exile writ small *and hence is also* the sufferings of humanity living east of Eden. Christ's resurrection is the return from exile *and so also* corresponds to the resurrection of all humanity and indeed the whole of creation (Romans 8). A further step would be to appreciate the relationship between the sufferings of Christ and the sufferings of the church. That the church participates in the apocalyptic sufferings of her Lord is a recurring theme in the New Testament (Mark 8:34-38; Rom 8:17; Phil 3:10; 2 Cor 1:5; 4:10-12; 1 Pet 2:21-25).

My contention is that these biblical-theological connections create a framework for some fruitful, imaginative, Christian *re*-appropriation of Lamentations. Lamentations concerns the devastation of the exilic experience from the perspective of those who have been left behind. It is the Holy Saturday of Israel's life caught between exilic death at the hands of Babylon and the desperate hope for resurrection. The future exile of Israel was seen by Leviticus as an enforced Sabbath rest for the land because Israel had neglected to observe the Sabbaths (Lev 26:34-35). So it is that Christ's death on Good Friday is followed by the "exilic," Sabbath rest of Holy Saturday. The framework outlined above allows a Christian reader to connect the suffering of Lamentations with the sufferings of humanity more generally and, in accord with the Rule of Faith, with the sufferings of Christ in particular. Locating the tears of Lamentations in these intercanonical flows allows us to read the tears of the world through the tears of Lamentations and vice versa. It also invites us to read Lamentations in the light of the cross and the cross in the light of Lamentations. The connections between Christ's suffering and that of the church would also help us to connect Lamentations to the plight of suffering Christians across the globe. The potential for fresh insight emerging from such imaginative theological engagements with the text is immense and very open-ended. Such engagements would be guided by a biblical theology which emerges from various texts in Scripture, but the possibilities for fresh interpretations, even within this Christian framework, are vast.

This approach helps address a concern raised by Linafelt, who protests against the privileging of the suffering man in Lamentations 3 to the relative neglect of Lady Jerusalem in chapters 1 and 2. He argues with some justification that this bias in part reflects the influence of Christian theology. The suffering man in chapter 3 seems a candidate for being a type of Christ, while Lady Jerusalem does not.[28] However, my suggested approach to Christian

---

28. Though it is surprising how the history of Christian reception of Lamentations 3 reveals that Christological interpretations were not dominant.

theological engagement with Lamentations does not require the marginalization of Lady Jerusalem, even if it does affirm the centrality of Lamentations 3. It invites the Christian reader to connect Christ's suffering not simply with the man in Lamentations 3 *but also* with the sufferings of Lady Jerusalem, the desolate, God-forsaken, naked, and publicly shamed rape victim whose husband is gone and whose children have been taken away by her attacker. Indeed, such avenues of exploration may be more creative for Christian theological reflection because they have been neglected in the past. So this linking of Jesus' sufferings with Jerusalem's is not an arbitrary move but one motivated by currents within parts of the Bible.

Lamentations then is to the exile and restoration of Israel what Holy Saturday is to the cross and resurrection of Christ. "Under the immediate impact of the catastrophe of 587 the collapse of Jerusalem was described [in Lamentations] in such a way that motifs from the [funeral] dirge enriched the communal lament. This was because the collapse of the city was experienced as its death."[29] Lamentations is the Old Testament equivalent of Paul's claim "that Christ died [and] . . . , was buried" (1 Cor 15:3-4) and the statement in the Apostles' Creed that Christ "was crucified . . . [and] descended into hell." What seemed to be the obscure link made in the Christian *Tenebrae* service between Christ and Lady Jerusalem turns out to reflect the kind of organic link with the original horizon of the text that I think a theological reading requires.

	Covenant Blessing	Destruction	Rubble	New Life
Humanity (and creation)	Humanity in Eden	Expulsion from Eden (judgment)	The groaning of humanity (and creation)	Resurrection (and new creation)
Israel (and the Land)	Israel living in Canaan in obedience to covenant	Babylonian destruction and exile (judgment) *(Lamentations)*	Aftermath of destruction *(Lamentations)*	Restoration of Israel, Jerusalem, and the Land
Christ	Christ throughout his ministry	Death (judgment)	Burial	Resurrection

29. Westermann, *Lamentations,* 11.

Expanding Contexts: Lamentations and Christian Anti-Semitism

This approach to Lamentations allows us to connect its words to suffering in all sorts of contexts. Lamentations can address, as Judaism has long acknowledged, the sufferings of Jews, not simply at the time of the Babylonian exile, but later at the hands of Rome and on through a history of anti-Semitic terror (shamefully often caused by Christians) that continues into the present time. Jewish liturgical usage reflects precisely this trajectory. But for *Christians,* the christological links I outline above should suggest that when the church persecuted the Jews, their (as yet unacknowledged) Messiah Jesus suffered alongside his afflicted Jewish brethren and the church played out the role of the despicable enemies from Lamentations! Jesus called out to the Christians, "Church, Church, why do you persecute me?"

In Christ, God was not merely incarnate in *human* flesh, he was incarnate in *Jewish* flesh. In Christ, God speaks his "Yes" to Israel, even in the face of Israel's "No" to Jesus. And in Christ's crucifixion God stands in solidarity with "crucified" Israel. Thomas Torrance wrote:

> In faithfulness to the God and Father of our Lord Jesus Christ the Christian Church can never be the same after the Holocaust, for all its understanding of divine revelation and salvation, mediated through Israel, must be, and cannot but be, affected by the *Eli, Eli, lama sabachthani?* in which Israel and Jesus Christ are for ever forged together in a new and quite irreversible way.[30]

These links allow contemporary Messianic Jews to draw remembrance of the historic sufferings of the Jews alongside not merely Lamentations but also the cross. Mark Kinzer, a Messianic rabbi, explains how the lectionary of *Besorah* used by some Messianic Jews makes precisely these connections:

> The cycle reaches its climax, with the narrative of Yeshua's death, between the 17th of Tammuz and the 9th of Av, when the Jewish calendar enters a period of mourning for the destruction of the temple, and three haftorahs of admonition are read. It reaches its joyful conclusion with seven readings related to Yeshua's resurrection, corresponding to the seven Sabbaths between the 9th of Av and Rosh Hashanah, when haftorahs of consolation from the latter chapters of Isaiah are read. The cycle thus points us to the truth that Yeshua, as the King of Israel and its representative, embodies in his person the meaning of the temple, the

---

30. Torrance, "The Divine Vocation and Destiny of Israel," 96. See also *Incarnation*, ch. 2.

holy city, and Jewish history as a whole. His suffering sums up and puri-
fies Israel's suffering, and his resurrection will bring about Israel's ultimate restoration. . . . Thus, the 9th of Av, the destruction of the two temples, and the book of Lamentations are all set in a liturgical framework
that connects them to the death of Yeshua.[31]

All this suggests the need for Gentile Christ-believers to hear Lamentations as
a word addressed, in the first instance, *by* the people of Israel to YHWH, and
written down *for* the people of Israel. Christians instinctively read the texts as
insiders — we hear our own voices in the anguished words of those in pain.
This is right, but I am proposing that there is a place for a different, far more
unsettling reading stance vis-à-vis the text.

The book speaks of the brutal violence of the nations against the Jews,
and it is sobering for Gentile Christians to read the text, not from the position
of suffering-Israel, but in *the role of the oppressive nations.* Read in this way,
the book serves to invite the communities that have persecuted Jews to listen
to the voices of their victims. Even a glancing familiarity with the shocking
treatment of Jews by Christians through the ages goes a long way towards indicating the potential power of such a reading strategy.

But, someone may protest, surely this is not to read Lamentations as
Christian Scripture, for it puts Christians on the outside looking in. So long as
this is not the only stance that Christian readers take to the text, I must beg to
differ. In this dangerous, almost prophetic mode the word of God functions
as a harsh word of rebuke, as a shocking exposure of an oft forgotten crime, as
a call to the painful task of listening to one's victims, and as an invitation to
repentance. Christian oppression of Jewish people may have been at its worst
in times gone by, but it is certainly not a thing of the past. Christians live with
the ever-present temptation to think that since the Messiah came God has
abandoned the Jewish people in favour of the church. This, to my mind, represents a fundamentally unbiblical ecclesiology, but it has been the theology
at the root of a lot of anti-Semitic attitudes and actions over the centuries.
Hearing Lamentations as a text *by Jews and for Jews* in which Gentile Christ-
believers have often shamefully enacted the role of the destructive nations
would actually be one very constructive, chastening reading strategy. The text
of Lamentations strikes a very different sound in the context of the church
when heard in such ways. Consider the different ways in which the nations
are related to Israel in the book:

---

31. Email 18 July 2008.

Some of the nations are those who were supposed allies, bound by treaties to support Israel if she was attacked. Yet, when the moment of truth arrived, they abandoned her to her enemies without a word of protest (1:2, 7; 4:17).

The attacking nation uses lethal violence against Jerusalem and her people (1:15; 2:4, 21; 4:1-10).

They enrich themselves on her wealth, stealing goods and property, and desecrating places and items of religious value (1:10; 2:6-7).

They expel her people (1:3, 5, 18).

They mock Jerusalem's suffering and rejoice in her downfall at their hands (1:7, 21; 2:15-17).

They fail to offer comfort to the suffering city (1:2, 9, 16, 17, 21).

It does not take much knowledge of Jewish-Christian relations throughout history to see how Lamentations might serve to expose past Christian acts for what they are. As such, Christians would be wise to pay careful attention to the traditional Jewish reading of the text on the 9th of Ab as a prism for understanding a wide range of Israel's sufferings. We need to hear that and acknowledge the legitimacy of that interpretation — *legitimacy retained within a Christian theological frame of reference.* If we who are Christians are not prepared to face our history and to allow Scripture to expose our infidelity, then what claims do we have to honor and tremble before God's word?

Expanding Contexts—Lamentations and Political Theology

Jewish approaches consider Lamentations in the light of the very concrete afflictions of the Jewish community through history, and they warn us against the tendency to simply individualize and spiritualize the significance of the book. This opens up the issue of how Lamentations might contribute to the broader project of political theology. Lamentations speaks of the destruction of Judah as a *political entity.* Its center of government, Jerusalem, is literally broken apart. The defensive walls, the gates, the citadels, the palaces, and its religious heart — the temple — are torn down (2:1-9). Her army is crushed (1:15, 20), and her political leadership — the king, princes, elders, and priests — are mostly killed or captured and deported (1:6; 2:2, 6, 9, 20; 4:20). Those that remain are in a broken condition (1:4; 2:10) or abused and possibly executed (5:12). The legal system has ceased to function without the leadership (5:14); the normal economic processes have collapsed, and starvation has set in (2:12, 20; 4:1-10; 5:2, 4-6). The people have lost control of their houses and land along with their access to free natural resources such as water and wood (5:2, 4). The kingdom and its princes have been brought down to the ground (2:2), and Jerusalem has been reduced from a "princess" on the international scene to a "forced laborer" (1:1); to "filth and refuse in the midst of the peoples" (3:45).

Christian readers, often more interested in individual spirituality or ecclesial practices, regularly miss the significance of the political suffering in Lamentations. But it is clear that Jerusalem's *political* decimation is a major focus of the poetry. In his book *Desire of the Nations,* Oliver O'Donovan has argued that Israel's political expression of God's kingship was manifest in three affirmations: first, YHWH gives Israel military *victory;* second, YHWH exercises just *judgment* through Israel's political leadership; third, YHWH grants political order and stability to Israel through *possession* of the promised land.[32] It takes but the reflection of a moment to see that Lamentations testifies to the loss of all three political aspects of God's rule in Israel. Israel had suffered a devastating military defeat, had lost the leadership that mediated public justice, and had lost control of its land (both as a national possession, 5:8, and the possession of individual families, 5:2). This was a total political, economic, and social meltdown! And Israel's prayers for restoration in Lamentations were not expressions of an apolitical hope, but rather of a hope with concrete social and political dimensions (5:21).

Lamentations will not be a key text for those reflecting on political questions such as the justification for and the nature of government, or the administration of public justice, or relationship between church and state. There are plenty of biblical texts that bear more directly on such issues. The role of Lamentations in political reflections must be of a different kind. Lamentations is not about providing theological categories with which to make sense of theoretical questions. Rather, it serves as a witness that demands the attention of all political-theological theoreticians. The poetry bears witness to the horror of political meltdown and, indirectly, to the goodness of political stability. It testifies to the real, concrete human suffering that follows social collapse.

Lamentations also plays its role as a part of the wider biblical critique of empire. The biblical literature, both Old and New Testament, is very positive about nations, but it is mostly very negative about empires.[33] Lamentations says nothing directly *about* empire, but it *portrays the impact of empire* upon the nation of Israel. The imperial use of massive lethal force to overwhelm

32. O'Donovan, *The Desire of the Nations,* ch. 2.
33. On empires, see O'Donovan, *The Desire of the Nations,* 70-72, 86-88. On nations, see Bretherton, "Valuing the Nation."

stubborn nations is presented *from the perspective of the victims.* Victors don't tell these stories, but conveniently brush them under the carpet. The poetry demands of its readers that they look at the broken body of Jerusalem and do not turn away; that they serve as her comforters standing in solidarity with her. It is always a temptation for the politically powerful to avoid looking at those adversely affected by their decisions. Lamentations calls to its users (God included) to look very hard indeed.

As part of a critique of empire, Lamentations functions as a witness against the use of excessive and indiscriminate military force to achieve goals. Those who suffer here are not simply the soldiers and leaders of Judah but the old people, the women, and the children. The empire used its power to win, *whatever the cost.* This book invites its audience to consider the cost and to weep.

Lamentations offers not merely a negative assessment of the imperial enemy, but also of the nations that had treaty obligations to help Judah in her time of need but who failed to do so (1:2; 4:17). The issue of broken treaties looms its head. Also negatively presented are those nations pictured as "walking by on the other side" — rubbernecking as they gasp at Jerusalem's decimation yet not lifting a finger to help (1:12, 17a). They are expected by Jerusalem and by the poet to serve as comforters, but a policy of noninvolvement prevails. Worse still are nations such as Edom that appear to have used the situation of Judah's "destruction" as an opportunity to enrich themselves at her expense (4:21-22). Such behavior is inexcusable. In these ways Lamentations portrays a range of bad political responses on the part of different nations to the suffering of Judah. These provide food for thought as we consider international relations today.

For Christians, reading the book in the light of the wider canonical story, the connections between Christ's suffering and the exilic sufferings of Israel are suggestive. If Christ himself embraces Israel's exile, then we are invited to consider Lamentations in the light of the cross and vice versa. For Christians used to seeing the cross simply in spiritual terms, this rudely reminds us that it was a highly political event. Jesus was *crucified* — the death assigned for *political* enemies of Rome, the imperial power of the time. The Nicene Creed makes this clear when it affirms that "he was crucified *under Pontius Pilate.*" He, like Jerusalem, was a victim of lethal imperial violence designed not merely to kill but to humiliate. There is a need for Christians to consider the implications of Jesus' standing in solidarity with political victims. And seeing the political implications of the cross opens up new political windows onto the resurrection and ascension. Here we are entering into a vast terrain well beyond the bounds of this commentary, but I hope that these brief gestures at least suggest avenues for fruitful exploration.

One such avenue is to use the text with a view to opening our eyes to contemporary political sufferings. As we have seen, the sufferings of the Jewish people past and present are very obviously relevant to reading the text today. But Israel's witness in Lamentations can serve to open our eyes to the plight of Gentile nations.

Lamentations can speak to the Jew but also, say, to the Palestinian suffering, in part, as a result of Israeli policies regarding the Occupied Territories.[34] "If you wish to really understand what is taking place in the Gaza Strip," says Catholic priest Fr. Manuel Musallam from Gaza,

> please open your Bible and read the Lamentations of Jeremiah. This is what we are all living. People are crying, hungry, thirsty and desperate. . . . Even if there is food for sale, people have no money to buy food. The price of food, of course, has doubled and tripled in the situation. They have no income, no opportunities to get food from outside and no opportunities to secure money inside Gaza. No work. No livelihood. No future. They have no hope and many very poor people are aimlessly wandering around trying to beg for something from others who also have nothing. It is heart-breaking to see.[35]

Colin Chapman, who lived for many years in Beirut, began to engage with Lamentations in this way in his article "A Lament over Lebanon," written on 22 July 2006 (ten days after Hizbullah's attacks on Israel and Israel's bombing campaign unleashed such devastation in Lebanon). He applied the descriptions of the devastated city and the humanitarian crisis in Lamentations to Beirut in 2006. The cries of pain in the biblical book served to articulate the anguish felt by many Lebanese. Chapman finally drew future hope in the midst of his despair from Lam 3:19-23:

> What kept me sane and enabled me to hold onto my faith during the dark days of the civil war in Lebanon [1975-1990] and through all that has happened in the Middle East since then has been the writings of the biblical prophets. There we find a world-view which sees all history in the hands of a holy and loving God who is at work both in judgement and in mercy, in and through all the terrible events that we witness.[36]

34. I affirm the right of the State of Israel to exist and to defend its citizens, and I am well aware of the complexity of the situation in the Occupied Territories. But I also think that friendship with Israel is compatible with robust critique of Israeli policies and actions.

35. Reported in the Independent Catholic News on 7/7/06 (http://www.indcatholicnews .com/urgecarit118.html).

36. Chapman, "A Lament over Lebanon," 6.

Chapman's engagement with Lamentations in the Lebanese context could have been taken further through the exploration of the christological connections outlined above.

Perhaps the most systematic attempt to grasp Lamentations in one hand and our current military conflicts in the other is found in *Lamentations: From New York to Kabul and Beyond* by the Jesuit priest and peace activist Daniel Berrigan. In the shadow of 9/11 he writes, "On those raw pages, I met — myself, ourselves."[37] In Berrigan's hands Lamentations becomes a powerful antiwar poem which exposes the dehumanizing of military conflict. To take but one example: commenting on Lam 4:2 in which precious children are like broken pots, Berrigan writes:

> The pots too are endangered — in the frenzy, they may well be reduced to shards. The poet is precise on every count and implication. In war, the children might be thought immune to the common fate. Not at all, he implies. He would have us look unflinchingly at the wars of our own times. Ancient times, our own times, one and the same: an abomination. We have seen in the Bible every crime consequent on war: betrayal of friends, hundred year conflicts going nowhere, extermination mandated from on high, sieges laid against cities, mothers resorting to cannibalism, helpless lepers caught between opposing armies, soldiers slaying their counterparts for entertainment of commanders . . . a history held up like an ensanguined mirror — of our own times.[38]

Lamentations can also address the sufferings of persecuted churches like those in Saudi Arabia, Pakistan, and Sudan, as well as the survivors of the Shoah, the Rwandan genocide, Darfur, or any number of other sufferings. It also allows us to connect all of these sufferings to those of Christ and consequently to invest all such situations with the hope that springs from his resurrection.

Lamentations and the Rule of Faith

So a crucial move towards a Christian theological interpretation is to use some of the canonical interconnections which will open up the text to re-readings. But theological interpretation is more than simply a biblical-theological interpretation. The canon *is* privileged in theological interpreta-

---

37. Berrigan, *Lamentations,* xviii. On Berrigan's interpretation, see H. Thomas, "Reading Lamentations with Daniel Berrigan, SJ."

38. Berrigan, *Lamentations,* 86.

tion and serves as a plumb line against which Christian readings are measured. However, the story of Christian theological reflection did not end with the writing of the biblical texts. In the early church various groups arose who were reading the same sacred books but were reading them in radically diverse ways. The matter became a serious concern in the second century when Gnostic groups were interpreting the Scriptures in questionable ways. In this context the proto-orthodox appealed to the Rule of Faith as a guide to legitimate biblical interpretation. The Rule of Faith was a summary of the key Christian beliefs passed on in those churches set up by the apostles. It is not enough, they said, simply to have all the correct sacred texts but also to understand them in the right way.[39]

The Rule of Faith is expressed in different ways in early Christian literature, but its basic content is straightforward and organized trinitarianly around the one God and Father; the one Lord, the crucified and risen Jesus Christ; and the one Holy Spirit. As with the later creeds, the story of Jesus is the focus of the Rule of Faith, and, as theological reading was guided by the Rule, Christian readers were led to maintain a tradition of reading, rooted in the New Testament, which saw all of the Scriptures as related to Christ in some way. What came to be called the Old Testament, no less than what became the New, speaks of Christ. So a robust *Christian theological* hermeneutic operates with a full-blown Trinitarian vision of God. How might that work?

Christ and Lamentations

Christ and Lady Jerusalem

If we recognize Jesus as Israel's Messiah, the one who represents the nation of Israel, then we can recognize in his suffering and death the exilic suffering and "death" of Israel. As we have already argued, this draws Jesus' cross alongside the motif of the destruction of Jerusalem so prominent in Lamentations, and it allows us to see Jesus, in some senses, *in the role of Zion* in Lamentations. It is important to qualify the way in which Jesus can be said to parallel Jerusalem in Lamentations 1–2. Jesus' suffering is *not* identical in every way to Zion's. Every experience of suffering is unique, and we need to recognize not only what different experiences of pain share in common but *also* the ways in which they differ. Honoring the *particularity* of suffering is as important as grasping the communion of suffering. Jesus' pain is *not* identical with Zion's pain. *Unlike*

39. On the Rule of Faith, see Wall, "Reading the Bible from within Our Traditions."

Jerusalem, Jesus did not sin but bore the sins of others. Jesus was *not* widowed, did *not* suffer the loss of children, and was *not* raped. Jesus' suffering was *not constituted by* the suffering of his followers as Zion's was constituted, in part, by the suffering of her population. These dimensions of Zion's agony are not incidental but fundamental. In the same way, there are aspects of Jesus' suffering which were not shared by Zion, and we need to honor the differences.

However, to honor only the differences and not the convergences is to err in the other direction. Jesus' suffering does run in parallel to Jerusalem's in numerous ways as he plays out his role as her representative. *Like* Jerusalem, tears were upon his cheeks as he prayed alone in the garden. *Like* Jerusalem, he knew betrayal by his "friends" who left him to suffer alone. *Like* Jerusalem Jesus was beaten, stripped naked, publicly humiliated, and afflicted. *Like* Jerusalem, he was reduced from a high and noble status to dust. *Like* Jerusalem, he bore the divine curse for covenant disobedience. *Like* Jerusalem, he was violently attacked by a pagan occupying force. *Like* Jerusalem, he felt abandoned by YHWH in the face of these pagan military oppressors. *Like* Jerusalem, he was mocked and despised by those who looked on at his destruction.

Lamentations at one point picks up a common Old Testament image of the cup of God's wrath (Isa 51:17-23; Jer 25:15-16, 27-29; 48:26; 49:12-13; 51:39, 57; Ezek 23:31-35; Hab 2:15-17; Ps 11:6; 60:3; 75:8; Obad 15-16; Zech 12:2). The judgment is expressed in the image of being made to drink from the cup, leading to drunkenness, staggering, "madness," vomiting, and falling. Judah has drunk from this cup, but after that it will be passed to Edom, her enemy (4:21; cf. Jer 49:12-13; Isa 51:17). The very same image is picked up in the Gospels. The suffering of Christ is spoken metaphorically as "this cup" (Mark 14:36), linking Jesus' suffering yet again to the cup of divine wrath that Judah drank from (a cup his followers would also have to drink from, Mark 10:38-39). The cup of wine at the Last Supper from which Jesus tells his disciples to drink quite possibly, *at one level*, also alludes to this cup of Jesus' suffering. Now these intertextual allusions open up the possibility of connecting the Christian Eucharist with the afflictions of Jerusalem in Lamentations. The bread and the cup are rich in complex symbolic overtones, but one of them is that of sharing in Christ's sufferings and death (and thus, indirectly, in Jerusalem's). We shall return to this idea later.

Jesus' crucifixion at the hands of Rome was a representative foretaste of Jerusalem's destruction at the hands of pagan Rome in A.D. 70, so our drawing Jesus' death alongside Jerusalem's destruction in Lamentations is not arbitrary. Thinking scripturally, we may see a *typological* relationship between all three. Precisely how this may impact the way we hear Lamentations will be discussed later.

Christ and the Destroyed Temple

Lamentations 2:15 provides one of only two relatively clear New Testament allusions to Lamentations:

> They clapped hands against you,
>   all those who passed by.
> They whistled and shook their heads, because of
>   Daughter Jerusalem.

Matthew 27:39 picks up on this in his depiction of those who passed by the cross of Jesus:[40]

> Those who passed by hurled insults at him, shaking their heads. "The one who destroys the temple and in three days rebuilds it, save yourself, if you are the son of God, and come down from the cross."

Here, reinforcing our earlier comments, Matthew portrays Jesus on the cross as playing out the same role as Lady Jerusalem. He is destroyed by foreign armies and mocked by those who walk past shaking their heads. Matthew also picks up on another theme from the chapter in the words spoken by the passers-by, namely the destruction of the temple. What the mockers fail to appreciate is that the temple destroyed and rebuilt in three days is Jesus' own body (cf. John 2:19-22). Thus Jesus is also seen to play out the role of the devastated temple in 70 A.D. and in Lamentations 2. This insight provides a rich resource for theological reflection.

To begin merely to pry open some of the possibilities here, let's consider what the temple represented in ancient Israel. It is widely recognized that temples across the ancient Near East were symbols of the cosmos and dwelling places for deities. Temples were not just very important buildings, but were seen as fundamental for the relationships between human communities and their gods. Similarly, the temple in Jerusalem was perceived as a microcosm of the whole created order (heaven and earth), with the divine presence dwelling at

---

40. Moffitt, "Righteous Bloodshed," 310-12, makes a strong case for the view that Matt 27:39 alludes to Lam 2:15 and not to Ps 22:7, as most scholars think. First, there is more verbal overlap with Lam 2:15 than Ps 22:7 (LXX 21:8). Second, Lamentations 2 and Matthew 27 have a destruction of the temple motif not found in Psalm 22. Third, while Matthew later quotes Ps 22:8, the words he puts in the mouth of the passers-by are not from the mockers in Psalm 22. Instead, their words pick up on a theme from Lamentations 2: the destruction of the temple. Finally, Moffitt has argued previously that Matthew has already connected Jesus' crucifixion with the shedding of righteous blood in Lam 4:13 that led to the destruction of the temple.

the heart of it (Ps 78:69). Gregory Beale has argued that the outer court represented the habitable world where humanity dwells, the holy place represented the visible heavens, and the holy of holies symbolized the invisible dimension of the cosmos where God and the angels dwelt.[41] The different elements of creation were represented in the temple: the wash basin referred to as "the sea" (1 Kgs 7:23-26), the stone altar referred to as "the bosom of the earth" (Ezek 43:14) which was made of earth or uncut stone (Exod 20:24-25). These likely symbolize sea and earth. The seven lamps in the holy place may have represented the heavenly lights visible to the naked eye (sun, moon, and five planets). The holy of holies, inaccessible to human eyes, was associated with God and his guardian cherubim. The curtains dividing the compartments of the temple were covered in lush vegetation and flying creatures. Given the significance of the temple, one can begin to appreciate the significance of its destruction. The razing of the sanctuary is, in microcosm, the end of the world! It is the destruction of symbolic earth and the symbolic heaven. It is the severing of the appointed ritual meeting place between the literal earth and the literal heavens.

Jesus looked to the future (from his point in history) and saw the Jerusalem temple facing destruction for a second time, now at the hands of Rome (Mark 13). As with the destruction recounted in Lamentations, this was also a judgment on Israel. But Jesus also saw his own death as symbolically related to the destruction of the temple. His own body effectively fulfilled the role of the temple by mediating the divine presence in the midst of Israel (John 1:14). Jesus' body replaced the temple of stone.[42] So Jesus' death could be spoken of as the destruction of the temple, and his resurrection was its rebuilding (John 2:18-22). When Jesus breathed his last, we see the Spirit leaving him and the temple curtain (symbolizing the visible heavens) torn from top to bottom representing the destruction of the old heavens and earth.[43] Jesus' death is symbolically the death of Israel, the death of humanity in general, and, more than that, *the death of the created order itself.* Heaven and earth symbolically end with the death of the Messiah-temple, and his resurrection is the foundation of renewed heavens and earth.

Turning back to Lamentations 2, what do we see in the weeping over the loss of the temple? Merely a ruined building? Can't we see a fracture in the relation between humanity and God as the meeting place is removed? Is there not a terrible symbol of cataclysmic cosmic upheaval? Could not an environmentally aware believer see in those scattered blocks of stone an image of the

---

41. Beale, *The Temple and the Church's Mission*, ch. 1.

42. See Hoskins, *Jesus as the Fulfillment of the Temple.*

43. So Johnson, "The 'New Creation', the Crucified and Risen Christ, and the Temple."

damage humans can do to the created order? Can't a Christian see a symbol of the death of Christ in those ruins? And can't we, by perceiving Jesus' role as the temple representing all of creation, find hope for our future in the fact that "in Christ" the temple/creation does not stay in ruins but is rebuilt?

Cosmos (God indwelling)	Subject to decay and "groaning" in frustration: passing away	"New" Heavens and Earth
Temple (God indwelling)	Destroyed (Lamentations)	Rebuilt
Christ (God indwelling)	Dead	Resurrection (= new temple/new creation)

Christ and the Valiant Man

Historically, Christians have sometimes seen the man in Lamentations 3 as a type of Christ. Of course, the man in chapter 3 is not presented as a savior figure, and he does not die to rescue the oppressed people. The poet was not thinking of him as a type of the Messiah,[44] and the implied readers would not see him as such. However, the first horizon (explored in the main commentary) and the link between the man and the Servant in Isaiah indicate that a typological reading of the text is not arbitrary, even if it goes beyond the expected interpretation. There are structural similarities between the man and Jesus that allow Christian readers to see him as playing out a role that is fulfilled in Christ. It is worth itemizing these briefly.

First, the connection between his suffering and Jerusalem's suffering is much like the link between Jesus' death and the crushing of the holy city. The man embodies the divine judgment on Jerusalem in his own story. Jesus' crucifixion at the hands of the Romans embodies the eschatological judgment of Jerusalem.

The man is metaphorically thrown into the pit of death, and God delivers him from that pit. The connection with Jesus' *literal* death and resurrection is clear. Rufinus saw in the words "they have cut off my life in the pit, and have laid a stone upon me," a plain prophecy of Christ's death and burial.[45] While that is going too far, the connection he makes is not irresponsible.

---

44. Although it is *possible* that he was presented as Israel's king, and, if so, this would strengthen a Christian reappropriation.

45. Rufinus, *A Commentary on the Apostles' Creed* 27. NPNF² 3, 553. Cyril made the same connection, *Lecture 13. NPNF²* 7, 91.

The current status of the man vis-à-vis his enemies is not unlike that of Jesus. On the one hand, he has been redeemed from the pit. On the other hand, his opponents are still out there and their full defeat is yet to come. This is close to the New Testament understanding of Christ as raised by God from the dead and reigning, but currently not all his enemies are yet under his feet. The final defeat of death and sin lies in the future (1 Cor 15:24-28).

The redemption of the man from his pit is presented as a sign of hope that God will do the same for the population at large. His past redemption is a sign of their coming redemption. So too, Christ's resurrection from the dead is presented as the firstfruits of a general resurrection of those who belong to him, a sign of the future of the people of God (1 Cor 15:12-22). What God did for the man he will do for Israel; what God did for Christ he will do for the church.

Valiant Man	Christ
Embodies the suffering of Jerusalem	Embodies the suffering of Jerusalem (and humanity)
In the pit (metaphorical death)	In the grave (real death)
Redeemed from the pit	Raised from the dead
His redemption is a sign of hope for Israel	His redemption is a sign of hope for Israel (and the world)
His enemies still plot against him	His enemies still fight against him
Final defeat of his enemies is future	Final defeat of his enemies is future

Does looking at chapter 3 typologically enrich our appreciation of Christ's death? I think so. Consider this question: Would it enrich our theological grasp of the crucifixion to see the man's lament in 3:1-18 as the kind of prayer that Jesus could have prayed on the cross? I am not asking this as a historical question — there is no reason to think that he did pray it — but as a theological one? *Could* he have, and, if he could, what would it tell us about Christ and his relationship to our situation? I suggest that an imaginative reading of Lam 3:1-18 as Christ's own prayer to his Father does indeed enrich our understanding of the depths of his despair and his solidarity with suffering humanity.

Christ and the Righteous Victims

The second New Testament allusion to Lamentations picks up on 4:13.[46]

46. The argument that follows is based on Moffitt, "Righteous Bloodshed."

[This was] because of [the] sins of her prophets
   [and the] iniquities of her priests,
who shed in the midst of her
   [the] blood of [the] righteous.

Jesus, in Matt 23:35, says,

> So that *all the righteous blood* that has been shed upon the land may come upon you from the blood of righteous Abel to the blood of Zechariah the son of Barachiah whom you murdered between the temple and the altar.

The expression "righteous blood" occurs only in LXX Joel 3:19; Jonah 1:14; and Lam 4:13, and only the latter passage shares with Matt 23:35 a focus on the reason for the destruction of Jerusalem and its temple. Lamentations 4:13 is explaining that a key reason for God's judgment on Jerusalem was that the leadership shed the blood of the righteous (LXX "righteous blood"). Jesus is explaining that the coming judgment on Jerusalem is because the leadership shed righteous blood. An allusion to Lam 4:13 makes perfect sense. What is interesting is the way that Matthew then goes on to present the killing of Jesus as the climax of this shedding of righteous blood and thus the sealing of the fate of Jerusalem. Pilate's wife urges him to have nothing to do with that "righteous man" (Matt 27:19), and Pilate declares, "I am innocent of the blood of this righteous one"[47] (Matt 27:24). The people reply, "His blood be upon us and upon our children" (Matt 27:25). So it is that the shedding of the blood of Jesus is the climax of the righteous blood-shedding that led to the fall of Jerusalem at the hands of Babylon and will lead to its fall again at the hands of Rome.[48]

---

47. Most versions have "this man," but there is a good case for adopting a variant Greek textual tradition of "this righteous one" (Moffitt, "Righteous Bloodshed," 317-19). Similarly, there are good grounds for adopting an alternative Greek textual tradition of Matt 27:4, in which Judas says, "I have sinned by handing over *righteous* blood" (as opposed to "innocent blood" in the normally adopted textual tradition); Moffitt, "Righteous Bloodshed," 313-16.

48. The comparison between Jerusalem and Sodom in Lam 4:6 was understood by Athanasius and Jerome to indicate that, by killing the Son of God, the sins of the Jews so far exceeded those of Sodom that the latter appeared positively justified by comparison; Athanasius, *Letter 10* [Easter 338], *NPNF*[2] 4, 530; Jerome, *Against the Pelagians* 1.17. *NPNF*[2] 6, 457. Great care is needed here, given the history of the idea of the Jews as Christ-killers. Holding Jews as a group responsible for the death of Jesus has been the source of unspeakable evil in history. Clearly, *certain* Jews did play a role in his death (as did certain Gentiles), and, according to Matthew's Gospel, the fall of Jerusalem was, in *part,* a divine judgment for that (hence, "and on our children"). However, it does not follow from this that all Jews, either at the time of Jesus or subsequently, can be considered responsible for Jesus' death. Traditional Evangelical piety would see all sinners (Jews and Gentiles) as culpable for his death.

While the killing of *Jesus* is not referred to in Lam 4:13, the text reinforces a principle (judgment for shedding righteous blood) that is ultimately exemplified in Jesus and the destruction of Jerusalem in A.D. 70.

Lamentations 4:13, however, should not be seen merely as a type of the shedding of Christ's blood. It is a general principle exemplified in Christ, but its impact is best experienced today by retaining that generality of reference. When leaders appointed to lead wisely and to do justice shed the blood of the righteous, they betray their calling and bring down divine wrath. The righteous might see in the text the fact that their loyalty to YHWH does not mean they will be spared suffering and death. But they may also see that their blood will be avenged and that God, in Christ, has stood in solidarity with them in persecution.

Christ and the Captured Messiah in 4:20

Lamentations 4:20 was important to early Christian interpreters of Lamentations and was almost always read christologically.[49] The Hebrew could be translated as follows:

> [The] breath of our nostrils, YHWH's anointed,
>   was captured in their pits —
> [He of] whom we said, "In his shade,
>   we will live among the nations."

Many of the early Christians understood the LXX as follows:

> The s/Spirit before our face, Christ the Lord,
>   was taken in our/their corruptions/snares,
> of whom we said, "In his shadow
>   we shall live among the Gentiles."

---

49. Aphrahat was unusual in resisting the christological reading of Lam 4:20. He is adamant that it referred to Israel's king only and *not* to Jesus. His reasoning is that Lam 5:16 refers back to 4:20 with the image of the crown falling from the head of the people. But, objects Aphrahat, "Christ has not fallen, because He rose again the third day"; *Select Demonstrations* 9. *NPNF²* 13, 355.

Perhaps the strangest christological appropriation of Lam 4:20 is that of Justin Martyr. Seeing signs of the cross hidden throughout creation by God, Justin draws attention to the human form. He sees the nose extending from the forehead as having the form of a cross. Through this sign of the cross, life-breath is drawn as the prophet said, "The breath before our face is the Lord Christ"; *The First Apology of Justin*, ch. 55. *ANCL* 11, 55. Understandably Justin's reading of the text did not initiate a fruitful tradition of reception.

This was taken by early Christians to indicate several things. First, it suggested an intimate association of some sort between Jesus Christ and "S/spirit." Tertullian saw an identification between Christ and the Spirit of the Creator: "The person of our Spirit, Christ the Lord."[50] Cyril explains that it is Christ's spiritual *nature* that comes out in Lam 4:20. The Father is spirit (John 4:24), *the Son is spirit* (Lam 4:20), and the Spirit is spirit.[51] This spiritual nature of Christ is applied to the Eucharist by Ambrose. In the sacrament we partake in the body of Christ — not bodily food but *spiritual food,* for "the Body of Christ is the Body of the Divine Spirit." He quotes Lam 4:20 to support this.[52]

Second, it was linked to Christ's death. Augustine took the verse to briefly show "that Christ is our Lord and that He suffered for us."[53] It was employed by Rufinus as part of an apologetic argument used in dialogue with Jews to show that the Christ was to suffer. "Thou hearest how the Prophet says that Christ the Lord was taken, and for us, that is, for our sins, delivered to corruption. Under whose shadow, since the people of the Jews have continued in unbelief, he says the Gentiles lie, because we live not in Israel, but among the Gentiles."[54] The linking of Lam 4:20 with the death of Jesus and a polemic against Judaism can also be seen in Cyril's *Catechetical Lectures.* There he contrasts the (spiritual) Jerusalem which now is (Gal 4:25) with the (earthly) Jerusalem which was. The Jerusalem-which-*is* worships Christ, but the Jerusalem-which-*was* crucified him. Thus Jeremiah lamented the destruction of earthly Jerusalem. "Christ the Lord was taken in our corruptions." As a result, citing 4:20b, "the grace of life is no longer to dwell in Israel, but among the Gentiles."[55]

What should we make of such appropriations of the text? The anti-Judaic overtones should not be retained today by Christians. More positive Christian attitudes towards Jews who do not believe in Jesus (i.e., the vast majority) are found in Romans 11. But what of the christological interpretation? Interestingly, even a contemporary critical scholar like Erhard Gerstenberger sees the Messiah in this verse as a *future* deliverer.[56] While I think that Gerstenberger is mistaken in this, the connection with Jesus is not unjustified.

---

50. *Against Marcion,* Book III. ANCL 7, 129.

51. *Catechetical Lectures* 34. NPNF² 7, 132. The same argument is in Ambrose (*Of the Holy Spirit,* Book I, 105. NPNF² 10, 107) and Gregory of Nyssa (*Against Eunomius,* Book 11, 14. NPNF² 5, 128). Interestingly, Basil sees Lam 4:20 as a reference to the *Spirit* as "the anointed of the Lord" rather than to Jesus; *On the Spirit,* ch. 19, 48, NPNF² 8, 30.

52. *On the Mysteries* 58. NPNF² 10, 325.

53. *The City of God* 33. NPNF¹ 2, 379.

54. *A Commentary on the Apostles' Creed* 19. NPNF² 3, 551.

55. *Catechetical Lectures* 7. NPNF² 7, 84.

56. Gerstenberger, *Psalms, Pt 2,* 499.

Indeed, a christological re-reading of the passage opens up interesting new ways of construing it. The capture of the king in 4:20 is the climax of the woes in the chapter: he who embodied the whole nation representatively has fallen to the foe. Immediately after this we have the unexpected oracle of salvation (4:21-22), with no hint in the text as to how one could move from the lowest pit to the highest point of hope in the book. What precipitates that shift? The reader is left to fill in the gap.

On a christological interpretation, the move from verse 20 to verse 21 makes perfect sense. The loss of the king of Israel to the pagan foe in 4:20 is simultaneously the climax of the exilic woes *and the means by which those woes come to an end.* That is not what the poet had in mind, but a Christian reader looking back with the advantage of hindsight can join the dots in this way. This introduces an interesting new theological perspective into Lamentations 4 not contained within the text, but one which can frame the Christian reading of the text. The violence of the enemy is engraved on the subjugated and broken body of the Messiah, and yet in the act of being overcome by evil the evil is itself overcome by nonviolence. A subversive, cruciform element is introduced in the reception of the text.

The Spirit and Lamentations

I have indicated how one may begin to connect *Christ* to the interpretation of Lamentations, but how is the *Spirit* connected with the sufferings of the book? Nothing in Lamentations will answer that question, and no other biblical text directly addresses it either. However, there is a Pauline text that allows us to begin to see how we can *imagine* an answer to it. In Romans 8, Paul connects the sufferings and groans of the church awaiting its full salvation with the sufferings and groans of creation awaiting its full redemption. The logic of the rest of the chapter would also suggest that Paul connected the church's suffering with Christ's (Rom 8:17). What is of special interest for us is the way Paul weaves the Spirit into this web. The Spirit, he says, is also groaning with the church and with creation, interceding from the depth of his being for their fullness of salvation. If we take this Pauline insight and connect it with our humanity-Israel-Christ-church links above, we create the space to see the Spirit in the sufferings of Lamentations. Paul gives us a way to see the Spirit as groaning with the sufferers in Lamentations, interceding and looking for the redemption of Jerusalem. We shall have more to say about this later.

I have argued that some of the theological connections made in canonical texts between the sufferings of Israel and those of humanity in general, of

Christ in particular, and even of the Spirit have the potential to put Lamentations in a new light. But not only do these "insights" put Lamentations in a new light: Lamentations can shed light upon the sufferings of humanity, of Christ, of the church, and of the Spirit. Lamentations may allow us to see the crucifixion stories from a new angle; we may also be equipped to understand the sufferings of Jews, of Christians, and of human beings in general in new ways.

Does Christian Interpretation Neutralize Lamentations?

One criticism of the kind of Christian interpretation I am advocating is that it robs Lamentations of its power. Lamentations is hard-hitting because it arises from the experience of suffering, and yet within its pages deliverance remains far off. There are multiple voices in the book, but the one that is conspicuous by its absence is that of YHWH. Once Lamentations is read through Christian theological lenses we insert YHWH's voice back into the text. We see that God actually stands in solidarity with Jerusalem in its sufferings through Christ and by his Spirit. We see that YHWH himself eventually provides the comfort so longed for by Jerusalem. But, the critic may argue, this domesticates the book and neutralizes its ability to address the bleakest of human situations.

Several things need to be said here. First, Christian readers need to appreciate *both* the canonical form of the text *and* the canonical context. It is the canonical context which allows us to read the book in the light of the cross and resurrection of Christ, but it is the canonical form which *preserves the voices of the sufferers as uttered on their Holy Saturday.* The canonization of the book in this form requires that we find a way to respect the integrity of that pain without allowing it to be lost in the canonical context. On the other hand, it needs to be acknowledged that respecting only the canonical form but not the canonical context fails to interpret the text as Scripture. It needs to be acknowledged then that Christians cannot read Lamentations with the same hopelessness felt by Lady Jerusalem because they know that Christ has been raised. The resurrection generates a hermeneutic of hope that can transform the darkness of Lamentations and infuse it with a brighter light than any found in the book itself. But, and this is important, it does *not* make the pain of Lamentations less dreadful and dark. It does not explain why the pain was as it was. It does not trivialize the suffering any more than the resurrection trivializes the cross. So, while a canonical interpretation of Lamentations will not allow destruction and death to have the last word, it can allow them a penultimate word.

The book of Lamentations speaks during a Holy Saturday experience and is then silent, *and the Bible preserves it in that form.* We have to wait for Isaiah 40–55 to hear the buildup to the "Easter Sunday" deliverance. The canon allows a pause between these two and does not seek to collapse them prematurely. Similarly, the disciples experienced the desolation and despair of Saturday before experiencing the joy of Sunday. A Christian theological reading of the book can bracket out for a moment the resurrection joy and allow the shock of the pain to have its full force. Often Christians themselves can feel the depths of the darkness in their pain as resurrection hope fades. However, this bracketing out of resurrection hope can only be temporary to allow the pain time to breathe. Ultimately, the Christian vision is *not* a tragic vision. The world cannot be the same after Easter, and sufferings cannot be seen as our final destiny.

I would like to seek guidance for handling this dilemma in Alan Lewis's book, *Between Cross and Resurrection.* Lewis was concerned that Christians move too quickly from Good Friday to Easter Sunday and pass over the "brief, inert void" of Easter Saturday. Lewis proposed that we need to stand imaginatively again on Holy Saturday and consider the view both ways, looking back to the Friday and forward to the Sunday. We start, he suggested, by trying to hear the crucifixion story again as first-time hearers would, not knowing that the resurrection is coming. "Far from being the first day, the day of the cross is, in the logic of the narrative itself, actually the last day, the end of the story of Jesus. And the day that follows it is . . . an empty void, a nothing, shapeless, meaningless, and anticlimactic: simply the day after the end."[57] On Holy Saturday "Death is given time and space to be itself, in all its coldness and helplessness."[58] The resurrection must be heard first of all as an unexpected and shocking event. Clearly then the Christian reader must look again at the cross event in the light of the resurrection and see it in new light, but this new understanding does not mean that we can leave behind the first hearing. "This is a story which must be told and heard, believed and interpreted, *two different ways at once* — as a story whose ending is *known,* and as one whose ending is discovered only as it *happens* . . . the separate sound in each ear creating, as it were, a stereophonic unity."[59] Holy Saturday serves to keep the crucifixion and resurrection apart *and* to hold them together.

For Lewis, God himself is convicted by Jesus' death because of the identity of the crucified one. Jesus was one who had known an intimacy of rela-

57. Lewis, *Between Cross and Resurrection,* 31.
58. Lewis, *Between Cross and Resurrection,* 37.
59. Lewis, *Between Cross and Resurrection,* 33.

tion with his Father in heaven unknown by any other human. For *him* to die a God-forsaken death is to imply that *God* has failed him. One is reminded of Lady Zion's "See, YHWH, and observe who it is that you have dealt with severely here" (Lam 2:20). It is important to ponder the implications of this for reading Lamentations. Lewis's respect for the integrity of Jesus' cry of dereliction and God's nonresponse is instructive for us as we seek to do justice to Lady Jerusalem's analogous cries of dereliction and YHWH's failure to reply to her.

The resurrection is the vindication not only of Christ (he really is the Son of God) but also of God (he really is the loving Father of Christ, of Israel, of humanity), and it offers hope not merely for Christ but for Israel, for humanity, for the cosmos. But the resurrection must not be seen to put the cross out of sight — resurrection is only reached through the cross, and "the only flower of victory is one which germinates and grows in the darkness of a tomb."[60]

The Anger of God and "The Day of YHWH"

Having sketched and defended a reception of Lamentations from a full-blown Christian perspective, it is time to move on and consider the central theological theme of divine fury. God's anger permeates the entirety of Lamentations, though its intensity glows white hot in chapter 2. Claus Westermann points out that "[a]t hardly any other place in the whole of the Old Testament is there so much talk of the wrath of God."[61] How can we think theologically on this matter?[62]

The Anger of God

The early church, like many of the more philosophically-minded pagans in the ancient world, took a polemical line against the deities of popular Greco-Roman religion. They argued that the Christian God was not like the pagan gods because he was impassible and so above the passions of envy, lust, and selfish desires.[63] But can an impassible God be angry? To some pagan philos-

60. Lewis, *Between Cross and Resurrection*, 77.

61. Westermann, *Lamentations*, 149.

62. A pertinent question in light of the fact that contemporary Christian systematic theology manifests an almost total neglect of the theme.

63. E.g., Justin Martyr, *First Apology* ch. 25, ANCL 7.

ophers, the Christians should have applied their critique of the pagan gods to their own Scriptures because the God of those Scriptures was a deity to whom morally objectionable emotions such as anger are ascribed.[64] An angry deity is an imperfect and false deity. Some early Christians followed the Stoic view that anger was a bad emotion and that consequently God was free from it.[65] Most of the Fathers, however, departed from a simplistic rejection of anger as an immoral emotion. They said that, while anger could be immoral, in certain forms and in certain contexts it was a necessary part of justice. Lactantius in his extended reflections on the anger of God maintained that *not to experience anger in certain situations was the morally deficient disposition.*[66] This connection with justice dominated Patristic understanding of God's anger.[67]

The Fathers took two different approaches to the interpretation of the language in Scripture about divine wrath. We could refer to them as the subjective and objective approaches. The subjective approach argued that God did not actually experience feeling angry but human beings experience the consequences of God's punishments *as if* God was feeling angry. Thus the language of divine wrath describes *how things look from our end of the telescope* and not how things are from God's end. Biblical language of God's anger is metaphorical and is the result of God accommodating himself to human language for the purpose of instilling piety in people. Anger should be ascribed to God not anthropopathically but, as John Cassian said, "in a sense worthy of God, *who is a stranger to all perturbations.*"[68] Cassian thought that it was fear of divine judgment that made humans *perceive* God's kindness and justice as wrath. So for the likes of Clement of Alexandria, Origen, and John Cassian, God justly punishes humans, and we experience this *as if* it was anger, but, strictly speaking, God *feels* no anger at all.

The objective approach, on the other hand, maintained that God actually did experience feeling angry but that the anger he felt was not like human anger. God is fully in control of his anger for, being "impassible," he has no *uncontrollable* passions. So divine "impassibility" does not rule out divine emotions but preserves divine control over the passions that humans cannot easily manage. God never becomes angry for no reason or for bad reasons. Indeed, according to Novatian, "God becomes angry not out of vice, but for the

---

64. E.g., Julian, quoted by Cyril in *Against Julian*, 171E.

65. E.g., Athenagoras, Aristides, and, in the third century, Arnobius.

66. *A Treatise on the Anger of God*, ch. 17. ANCL 7.

67. See Gavrilyuk, *The Suffering of the Impassible God*, 51-60, for the discussion on patristic views on God's anger on which my reflections are based.

68. John Cassian, *Institutes of the Coenobia*, book 8, ch. 4. Cf. $NPNF^2$ 11, 258.

sake of healing us."[69] And how does God experience his anger? Not, says Augustine, in the way that we do. When we feel anger we experience annoyance. God does not. "He is angry without being emotionally upset."[70] God experiences anger in a manner appropriate to his divine being, and we must retain a reverent agnosticism about what that is like.

We should not overlook the agreement between these two approaches. Both agreed that God's "anger" is a manifestation of divine justice, that it is experienced by humans as punishment, and that whatever it is like for God to be angry, it is not the same as what it is like for humans. So the early church was very clear that biblical language about God's anger should *not* be understood as the deity losing his temper. As Walter Kaiser writes, "God's anger is never explosive, unreasonable or unexplained. It is rather His firm expression of real displeasure with our wickedness and sin. Even in God it is never a force or a ruling passion; rather it is an instrument of His will. And His anger has not, thereby, shut off His compassion to us."[71]

More than this, we need to appreciate that the divine anger in Lamentations is God's response to Judah's *covenant* violations. "When a term for wrath is combined with a designation of God we usually find יהוה.... It shows that the idea of wrath is closely bound up with belief in the covenant."[72]

Returning to Lamentations 2, how should we try to make sense of the language about God's fierce anger that we find there? Norman Gottwald speaks of the way in which the Hebrew Bible never surrendered the destructive or "demonic" characterization of YHWH but that it did ethicize it by subordinating it to God's righteous purposes.[73] So, as in the church fathers, God's anger is a righteous response to evil. Does anger language tell us about God's emotional state? Westermann suggests it does not refer to an inner disposition of God such as an inner feeling. Rather, it describes the concrete actions of God that are experienced by people as a damaging blow. God's anger, in this instance, *is* the devastation of Jerusalem.[74] This is a contemporary version of what we have described as the subjective approach to divine anger found early in Christian theology. So while the chapter describes God *as if* he was a man who had gotten so angry that he simply smashed everything in sight, it would be wrong to take that language in a simplistic way. The language communicates how the punishment of God *felt* to those on its receiving end.

---

69. Novatian, *A Treatise Concerning the Trinity,* ch. 5. ANCL 5.
70. Augustine, *On Patience,* ch. 1. Cf. *NPNF*[1] 3, 527.
71. Kaiser, *Grief and Pain,* 62.
72. Fichtner, "The Wrath of God," 396.
73. Gottwald, *Studies in the Book of Lamentations,* 88-89.
74. Westermann, *Lamentations,* 150.

I find the above approach helpful, but there is a problem with reading Lamentations' portrayals of God's anger in the light of a fully formed perfect-being theology. In one sense to do so is justified because God *is* perfectly righteous. Nevertheless, the approach fails to step inside the perspectives of the speakers, and thus it fails to feel the problem of divine justice they feel. Granted that God may not *actually* have behaved inappropriately (for that would be impossible), it might *feel* that way to the sufferers. So while the anger language is metaphorical or analogical when applied to God, its power is drawn from the raw reality of the experience of violent anger. God is certainly not someone who has lost his temper, but Lamentations does present him *as if* he was *because that was how it felt*. F. W. Dobbs-Allsopp writes, "Here we do not meet the kindly and compassionate God so often preached in church and synagogue. Nor do we even have to do with the fearsome but righteous God of justice whose punishments, though severe, are always just and appropriate. Rather, here [Lam 2:4] the only presence of the deity available to the poet (and reader) is that which is manifested in the raw and malevolent power of an enemy."[75] Due weight must be given to the highly emotive text of Lamentations. Consequently, we need simultaneously to allow the language space to shock us with a portrayal of God as a violent aggressor bent on harm and, at the same time, to recognize that such language cannot be simply collapsed into the literal reality about God. Taking this stereophonic approach allows us to take the *human experience* of God's wrath seriously (remembering that *Scripture itself* authorizes such "blasphemy") and also to recognize that God is not literally someone struggling to control violent impulses.

In his anger God *forsakes* Judah. This is strong language that resonates powerfully with the sense of divine absence. The torah and prophets are stilled in 2:10, and that dreadful divine silence is inscribed in the book of Lamentations through its missing words. Where is the God who speaks? He is not here. He has abandoned us. Lamentations drives us to ask, What does it *mean* for God to "forsake" Judah? to "abandon" Israel? to "reject" his people? It seems like the language of terminated relationships, but, when read contextually, it does not mean ultimate, final, or irrevocable abandonment. God's forsaking may have felt never-ending to those living through it (Lam 5:20), but Second Isaiah says that in the big picture it can be seen that the anger only lasted for a brief time (Isa 54:7-8). The abandoning was real but temporary. Mercy, not anger, is God's deepest orientation towards his people. Anger is never the end of the story. Judah's was an "abandoning" situated within a deeper covenant commitment according to which God's people can be "for-

75. Dobbs-Allsopp, *Lamentations*, 84.

saken" but never Forsaken; "rejected" but never Rejected; "abandoned" but never Abandoned. Wrath and rejection take place *within* God's covenant relationship with Israel. This was recognized within the rabbinic reception of Lamentations.

> The theme of *Lamentations Rabbati* is Israel's relationship with God, and the message concerning that theme is that the stipulative covenant still and always governs that relationship. . . . This is the one and whole message of our compilation, and it is the only message that is repeated throughout; everything else proves secondary and derivative of the fundamental proposition that the destruction of the Temple in Jerusalem in 70 C.E. — as much as in 586 B.C.E. — proves the enduring validity of the covenant, its rules and its promises of redemption.[76]

In the same way, God is "absent" *in the sense that* he is not acting to bless his people and protect them from their enemies. But God is not "absent" in any metaphysical sense. Indeed, if anything, the problem is not that God is absent so much as that he is *present as enemy-of-Israel.* And even this language must be understood carefully. It feels like he is acting *as if* he were an enemy bent on their ruin. The deeper reality is that God is not bent on the ruin of Judah at all. This is brought out by the Targum, which exploits the preposition כ/*k* ("like") in 2:4a and 5a: "*like* an enemy." YHWH, according to the Targum, is indeed *like* an enemy, but is *not actually* an enemy.[77]

All this language must be heard at two levels. First, it must be heard as shocking, visceral, and raw depictions of God's treatment of Judah as seen by those on the receiving end. Second, it must be understood in a manner appropriate to the God revealed in the Scripture as a whole. To do the former but not the latter would yield an unworthy perspective on God, but to do the latter without the former would yield an orthodox God at the price of failing to do justice to the biblical text or our experience of pain.

The Day of YHWH, Final Judgment, and the Cross

The world-shaking nature of the fall of Jerusalem is clear in the application of the "Day of the Lord" motif. The coming Day of YHWH was quite likely orig-

---

76. Neusner, *Introduction to Rabbinic Literature,* 510-11.

77. *Tg. Lam.* 2:4-5. Of course, Lamentations is ambiguous here (does the כ/*k* in 2:4a, 5a mean "indeed" or "like"?), and the Targum is disambiguating the text to offer theological clarification; Thomas, "Poetry and Theology in Lamentations," 173-74.

inally understood as doom for the nations and blessing for Israel,[78] but the prophet Amos reversed that perception:

> Woe to you who desire the day of the Lord!
> Why would you have the day of the Lord?
> It is darkness and not light. (Amos 5:18)

Amos, and later prophets, saw it as a "day" for the destruction of evil, not only among the nations *but also in Israel.* Lamentations too sees it as a "day" of fierce judgment (1:12; 2:1; 2:21-22). The battle motif is prominent in "Day of YHWH" texts, as Lamentations 2 illustrates. The invincible YHWH *fights against* his people and none can stop him.

Unusual in Lamentations is the designation of the Day of YHWH as *past* (cf. Isa 22:1-4; Jer 46:3-12). Clearly then, it was not seen as the end of history but as a time when God acts openly to bring judgment *in* history. Thus it can recur in different periods of time. Indeed, Lamentations contains prayer for, and an expectation that, the nations who oppress Israel shall taste that "Day" for themselves in the near future (1:21-22; 4:21-22). So the Day of YHWH is not, in Old Testament theology, a single one-off judgment at the end of the world.[79]

←——— Lamentations looking *back* to the Day of the Lord for Judah
Lamentations looking *forward* to the Day of the Lord for Enemies ———→

The New Testament takes up the motif of "the Day of the Lord" and applies it to the Parousia of Christ. This is the ultimate Day of the Lord that all the previous Days of the Lord had pointed towards. While Lamentations is emphatically not about *the* end of the present evil age, it can be reappropriated as a type of the final Day of the Lord.[80] God's judgment on Jerusalem is a picture of God's final judgment on a fallen world. Here it has to be emphasized that the New Testament and the Christian tradition have been just as insistent as the Old Testament that God will act in space-time history to punish sin, whether it be that of Israel and Rome at — from the perspective of New Testament au-

---

78. And it could be this on various different views of its historical origins — a subject on which there is no scholarly consensus. See Boase, *The Fulfillment of Doom?*, 106-13, for a helpful brief survey of different scholarly views on the origins of the motif.

79. For a detailed and nuanced analysis of the similarities and differences between the Day of YHWH motif in Lamentations and earlier prophetic literature, see Boase, *The Fulfillment of Doom?*, ch. 3.

80. Rightly Kaiser, *Grief and Pain*, 56.

thors — some point in the not too distant future, or the world more generally on the final day of judgment. The message of Jeremiah in the first part of his ministry was equivalent to the Christian call, "Be reconciled to God. . . . Behold, *now* is the favorable time; behold *now* is the day of salvation" (2 Cor 5:20b; 6:2b). But the "day of salvation" was not held open forever, and Jeremiah records how Judah passed beyond the point of no return, making the day of wrath inevitable. Lamentations provides a portrait of the *aftermath* of the Day of the Lord for those subject to punishment. As such it serves as a type of what Christians call "hell." The *actual* "second death" will be the eschatological climax of divine judgments in history and hence not identical with them. Nevertheless, hell is not utterly discontinuous with historical divine judgments. Judah suffers "hell" in exile and Jesus suffers hell on the cross.[81]

Israel	The Day of the Lord (darkness not light)	Destruction of Israel and exile (and its aftermath in the ruins). Godforsaken
Christ		Destruction on the cross (and its aftermath in the realm of death). Godforsaken
The world		Judgment (and its aftermath in hell). Godforsaken

Calvin (and the subsequent Reformed tradition), instead of interpreting the descent of Christ into hell as an event that occurs after the crucifixion, sees it as a theological comment on the nature of the crucifixion. On the cross Jesus suffers the second death. So the creed states that Christ was "crucified," indicating his outward suffering in the sight of men. It also says that he "descended into hell," which describes "that invisible and incomprehensible judgment which he underwent in the sight of God."[82] The theology of descent into hell is, for Calvin, grounded in the cry of dereliction. Christ's dreadful feeling of being God-forsaken and God's silence in the face of Jesus' cries are nothing less than the experience of hell. The doctrine of the *descensus ad inferna* is a powerful interpretative tool for understanding the wrath of God experienced by Jesus on the cross, and its biblical foundation is found in the Passion narratives as much as in the "standard" texts (Acts 2:27; Rom 10:6-7; Eph 4:8-9; 1 Pet 3:18-20; 4:6). In the tradition of Calvin, Karl Barth writes that Christ "must suffer the sin of many to be laid upon Him . . . , in order that He may bear it away . . . out into the darkness, the nothingness from which it

---

81. On Jesus' experience of hell on the cross see especially Lauber, *Barth on the Descent into Hell.*

82. Calvin, *The Institutes of the Christian Religion,* II.xvi.10, 516.

came and to which it alone belongs. . . . For this, in our flesh, according to His human nature, as the Son of David, He must be the Rejected. He must be delivered up by His people to the heathen, descending into hell, where He can only cry: 'My God, my God, why hast thou forsaken me?'"[83]

Christ's experience of hell, however, while incorporating Jesus' experiences on Calvary, also includes the apparent triumph of death itself and consequently takes in Easter Saturday. Here Hans Urs von Balthasar is more helpful than Calvin and Barth. For Balthasar, Easter Saturday is about Jesus' solidarity with the dead: his passive "being with the dead."[84] If Christ's actually *being dead* is not included in his "descent into hell," then he has not experienced the full reaches of Godforsakenness. "If Jesus has suffered on the cross the sin of the world to the very last truth of this sin — godforsakenness — then he must also experience, in solidarity with sinners who have gone into the underworld, their — ultimately hopeless — separation from God, otherwise he would not have known all the phases and conditions of what it means for man to be unredeemed yet awaiting redemption."[85]

In the spirit of "providing christological answers for eschatological questions,"[86] one has to ask first how a theology of "hell" can be developed that is consistent with these insights. While much contemporary theology has little interest in the theology of hell, it seems to me that it is a fundamental strand within New Testament and historic Christian theology and simply cannot be jettisoned. Can Lamentations, read through the cross, contribute to our contemporary Christian reflections on the "hell" that many people suffer around us and the final reality of hell that we believe is still future? Perhaps the following thoughts might have the potential for development.

The fact that Lamentations focuses on the *suffering* of those in "hell" rather than their sin (though the sin is certainly clearly asserted) and seeks to elicit compassion for them suggests an appropriate Christian attitude towards those who suffer "hell" both now and in the eschaton. The classical Christian theology according to which the redeemed saints in heaven look on the torments of the damned and joyfully worship God for his perfect justice is simply inappropriate. God himself does not delight in afflicting people, *even if he is acting justly* (Lam 3:33). Lamentations calls not for gloating or celebration but compassion for the "damned."

Second, does the nature of God, as revealed in Lamentations 3, hold out

---

83. Barth, *Church Dogmatics*, II/2, 365.

84. Balthasar, *Mysterium Paschale*, 150.

85. Balthasar, *Explorations in Theology*, 4:408. On both Barth and Balthasar, see esp. Lauber, *Barth on the Descent into Hell*.

86. Moltmann, *The Coming of God*, 250.

hope for all who experience the Day of YHWH? "For the Lord will not cast off *forever,* but, *though he causes grief, he will have compassion* according to the abundance of his steadfast love" (Lam 3:31-32). Does the message of comfort and restoration given in Isaiah 40–55 in reply to Lamentations' cry of pain, have hopeful implications for those who taste "hell" both now and perhaps even in the "Lake of Fire"? Does the resurrection of Christ from death indicate that the human predicament cannot ever pass to a point beyond the redemptive reach of God? Where sin abounds might grace abound all the more?

Third, is it not inappropriate to voice our honest feelings to God about the torments of "hell" and to ask God to deliver people from their "hells"? It is interesting to consider in this regard the second-century Christian book, *St Peter's Apocalypse.* It speaks in very graphic terms of the punishment of sinners in hell. Their sin is very serious, and their punishment is very harsh. Then, in 14:1, the Greek text says,

> Then I will grant to my called and elect ones whomsoever they request from me, out of the punishment. And I will give [those they pray for] a fine . . . baptism in salvation from the Acherousian lake . . . , a portion of righteousness with my holy ones.[87]

If the resurrected victims of those in hell are prepared to forgive their enemies and ask for divine mercy, then God will hear those prayers and take the damned, via a purgatorial lake, to redemption. Now, I am not suggesting that *St Peter's Apocalypse* has any authoritative status in Christian theology. I merely suggest that glimmers of hope after hell are not simply the desperate grasping of modern Christians. Indeed, I am suggesting that Lamentations might contribute towards biblical foundations for such hope. I have developed the broader theological and biblical bases for such eschatological hope at length elsewhere.[88]

Theodicy and Divine Suffering

One issue that has troubled Jews and Christians has been the ongoing and terrible suffering with which history is saturated. How could God have al-

---

87. This discussion of St Peter's Apocalypse is drawn from Ansell, *The Annihilation of Hell,* ch. 1.

88. See *The Evangelical Universalist,* a book I wrote under the pseudonym Gregory Mac-Donald (a combination of two Christian universalists, Gregory of Nyssa and George MacDonald).

lowed such affliction? The attempt to justify God's actions in the face of suffering and evil is known as theodicy, and in the contemporary debate the issue is framed in terms of the compatibility of evil and suffering with the existence of an omniscient, omnipotent, omnibenevolent God. Atheists often argue that suffering either makes such a God's existence impossible[89] or, more modestly, highly improbable.[90] It seems to me that neither conclusion can be demonstrated.[91] But Lamentations is engaging evil and suffering in a very different way from contemporary philosophy. The nonexistence of God is not even contemplated. Of course God exists! God is the one assaulting them! Lamentations does wrestle with the issue of God's *justice*, but in the end it does not deny divine justice, nor does it explain how justice is compatible with their experience. Lamentations is not concerned with solving the philosophical-theological problems of pain or justifying God in the face of evil.[92] Its main contribution lies in a different area. To begin to open up that contribution it will be helpful to start with the partial theodicy that *is* present in Lamentations, namely that suffering is a just punishment for sin.

One way of seeking to explain human suffering has been in terms of divine retribution for sin. In an Old Testament context this must be understood in terms of God's covenant with Israel. If they were to break God's covenant law, then divine curses would come into operation as punishment. This theology underpins much of the Old Testament literature and is clearly at work in Lamentations. However, to see Lamentations as a theodicy would be a mistake. It goes a little way towards a theodicy but hardly provides a neat justification for suffering. Indeed, Lamentations itself exposes some of the inadequacies of this as a theodicy. It recognizes that the righteous can suffer and die *in spite of* their loyalty to the covenant (4:13b). Also, the implicit complaint against God in the book is that the punishment seems to exceed the crime. It is too deep, cutting the nation to the heart. It is too wide, taking in innocent

89. E.g., Mackie, *The Miracle of Theism*, ch. 9.

90. See the essays by Rowe, Draper, and Gale in Howard-Snyder, *The Evidential Argument from Evil*.

91. On deductive arguments see Plantinga, *God, Freedom and Evil*. On inductive arguments see the essays by Plantinga, Wykstra, and van Inwagen in Howard-Snyder, *The Evidential Argument from Evil*.

92. John Howard Yoder, in "Trinity Versus Theodicy," argues that the biblical God is not subject to human judgment, and thus any attempt to judge whether God measures up to our standards is both impossible and idolatrous. However, he argues that there is a place for the protest against YHWH in the mode of the Jewish complaint against God. This lamenting is neither theodicy nor a rejection of God. It speaks its agonizing protests from the position of faith in, and relationship with, YHWH. It denounces YHWH, *then worships him* because it recognizes that God's ways transcend human minds.

children. It lasts too long. "Although the event was recognized as punishment, it remained incomprehensible in its severity."[93] This may be a just punishment *when considered at a group level,* but when we consider the impact on individuals it is clear that it is an imperfect justice. The righteous suffer alongside the guilty (Ezek 21:3-4). That is the issue with the suffering children; they did not sin, yet they suffer terribly. Whatever God is doing in the destruction, saying that it is a punishment for sin is an inadequate theodicy, *even if it is true.* No adequate theodicy is given in this book or anywhere else in the Bible. It never tells us why the people suffer for as long as they do or in the way that they do, why the righteous are killed, or why the children starve to death in the laps of their mothers. Instead, it is more concerned to express an unsystematic cluster of human responses to suffering.

On the other hand, it is equally mistaken to see Lamentations as a straightforward *anti*-theodic protest against divine injustice. As Heath Thomas notes,

> The appeal in 2:20 is for Yahweh to recognize *his own* complicity in this violence, and desist. . . . God may be put 'in the dock' in 2:20 for his actions, but in 3:59 and 5:1, it is precisely Yahweh, his justice, and his gracious actions by which the appeal functions rhetorically. . . . Thus, far from asserting a uniform theological vision, it appears that theodicy and anti-theodicy work alongside one other, ambiguating and enlivening the theology of the book for the reader.[94]

Protesting God and justifying God are held together in tension.

Might there be another way into reflecting on God's relationship to the sufferers if we shift attention from God-standing-over-against-the-afflicted to God-standing-with-the-afflicted? For the Christian who believes that "*God was in Christ,*" this puts Lamentations in a surprising new light. God stands not only as judge, but also as the Judge judged in Jerusalem's place; not only as the one who breaks, but also as the one who is broken.[95] How did God respond to Jerusalem weeping? At first he responded to her cries with a dreadful silence, but later, in Christ, he responded by standing right beside her and weeping with her — not simply as one who *understands* her pain, but as one who representatively *participates in* her pain. That is not a divine response ei-

---

93. Westermann, *Lamentations,* 153.

94. Thomas, "Aesthetic Theory of Umberto Eco," 18.

95. Against Fiddes, who insists that God *only* stands on the side of the sufferers and is not in any way a cause of the suffering; *Participating in God,* ch. 5. Lamentations does not let God off the hook that easily.

ther Jerusalem or the narrator could ever have imagined, but it does open avenues for Christian reflection. I believe that God does "suffer," in his divine being, when his people suffer. He is "grieved" to see them in pain, even if he himself has inflicted it.[96] This is reflected in rabbinic Jewish writing on Lamentations. *Lamentations Rabbah* pictures the following scene in heaven:

> At that moment the Holy One, blessed be he, wept, saying, "Woe is me! What have I done! I have brought my Presence to dwell below on account of the Israelites, and now that they have sinned, I have gone back to my earlier dwelling. Heaven forfend that I now become a joke to the nations and an object of ridicule among the people." . . . When the Holy One, blessed be he, saw the house of the sanctuary, he said, "This is certainly my house, and this is my resting place, and the enemies have come and done whatever they pleased with it!" At that moment the Holy One, blessed be he, wept, saying, "Woe is me for my house! O children of mine — where are you? O priests of mine — where are you? O you that love me — where are you? What shall I do for you? I warned you but you did not repent."[97]

However, we must beware of imagining that God is just like us and should remain reverently agnostic about what it is like for *God* to "suffer."[98] But in Christ something radically different happens: God suffered *in the flesh.* That is to say that the divine Logos was subject of the *human suffering* of Jesus. In Christ God experienced human suffering, not simply as a divine sympathizer who stands beside us, but *as a human who suffers with, as, and for us.* This is beyond mere divine sympathy and places God in shocking proximity to our broken condition. This is God on the inside. So here is the question — can you read some of the words of lamentations *as God's own words,* and, if you

---

96. Gerstenberger's proposal that it is YHWH himself who speaks in 2:11-12 in a manner akin to Jer 4:19-22 and 6:11-12 seems somewhat implausible; *Psalms, Part 2,* 487-88. However, it may be that a subsequent theological reflection may see the appropriateness of such a connection. We may see a blurring between the narrator's anguish and God's own anguish over the destruction of his beloved city.

97. *Lam. Rab.* XXIV.ii.1.1-2.C-D.

98. It seems to me that *absolute* impassibility would represent an imperfection in God, not a perfection (and arguably the church fathers did not teach *absolute* impassibility). It is true that the triune God does not *need* the world in order to be love. Creation is not a *necessary* act on God's part. It is, nevertheless, a *fitting* act for the self-giving God. Once God has chosen to create, then, given that God *is* love, he will love his creation. For God not to love his creation would be for God to fail to be God — impossible! And while divine love for creation is not necessarily suffering love, it seems to me that *if* creation suffers, *then* the divine lover will experience something *analogous to* suffering love. God cannot be indifferent to the suffering of his creatures.

can, what does it do to your theology? Caution is needed here. God, in Christ, did not sin and did not need to repent, so not all of the words could be spoken by him.[99] However, God, in Christ, did experience the punishment of Israel (and the world) from the inside.

The Spirit of God also participates in Jerusalem's sorrows. Earlier I argued that Romans 8 provides a basis for seeing the Spirit as groaning with all those who groan as they yearn for liberation. Jerusalem groans at her humiliation and turns away her face from onlookers (1:8c), just as her priests groan at the cessation of temple festivals (1:4b) and her people groan as they search for food (1:11a). This groaning looks back (mourning what is lost), looks around (expressing despair at the current situation), and looks forward (yearning for a reversal of the calamity). So also the Spirit, participating in the groaning of creation, groans as he looks back and looks around seeing a shattered world, but he also groans like a woman in childbirth looking forward, bringing to birth a new creation. The Spirit's groaning, while a participation in creation's groaning, also transforms it. It is a hope-infused groaning which looks to the future with confidence. The Spirit can enable our groaning to become a participation in his groaning. That is to say, Spirit-transformed groaning is still an expression of pain at the current situation, but it is not an expression of hopelessness.

There is then a fascinating Christian mode of lament in the pneumatic gift of speaking in tongues. Glossolalia is often seen as a triumphant, joyous act — and it can be. But, as the Pentecostal systematic theologian Frank Macchia observes, Romans 8 surprisingly presents the charismatic gift of glossolalia

> as deep and agonizing groans of human weakness that are changed by the Spirit of God into a cry for redemption, and even a foretaste of this redemption in the here-and-now. . . . Rather than tongues being a sign of an escape from this world into heights of glory, they are expressions of strength in weakness, or the capacity to experience the first-fruits of the kingdom-to-come in the midst of our groaning with the suffering creation. They bring to ultimate expression the struggle that is essential to all prayer, namely, trying to put into words what is deeper than words. They express the pain and the joy of this struggle. They are, in the words of Russell Spittler, a "broken language for a broken body until perfection comes." As such, tongues edify the soul and confront the church with a "sacrament" of the presence of God to empower and heal us as we

---

99. Though one might wish to ponder John McLeod Campbell's idea that at the cross Jesus vicariously repented on behalf of humanity (on which see Stevenson, *God in Our Nature*).

groan in solidarity with the needy and the lost in anticipation of the redemption-to-come.[100]

Finding a language for pain is one of the needs for those afflicted. Here is a pneumatic gift of lament that can play a role parallel to more conventional modes of lament. Yet this gift of inarticulate groans is simultaneously a gift of hopeful expectation for resurrection.

> Because the Holy Ghost over the bent
>   World broods with warm breast and with ah! bright wings.[101]

These reflections on the "suffering" God are not intended as a theodicy. They do not *explain, excuse,* or *justify* God in the face of horrors, but they do relocate God in relation to us. They point to what Paul Fiddes refers to as a "theodicy" of consolation. "No attempt is being made to argue that the suffering of God somehow accounts for human misery. But believing that God suffers in God's own self and so understands their predicament at first hand may in the end be more convincing to sufferers than any formal theodicy can be."[102] He is with us in the pit, seeking to turn our hell to heaven.

Lamentations has much to offer the actual *practice* of Christian lament — practical theodicy if you will — but before outlining that we need to explore the place of lament more generally in Christian spirituality. Can Christian theology even create space for lament?

The Place of Lament in Christian Spirituality

It is often observed that lament was embraced within the worship of Israel but that the Christian church has been far more ambiguous about it.[103] Should laments form part of Christian spirituality? The question is not as simple to answer as it is to ask.

The earliest Christians knew suffering in various shapes and sizes. Like the ancient Israelites in Lamentations, Christians in the earliest churches were

100. Macchia, "Groans Too Deep for Words," section 4. See also Macchia, "Sighs Too Deep for Words," 47-73.

101. Gerard Manley Hopkins, "God's Grandeur" (1877).

102. Fiddes, *Participating in God,* 155.

103. See, e.g., Wolterstorff, "If God Is Good and Sovereign," on the discomfort about lament felt by Augustine (to lament indicates an inappropriate attachment to the things of this world) and Calvin (we already know why we are suffering — God is teaching and blessing us through it — so there is no mystery).

sometimes imprisoned, went hungry, were beaten, and even killed. In some localities hostility against the church would flare up from time to time, making life very difficult. Social shaming and humiliation were not infrequently their lot. The New Testament makes no claims that Christian existence is pain-free, so while believers are to "rejoice with those who rejoice" in the church, they are also to "weep with those who weep" (Rom 12:15). Christians can be hurt, and fellow believers are called to stand in solidarity with them.

So far as we can tell, the early churches practiced conventional customs of mourning. Thus, when Stephen was martyred we read that "devout men buried Stephen and made *great lamentation* over him" (Acts 8:2), and when Dorcas died we are told that the widows *wept* and displayed her works (Acts 9:36f). Jesus himself wept at the death of Lazarus (John 11:35) and over the coming destruction of the Jerusalem of his day (Luke 19:41-44).

> Jesus is not so much confirming that Jerusalem's fate will be a righteous punishment of God upon a sinful city as he is raising a lament over the suffering that the destruction will bring upon the city's inhabitants. In the tears that Jesus sheds over this city, the divine compassion towards those who must suffer is more pronounced than the divine wrath that makes such a punishment necessary.[104]

This embracing of lament by Jesus is reinforced as he is led to the cross.

> And there followed him a great multitude of the people and of women who were mourning and lamenting for him. But turning to them Jesus said, "Daughters of Jerusalem, do not weep for me, but weep for yourselves and for your children. For behold, the days are coming when they will say, 'Blessed are the barren and the wombs that never bore and the breasts that never nursed!' Then they will begin to say to the mountains, 'Fall on us,' and to the hills, 'Cover us.' For if they do these things when the wood is green, what will happen when it is dry?" (Luke 23:27-31)

Jesus is saying that his crucifixion by the Romans on a false charge of rebellion (he is the green wood) is a sign of the fate in store for the whole nation that is setting itself on a collision course with Rome by means of militant rebellion (Israel is the dry wood ready for burning). The whole city will be "crucified," and Jesus is saying that, as in the book of Lamentations, weeping and lamenting are an apt response to such horrors.

Also relevant for our reflections is the acute mental suffering Paul testi-

---

104. Westermann, *Lamentations*, 232.

fied to in 2 Corinthians. Richard Dormandy has argued at length that in 2 Co-rinthians Paul is in the process of recovering from a crisis of severe emotional suffering. He itemizes the following aspects of the loss Paul had suffered:

> He has, like a star footballer, lost his winning streak and has had to face failure (4:3). With this he has lost his standing and reputation (13:7). He has lost his status and authority in Corinth (10:1). Possibly he has lost his physical or mental health (7:5). He has lost his heart for evangelism be-cause he is overwhelmed by the presence of the problem in Corinth (2:12-13). . . . He speaks of death as a relief . . . (5:1-4). He is aware of the power-lessness of his prayers (12:8), which may have been a contrast with the past (12:12), and his weakness in general (12:9-10).[105]

The recent loss above may have compounded earlier losses: the split with his friend Barnabas and the growing isolation from his spiritual home (the church in Antioch). As Paul writes 2 Corinthians, he has begun his journey of recovery, but we see his wounded soul laid bare. The straw that broke the camel's back was an unspecified situation in Asia (imprisonment? illness?) that was too much for him to cope with. Whatever the crisis was, it was a near-death experience. He wrote:

> We do not want you to be uninformed, brothers, about the hardships we suffered in the province of Asia. We were under great pressure, far beyond our ability to endure, so that we despaired even of life. Indeed, in our hearts we felt the sentence of death. But this happened that we might not rely on ourselves but on God, who raises the dead. He has delivered us from such a deadly peril, and he will deliver us. On him we have set our hope that he will continue to deliver us, as you help us by your prayers. (2 Cor 1:8-11)

Paul is writing from a position in which he has begun to experience deliver-ance. What is interesting is the way he describes his suffering prior to that: "We were under great pressure, *far beyond our ability to endure, so that we de-spaired even of life.* Indeed, in our hearts we felt the sentence of death." He is very open about the fact that when he was in the midst of this experience he was not positive about receiving God's deliverance. If the "thorn in his side" spoken of in 2 Cor 12:7-9 refers to the same affliction, then we know that on three occasions Paul cried to the Lord for deliverance and on each occasion he

---

105. Dormandy, *The Madness of Saint Paul*, 192. Dormandy also examines evidence that Paul may have suffered from depression.

was not delivered. And it was in this situation that Paul came to experience God as "the God of all comfort who comforts us in all our affliction" (2 Cor 1:3-4). This ties in directly to the theme of God-the-comforter in Isaiah 40–55 and back further into Zion's experience in Lamentations of no-comfort. Thus, Paul found himself *as a Christian* in a situation in some ways analogous to Zion's, and his prayers for deliverance went unanswered. *Then* he found the comfort of God.

While the New Testament bears witness to the real pain and suffering of Christians which can come out in prayer, we have little evidence of laments of complaint. The believer sometimes called to God for deliverance and may have been perplexed at why the suffering lasts so long, but there is no hint of any accusation that God has behaved wrongly. Indeed, the Psalter is the most quoted Old Testament book in the New Testament, and so it is interesting to note the lack of New Testament references to lament psalms. Although direct references to biblical laments are few and far between in the New Testament, we do find their influence in some of the motifs and vocabulary used in the New Testament. For instance, the agonizing question, "How long, O Lord?" so common in biblical laments is echoed on the lips of the martyred saints in Rev 6:9-10.[106] Similarly, the "groaning" of creation, church, and Spirit in Romans 8 may be seen as a lament of sorts.

But let's backtrack: Christian reflection on the place of lament must begin with Christ. Of particular interest is the fact that a complaint psalm is found on the lips of Christ on the cross (Ps 22:1). It is important to appreciate that this Psalm was not incidental to the crucifixion narratives but was fundamental, in Matthew, Mark, and John at least, in shaping them. The use of this psalm in the early church for interpreting the story of Jesus is also testified to by the linking of the praise section in Heb 2:12 (Ps 22:22 in particular) to the solidarity in which the human Christ stands with us. Hebrews 5:7 also seems to have Ps 22:1-2 & 24 in mind when the author writes, "During the days of Jesus' life on earth, he offered up prayers and petitions with loud cries and tears to the one who could save him from death, and he was heard because of his reverent submission." If Ps 22:24 is in mind here, then this would directly link the praise section at the end of the Psalm with the resurrection: a very natural hermeneutical move for those who have made the connection between the suffering of the psalmist and the suffering of Christ.

---

106. On top of the laments to be mentioned in the main text, we might note the quotation from Ps 69:9 in Rom 15:3: "For even Christ did not please himself but, as it is written: 'The insults of those who insult you have fallen on me.'" Here Christ is seen as the speaker of the lament. Also, the quotation from the lament in Ps 2:1-2 in the believers' prayer in Acts 4:23-30: "Why do the nations rage and the people plot in vain?"

Next we need to note the contradiction between Ps 22:1-2:

> My God, my God, why have you forsaken me? Why are you so far from saving me, so far from the words of my groaning? O my God, I cry out by day, but you do not answer, by night, and am not silent.

and 22:24:

> For he has not despised or disdained the suffering of the afflicted one; he has not hidden his face from him but has listened to his cry for help.

This suggests that the Psalmist's perception of the situation has changed. He is in terrible suffering and feels abandoned by God (22:1-8, 12-18). He calls to YHWH for salvation (22:9-11, 19-21) and then, perhaps after receiving some salvation oracle from the priest, takes on an attitude of confidence that God has heard him and will deliver him (22:22-31). The same pattern is seen in the story of Jesus on the cross. Mark 15:25 sees Jesus on the cross from the third hour (about 9 A.M.). From the sixth hour (12 NOON) until the ninth hour (3 P.M.) a darkness descends over the land (Mark 15:33; Matt 27:45; Luke 23:44). During this period of six hours Jesus has been experiencing the suffering of the righteous individual in the Psalms. Indeed, the suffering extends back through the tears of Gethsemane to the decision to go to Jerusalem knowing what lay ahead. At about 3 P.M. Jesus cried out in a loud voice, "My God, my God! Why have you forsaken me?" When groping around for words to express the feelings of grief at his perceived abandonment by the God whom he had worshipped from birth, it is no surprise that these words came to mind. Jesus was saturated in the Scriptures of Israel and cannot have missed the parallels between his predicament and that of the psalmist.

What is interesting is that the cry of dereliction comes not long before Jesus dies. This is not a period of doubt he went through near the beginning of his time on the cross and quickly got over. This was a simmering, growing despair held back in dignified silence until he can hold in no longer. For Matthew and Mark, it is the last thing they record Jesus saying before his crying out in a loud voice and dying. Luke and John record more positive last words ("Father, into your hands I commit my spirit," Luke 23:46; "It is finished," John 19:30).

While we need to respect the different emphases of the different Gospels, it is perfectly possible to imagine Jesus drawing hope and inspiration in the midst of his despair from the ultimate deliverance experienced by the psalmist that he has so identified himself with. But even if we use Psalm 22 to hold together the dark words of Jesus recorded in Matthew and Mark with the positive, final words in Luke and John, we must emphasize that (i) the darkness of his suffering expressed in the cry of dereliction was not a momentary doubt but a growing and prolonged anguish, (ii) the darkness experienced was not some Scripture-quoting ritual done for show but a genuine expression of how Jesus felt, (iii) that Jesus was not *abandoning* God in this prayer (for the psalmist, as for Jesus, God is still "*my* God," the one to whom they turn for deliverance), and (iv) that the positive change in Jesus' final moments may well have been influenced by the end of Psalm 22.

Now where does this story place the Christian vis-à-vis the laments of Israel? Jesus himself takes the prayer tradition of complaint against YHWH upon his own lips.[107] Jesus prays the lament *as his own prayer*. He stood as Israel's messianic representative, suffering *and lamenting* with his people Israel. He stood as the Adamic representative of the whole of humanity, suffering *and lamenting* with those broken upon the wheel of life. This must, for the Christian, legitimate Israel's worship tradition of lament.

But the situation is more complex for the Christian than this might suggest. On the following Sunday Jesus was raised from the dead, and at that point the praise section at the end of Psalm 22 was more fitting for the situation. Lament is appropriate on the cross, but not by the empty tomb. So where do Christians stand now in relation to the cross and its cry of dereliction and the resurrection with its song of joy? Is lament appropriate this side of Easter?

It is widely recognized that the New Testament has what is sometimes referred to as an inaugurated eschatology. Appreciating how this works is fundamental for Christian reappropriation of Israel's laments, so it will be necessary to explain it briefly. The inaugurated eschatologies of the New Testament documents represent a Christian adjustment of some contemporaneous Jewish apocalyptic eschatologies. According to these Jewish apocalyptic stories, the current situation in which Israel found itself was one of crisis. Pagan nations ruled over the people of God and persecuted them. The present age was one of darkness, suffering, and death for the saints. The apocalyptic hope was for the in-breaking of the kingdom of God. God has allowed his enemies time to afflict his people Israel, but their time is running out. The Lord will bring their reign to an end and will vindicate his people before the world. So the story is clear: for Israel there is suffering now and glory later.

This basic story was picked up by the Christians: currently the community will suffer for its allegiance to the Messiah, but their vindication is coming, so they must hang in there. But for the church, the situation was more complicated than that. The story of their suffering and vindication had already

---

107. The lament Psalm 69 was also seen as speaking in the voice of Jesus (cf. Rom 15:3; John 2:17).

been played out in the life of their representative, the Messiah Jesus. His death embodied the sufferings of God's people at the hands of oppressors. His resurrection was their vindication/justification. The resurrection of Christ was the in-breaking of their future deliverance. So for the early church, the new age had *already* arrived. New creation had come. The current age was no longer simply the present evil age. It was instead a time of paradox and overlap. It was still a time lived in the shadow of the cross (when suffering and sin and death awaited their final defeat), but the future salvation had begun to infiltrate. The gospel message had an inbuilt element of certainty about the glorious future because that future was already present in Christ's resurrection.

Matthew Boulton has helpfully suggested a way of linking Jesus' use of Psalm 22 to the inaugurated eschatology of the New Testament. He maintains that in Psalm 22 there is a negation of the God of glory but a clinging to God's promise of salvation. In Boulton's view, the Psalm does not end with salvation but with a vow to praise in light of the promise of salvation. The vow to praise is "an eschatological form of speech, a present trace of a future event, a foretaste, both present and absent, 'already' and 'not yet' in play."[108] Jesus' use of the psalm, liturgically commemorated in Holy Week, has implications for the pattern of Christian worship itself.

> Jesus' citation of Psalm 22 fashions Easter's 'hallelujah' — and with it all proper Christian praise — into an eschatological act, a gesture at once indicating decisive divine victory ('He is risen!') and the ongoing facts of crisis and suffering, which is to say, the fact that divine victory if nonetheless forthcoming, nonetheless 'not yet.' . . . Christian praise is properly eschatological praise, jubilant insofar as it witnesses to divine victory and deliverance, anguished insofar as it witnesses to creation's ongoing need of the same.[109]

Lament serves as a complaint against God, but also as a turning towards and clinging to the divine promise thus reconfiguring praise as an "impossible" revival of hope in the midst of darkness. "Christian doxology is properly offered by way of cruciform lament, continually reworked into Easter's 'hallelujah' by way of human anguish and indignation, which is to say, continually reworked into eschatological praise by way of unabashed Christian lamentation."[110]

So where in the story of God's people found in the Scriptures (our Old Testament) would the early Christians have placed themselves? With Lamen-

108. Boulton, "Forsaking God," 70.
109. Boulton, "Forsaking God," 74-75.
110. Boulton, "Forsaking God," 78.

tations? Yes, in that they were experiencing affliction at the hands of their enemies. Yes, in that they were groaning in pain as they awaited final deliverance. But the resurrection of Christ and the giving of the Spirit served as signs that God had acted decisively to redeem them, and this places them in a different location from the speakers of Lamentations — *after* the pain of divine silence. The Christians associated themselves most closely with the Israel addressed in Isaiah 40–55. Second Isaiah's words were directed to a people still in exile, but they were words of comfort heralding the certainty of immanent salvation. The words of Isaiah 40–55 seemed to speak directly to the Christians' own situation. Suffering? Yes, for a while, but the light of dawn is already breaking over the horizon and the coming of the sun is certain.

This death and resurrection of the Messiah put the understanding of suffering in the New Testament in a different light from that found in Lamentations. The Christians made sense of their own suffering in the light of Christ's suffering. Christ was *not suffering for his sin* but was innocent like the righteous sufferers in the Psalms and Lam 4:13. The community of Christ was similarly persecuted for righteousness' sake and *not as a divine punishment.* So it is no accident that when Paul appropriates a communal lament psalm (Psalm 44) in Rom 8:36, it is the only communal lament in which the *innocence* of the suffering community is pleaded. For Paul, the suffering of the innocent community in that psalm finds its parallel in the innocent suffering of the church. The difference is that the psalmist cannot understand why God would allow his people to suffer when they have been faithful to the covenant. For Paul, making sense of the psalm in the light of Christ's suffering, persecution is part of the calling of those who identify with the bleeding Messiah. This is not the way in which the voices in Lamentations understand their suffering. They are not the sufferers of Psalm 44 who have remained obedient to the covenant. They are being punished by God for their persistent and prolonged breach of the covenant. How can a Christian relate to *that?*

We have found the following disanalogies between the situation the church believes itself to be in and the situation the speakers of Lamentations believed themselves to be in. First, the suffering in Lamentations is seen as divine punishment for covenant *violation,* while the persecution of the church in all its diverse forms is seen as resulting from their covenant *obedience* to Christ. Second, while Lamentations does contain hope that the suffering will come to an end, it is a muted hope overlaid by grief. The resurrection of Jesus injected Christian suffering with a stronger tone of *certainty* of the future. Third, in Lamentations the suffering is understood as purely negative, while the identification made by the Christians of their sufferings with those of Christ transformed their theological imaginations, enabling them to see the world in subversive ways. Their public humiliation at the hands of the world became, in their reconfigured worldview, a badge of honor, of their loyalty to the Lord, and a sign that if they have suffered like him then they will reign with him (Rom 8:17). The story of Jesus' death and resurrection is their own story, and as they share in his sufferings they will share in his resurrection. Given this, we may ask whether a Christian could find a word from the Lord in the book of Lamentations.

First, and perhaps most obviously, Christians can see the sufferings of Christ typified in Lamentations. The rationale for this has already been spelled out.

Second, and following on from the first point, Christians can see their sufferings in Lamentations even though they may not be being punished for their sin. The early Christians had a strong sense of their spiritual unification with Christ and saw their persecution as a participation in the persecution of Christ, the righteous sufferer *par excellence.* Consequently, although the Isaianic Servant's role is fulfilled by Christ, the early Christians also felt a liberty to see the Servant's role as applicable to the calling of his body, the church.[111] In just the same way it may be that some Christian readers will see the story of the church etched in the story of the *geber* in Lamentations 3. The fact that persecuted Christians share in Christ's afflictions (which were the afflictions of Jerusalem) creates a space for Christians to see their persecution *partially* reflected in the poetry of Lamentations.

Third, many of the sufferings that Christians and churches experience are not a result of their loyalty to Christ but are simply part of the tragic fabric of a fallen world. Most of the New Testament teaching on suffering, because of its focus on being persecuted for the faith, does not directly address this situation.[112] Romans 8:18-30 offers a wider perspective which sees the grieving of Christians as part of the grieving of the whole created order. The suffering which causes Christians to "groan" is the general frustration and pain of living in a broken creation in bondage to decay and death (cf. 2 Cor 5:1-5). And in that text lie the seeds of a Trinitarian theology of lament. Not only does God participate, in Christ, in our sorrow, lamenting for and *as* us, but through the Spirit God laments for and *with* us. The Spirit groans for a broken world, bearing witness to God's own "grief" at the fractured nature of the world and the torment in it. This pneumatic groan is simultaneously a

---

111. See Wagner, "The Heralds of Isaiah."

112. Though see Jervis, *At the Heart of the Gospel,* ch. 4. Jervis argues that Romans provides a theology that embraces both suffering *with* Christ (persecution) and suffering *in* Christ, which reconfigures all our suffering so that we see it in a new light.

prayer to the Father to bring creation through to resurrection. Through the lament of the church the Spirit can intercede through us for deliverance of creation. This pneumatic gift of moaning is both an expression of pain and of hope for resurrection.

The idea of lament as an expression of grief and expectation is well put by Nicholas Wolterstorff in his comments on Matt 5:4, "Blessed are those who mourn, for they will be comforted." Who are the mourners? "The Mourners are those who have caught a glimpse of God's new day, who ache with all their being for that day's coming, and who break out into tears when confronted by its absence. . . . The mourners," he writes, "are aching visionaries," and as such their groans serve as prayers for salvation.[113]

Christians can suffer like anyone else and in times of loss can feel deeply perplexed and let down by God. Even belief in hope beyond death may not bring the needed consolation. As Jamie Grant observes:

> For the Christian, neither hope in Christ nor certainty of ultimate divine resolution to our problems in any way denies the human need for lament. Lament is not based on the psalmist's lack of future hope, lament is grounded in the psalmist's present experience of life with God in the world. Lament is intrinsic to humanity living in relationship with God in his good but fallen world. . . . The knowledge that everything will be alright does not change the fact that, in our humanity, we need to respond before God to those present realities that are not alright.[114]

The Psalmist asks, "Why?" and "How long?" but neither question need indicate a lack of hope for an ultimate salvation. Lament is thus not inappropriate as a mode of engaging with God in this now-and-not-yet period. After the death of his son in a climbing accident, Wolterstorff wrote:

> Elements of the gospel which I had always thought would console did not. They did something else, something important, but not that. It did not console me to be reminded of the hope of resurrection. If I had forgotten that hope, then it would indeed have brought light into my life to be reminded of it. But I did not think of death as a bottomless pit. I did not grieve as one who has no hope. Yet Eric is gone, *here* and *now* he is gone; *now* I cannot talk with him, *now* I cannot see him, *now* I cannot hug him, *now* I cannot hear of his plans for the future. *That* is my sorrow. A friend said, "Remember, he's in good hands." I was deeply moved. But

---

113. Wolterstorff, *Lament for a Son*, 85-86.
114. Grant, "Psalm 44," 10-11.

that reality does not put Eric back in my hands now. That's my grief. For that grief, what consolation can there be other than having him back? . . .

I have no explanation. I can do nothing else than endure in the face of this deepest and most painful of mysteries. I believe in God the Father Almighty, maker of heaven and earth and resurrecter of Jesus Christ. I also believe that my son's life was cut off in its prime. I cannot fit these pieces together. I am at a loss. I have read the theodicies produced to justify the ways of God to man. I find them unconvincing. To the most agonized question I have ever asked I do not know the answer. I do not know why God would watch him fall. I don't know why God would watch me wounded. I cannot even guess. . . . My wound is an unanswered question. The wounds of all humanity are an unanswered question.[115]

There will be times in which psalms of individual and communal lament will be the appropriate way of relating to the Lord honestly. While we may see lament as an act of unbelief, this is not the case. Lament is not a severing of relationship with God but takes places precisely *within* that relationship.

The lament is the response of one who cares enough to take the meaningless before God. That is an act of faith. To take our honest questions to God is not an act of defamation toward the character of God, but an act of affirmation. Why are there wrongs in this in-between time? Why are they so severe? How long must we endure? These are within the context of faith-struggle in this in-between time. And if Christians can muster at least as much faith as the Old Testament Psalmist and Prophets, then the release of such questions finds its form in the lament.[116]

Elie Wiesel noted that "[t]here is a certain power in the question which isn't found in the answer."[117] Lament explores the power of asking the kinds of questions for which adequate answers are hard to imagine. The Lament tradition, says Walter Brueggemann, kept covenant interaction between God and Israel alive. Without lament the human partner in the relationship becomes voiceless in dark times: "covenant minus lament is finally a practice of denial, cover-up, and pretense."[118] God does not require Israel to be "Yes-Men" who only know how to give thanks. Even the dangerous questioning of God's own justice is permitted. "A community of faith which neglects laments soon con-

---

115. Wolterstorff, *Lament for a Son*, 31, 67-68.
116. Resner, "Lament," 131.
117. Wiesel, *Night*, 16.
118. Brueggemann, "The Costly Loss of Lament," 60.

cludes that the hard issues of justice are improper questions to pose at the throne, because the throne seems to be only a place of praise."[119]

This insight acts as a corrective to a certain pious Christian discomfort with, and distortion of, Lamentations. For instance, St. Gregory's *Pastoral Rule* interprets the profuse weeping in Lam 3:48 as weeping over the defilements of former *sins*, whereas it is actually a lament over the *sufferings* of Zion.[120] This tendency to see repentance where it is not to be found can also be seen in Ambrose, who quotes Lam 2:10-11 to illustrate (along with 1:2, 4, 16, 20) the repentant posture of the elders.[121] Now, in no way do I wish to undermine the importance of repentance (3:40-42), but we need to acknowledge when the tears of lament are tears of pain, frustration, and anger rather than tears of pious repentance. And we need to recognize the legitimacy of such tears.

The giving of voice to sufferers is emphasized by Barbara Bozak. She observes that the experience of powerlessness and the loss of voice are central to many forms of suffering. Laments are the prayers of the disorientated and reflect an honest response to the different aspects of pain (physical, psychological, and social). They can play a role in the process of healing because they can help the sufferer to "find a language of lament, a cry of pain, words which begin to express what is happening in his or her life."[122] There is more to lament, however, than the expression of pain and anger. Will Soll reminds us that "we stop short of a full understanding of the lament psalms if we make them nothing more than a vocabulary of complaint. For the lament is not merely an articulation of unhappiness; it seeks, in the midst of unhappiness, to recover communion with God."[123] This is certainly the case in Lamentations. The book was not created simply to express grief and anger at God. It was primarily there to inspire God to bring about a change in Judah's circumstances. In Lamentations the graphic scenes of suffering are there, not merely because the people need to speak their pain, but mainly because the underlying hope is that YHWH is fundamentally a God of compassion: if his attention is drawn to the dreadful suffering, then, it was hoped, he will be moved to act salvifically. Even the articulation of complaint is a step on the way out of the darkness.

While the exact words of Lamentations may not express precisely how we feel because our situations will never entirely parallel theirs, we can still draw in-

---

119. Brueggemann, "The Costly Loss of Lament," 64.

120. *NPNF²* 12, 60.

121. Ambrose, *Concerning Repentance*, *NPNF²* 10, 351. Seeing a call for Zion's repentance in the words of 2:18 is less obviously inappropriate. See Cyprian, *Exhortation to Repentance*, *ANCL* 13.2, 267; John Cassian, *The First Conference of Abbot Isaac*, *NPNF²* 11, 397.

122. Bozak, "Suffering and the Psalms of Lament," 328.

123. Soll, "The Israelite Lament," 79.

spiration from the brutal honesty of the prayers. We can still relate to the bringing of pain before God and to the conflicting emotions. Indeed, Christians can sometimes lose sight of the certainty of resurrection and can wonder if their future is one of unending darkness. In such places of pain Lamentations can be an inspiration. Christ has been in that place of God-forsakenness too. He has stood in the darkness alongside us and called out our words of lament, "Why have you forsaken me?" Even in the experience of feeling forsaken, God is with us.

To see such a Christian appropriation of Lamentations consider St. John of the Cross's interesting and suggestive use of the *geber*'s lament in 3:1-19. The words are understood to describe "the dark night of the soul." He quotes extended sections from those verses on several occasions in which he is detailing the grievous afflictions of this spiritual state.[124] He says that he "can think now of no way to describe this state of oppression, and that which the soul feels and suffers in it, save by using these words of Jeremiah which refer to it."[125] Clearly Lamentations 3 was a key biblical text for St. John. "All these complaints Jeremiah makes about these pains and trials, and by means of them he most vividly depicts the sufferings of the soul in this spiritual night and purgation. Wherefore the soul that God sets in this tempestuous and horrible night is deserving of great compassion."[126] For St. John of the Cross this terrible dark night was intended by God for the *good* of the soul, as painful medicine to bring it to health, but for the soul in this state it is hard to perceive it that way. The soul is

> unable to raise its affection or its mind to God, neither can it pray to him, thinking, as Jeremiah thought concerning himself, that God has set a cloud before it through which its prayer cannot pass [Lam 3:44] . . . it thinks that God neither hears it nor pays heed to it . . . [he then quotes Lam 3:9]. In truth this is no time for the soul to speak with God; it should rather put its mouth to the dust, as Jeremiah says, so that perchance there may come to it some present hope [Lam 3:29], and it may endure its purgation with patience.[127]

The soul can do nothing, not even pray, but be passive; *God* is the one who is working on it.

St. John's interpretation of Lamentations 3 is helpful. It seeks to take with full seriousness the real horror of the man's sense of alienation from

---

124. *Dark Night of the Soul*, chs. 1, 8; *Living Flame of Love*, stanza 1.17.

125. *Living Flame of Love*, stanza 1.17.

126. *Dark Night of the Soul*, 7:3.

127. *Dark Night of the Soul*, ch. 8.

God and victimization by God. It also seeks to understand those sufferings as intended by God for good not ill, even if they do not feel that way to the sufferer at the time. That interpretation is sensitive to the overall shape of 3:1-39. The interpretation cashes in on the fact that the sufferer in Lamentations 3 is an individual, for the "dark night of the soul" in St. John's theology is something suffered by individuals, not communities. However, we might wish to extend his thought at this point and consider the cases of a dark night of the soul suffered by an entire faith community. Is that not exactly what we find in Lamentations? Indeed, as Dobbs-Allsopp argues, "It is precisely as a counterweight to the individualism that pervades our culture that Lamentations' thoroughgoing [communal] choral sensibilities are well poised to serve the church. For Lamentations ultimately crafts and frames its response to catastrophe in and through a communal idiom."[128]

Finally, there will be some situations in which Christians and churches suffer, not out of loyalty to Christ, but because they have sinned. The New Testament is quite clear that God may execute judgment in the present age on whole churches (Rev 3:16) as well as individuals (Acts 5:1-11; 1 Cor 11:30). In this regard, it is fascinating to see that Eusebius quotes Lam 2:1-2 and applies it to the destruction of churches in persecution in 302/303 A.D. This destruction was, according to Eusebius, due to divine judgment on the churches for internal strife and conflict between leaders who cast aside the bond of piety and acted like power-crazed tyrants.[129] In the persecution, houses of prayer were torn down, Scriptures were burned, church leaders hid and, when caught, were mocked by passers-by. Clearly Eusebius saw situations in which churches suffer *for their iniquity* much as Jerusalem did in Lamentations.

For those Christians experiencing divine punishment for sin, the words of Lamentations will resonate with their own situation. Calvin, in his lectures on Lamentations, certainly felt free to see in the book warnings to his Christian audience of the reality of divine judgment on the church or the Christian that sins in the way Israel did, and also a model of how to lament in a godly way (i.e., without raging against, and blaspheming, God but acknowledging his righteous punishment and humbling ourselves before him). For instance, commenting on 1:17, he writes:

> Now, if such a thing happened to the ancient church [i.e., Israel], let us not wonder if at this day also God should deal with us more severely than we wish. It is, indeed, a very bitter thing to see the church so afflicted as to

---

128. Dobbs-Allsopp, *Lamentations*, 135.
129. *Church History, NPNF*[2] 1, chs. 1-2, 324.

have the ungodly exulting over its calamities, and that God's children should be as the refuse and filth of the world. But let us patiently bear such a condition; and when we are thus contemptuously treated by our enemies, let us know that God visits us with punishment, and that the wicked do nothing except through the providence of God, for it is his will to try our faith, and thus to shew himself a righteous judge: for if we rightly consider in how many ways, and how obstinately we have provoked his wrath, we shall not wonder if we also be counted at this day an abomination and a curse.[130]

In a similar way, Matthew Henry, commenting on Lam 4:1-12, wrote, "Beholding the sad consequences of sin in the church of old, let us seriously consider to what the same causes may justly bring down the church now." And in the nineteenth century Eduard Nägelsbach wrote

Truly, since the Lord could destroy Jerusalem . . . without being unfaithful to His promise given to the Fathers, even so He can remove the candlestick of every particular Christian church, without breaking the promise given to the church at large, that the gates of Hell shall not prevail against it.[131]

Other Christian writers see the potential applications of Lamentations in similar ways. St. Gregory in his *Pastoral Rule* quotes Lamentations 2:14 about the prophets who don't challenge sinners. Christian leaders, he says, must care for their flock by prophetically speaking out against sinful people.[132] And Gregory is well aware that Christian leaders *do* fail in their callings. The *Pastoral Rule* provides an allegorical interpretation of Lamentations 4:1 in which the dimmed gold is holiness, the changed pure gold is reverence, the stones poured out on the streets are persons in sacred orders and the streets on which they are poured out are the latitudes of life. So the verse is seen to speak of what happens when "a life of holiness is polluted by earthly doings" (gold dimmed) and "when the previous reputation of persons who were believed to be living religiously is diminished" (most excellent color changed); when those who should have been at the heart of the holy place (both the stones from the High Priest's vestments and the building blocks of the temple) seek out the broadways of secular causes outside (the streets).[133]

---

130. *Lecture 3* on 1:11-18. On Calvin, see Wilcox, "John Calvin's Interpretation of Lamentations."

131. Nägelsbach, *The Lamentations of Jeremiah*, 61.

132. *NPNF²* 12, ch. 4, 11.

133. *NPNF²* 12, 18.

Charles Spurgeon, preaching on Lam 2:19 just before midnight on New Year's Eve 1855, was inspired to see the narrator's appeal to Zion to weep and plead for her children as reversible in the situation of his day. The sons of Zion must weep and plead for their mother (the church), for she has abandoned sound preaching and gospel truth:

> Methinks I might become a Jeremy to-night, and weep as he, for surely the church at large is in almost as evil a condition. . . . Arise, ye sons of Zion, and weep for your mother, yea weep bitterly, for she hath given herself to other lovers, and forsaken the Lord that bought her. I bear witness this night, in the midst of this solemn assembly, that the church at large is wickedly departing from the living God; she is leaving the truth which was once her glory, and she is mixing herself among the nations. Ah! beloved, it were well if Zion now could sometimes weep; it were well if there were more who would lay to heart the wound of the daughter of his people. How hath the city become a harlot! how hath the much fine gold become dim! and how hath the glory departed! Zion is under a cloud.[134]

The above serve merely to illustrate some of the diverse ways in which Christians have heard the word of the Lord addressed to them through the text of Lamentations.

Having found space within Christian theology for lament we can return to the issue of responding to suffering and ask how Lamentations can guide the Christian *practice* of lament.

Lamentations and the Practice of Theodicy

In his book *Raging with Compassion,* John Swinton argues that seeking to *explain* evil and suffering, in the way Christian theologians and philosophers often have, is both futile and, at times, positively *un*helpful. A more biblical and pastoral way of responding to evil is not to provide a theoretical account of why it occurs but "rather to develop forms of community within which the impact of evil and suffering [can] be absorbed, resisted, and transformed."[135] As Wendy Farley comments, "Suffering yearns more for experiences of healing presence than for logical arguments. Theory can provide some meaning to suffering, but it is in compassionate relationship that suffering discovers

134. Spurgeon, "Watch Night Service."
135. Swinton, *Raging with Compassion,* 35.

redemption."[136] As a practical theologian, Swinton wishes to recommend to the church various Christian *practices* (lament, forgiveness, thoughtfulness, and hospitality) which serve as "practiced acts of resistance" and "gestures of redemption." The goal of these practices is to help people respond to evil and suffering "in ways that are faith-enhancing rather than faith-destroying."[137]

The raw psychological impact of suffering — both communal and individual — is scratched into every page of Lamentations. Psychological studies on phases in the grief process and post–traumatic stress disorder in refugees highlight how the poems of Lamentations display a wide range of responses to trauma. We see shock (1:4), denial (3:39), isolation (1:2, 9, 16, 21), anger (2:20), bargaining (2:18-19; 3:40-42), depression (5:15), memories of happier times (1:7), shame (1:8), search for the guilty (4:12-13), laying blame (5:7), weeping (3:48-51), and controlled grief (in the act of writing the poems).[138] It is worth our while to ask what practical strategies the book of Lamentations presents for dealing with catastrophic suffering. Among them one might find the following:

Space for Silence

Lady Zion sits in silence for much of the time as do her inhabitants. Consider 2:10:

> The elders of Daughter Zion are sitting down in stunned silence;
> They put dust on their heads, they are dressed in sackcloth.
> The maidens of Jerusalem press their heads to the ground.

The human response to grief is often one of stunned silence. Swinton points to the often unnoticed fact that Jesus' six hours on the cross were spent, for the most part, in silence.[139] We so focus on his words from the cross that we miss the significance of the quiet spaces between them.

> We can understand the words of Jesus only in the light of his silence. If we are to transform and resist evil, we must understand the imposed silence

---

136. Quoted in Swinton, *Raging with Compassion*, 69.

137. Swinton, *Raging with Compassion*, 76.

138. See, e.g., on the application of Elisabeth Kübler-Ross's work on grief, Joyce, "Lamentations and the Grief Process"; and Reimer, "Good Grief?" Both helpfully identify how Lamentations manifests different psychological stages of grief (which need not occur in any set order). For an application of post–traumatic stress disorder in refugees, see Smith-Christopher, *A Biblical Theology of Exile*, 75-104. For the best overview of all recent psychological studies of Lamentations, see Thomas, "Current Trends."

139. Swinton, *Raging with Compassion*, ch. 5.

that accompanies evil and suffering before we can break that silence. We can understand the experience of suffering only when we learn how to listen to the silence, when we learn to interpret and understand the meaning of silence and the dangers of breaking that silence with words that can be harmful even when intended to be healing. . . . Jesus' silence and alienation legitimate the experience of suffering.[140]

Lamentations, as a book, represents a breaking of the silence — an attempt to articulate a suffering that is beyond words. However, we need to appreciate that the articulation of suffering in the poems in Lamentations was not the *first* reaction to the pain and that the poems recall the initial silence and the ongoing periods of silence. Silence, as Calvin Seerveld notes,

> is the mark of a person's being a single, self-conscious, individual creation. This is why when a person is threatened with shame, with public exposure . . . when what is closest to one's very self is to be violated, then as a last resort a person withdraws, pulls back into one's cloak of silence, trying to keep intact and out of reach at least something that is one's own. . . . Silence gives a person room to move around in oneself, [and] presents a reserve for regrouping one's forces.[141]

A Time to Weep

Zion weeps bitterly through the night and sits with tears running down her cheeks (1:2, 16). The inhabitants of the city weep (1:4b-c), as does the narrator (2:11; 3:48-51). The sheer gut-wrenching depth and physicality of this weeping is clear from 2:11.

> My eyes were worn out from tears,
> My stomach churned.
> My liver bile was poured out on the ground.

Articulating Suffering

Lamentations provides some of the words to articulate Judah's grief in the aftermath of Babylonian decimation. It provides long descriptions of the multiple and diverse horrors that are suffered and their impact on the soul of the community. As part of a journey of healing, pain must be named and owned without denying it, comparing it, or trivializing it.

---

140. Swinton, *Raging with Compassion*, 100-1.
141. Seerveld, "The Meaning of Silence," 298-99.

Bearing Witness to Suffering

Zion testifies to those who pass by about what has befallen her (1:12-16, 18-19). In the same way, the narrator acts as a witness to her grief and compels his audience to consider it. The man in chapter 3 bears blunt witness to his pain (3:1-18), as do the community in chapter 5 (5:1-18). Dealing with pain is more than being able to articulate it to ourselves — we need *others* to see and hear to reintegrate us into a wider community.

Comforting the Broken

What added insult to Zion's injury was the fact that there was no one to comfort her. Nobody would draw alongside her and sit with her in her sorrow. There was nobody to behold with kind eyes her condition and listen to her lament. The narrator himself is moved to take on this mantel (2:13). The poet knows that those who grieve should have a comforter and uses the poem to invite the readers of the book to play that role. Very clearly then, Lamentations is advocating the practice of weeping with those who weep (Rom 12:15). Practical and heartfelt compassion for those in pain is the way of Lamentations. The characters in the book who look on at Zion's pain and mock (1:21; 2:15-16) are treated as behaving wickedly.

Remembering Suffering

Lamentations, as a book, memorializes the grief of the city, and the ongoing Jewish liturgical use of the book embodies this refusal to forget. The connections we noted earlier between the cup of God's wrath that Judah had drunk and the cup through which Christians recall Jesus' death in Holy Communion are suggestive here. The ritual of the Eucharist compels Christians to remember the broken and tortured body of Christ. Recognizing the solidarity in which Christ stood with suffering Israel and damaged humanity liberates us to see in this cup a space for the remembrance of the brokenness of our world. Of course, Christ's death is unique (only he died for the salvation of creation), but in that death he embraced the fate of humanity. So perhaps the Christian celebration of communion can become a space in which we refuse to forget the "crucifixion" of creation, of humanity, of Israel as we recall how Jesus alone took that judgment *to its limit and exhausted it.* Perhaps Holy Communion could become a time for Christians to "remember" the sufferings of the world in the sufferings of Jesus.

Prayers of Protest and Petition

Wolterstorff wrote that "Lament is more . . . than the voicing of suffering. The mere voicing of suffering is complaint, not lament. Lament is a *cry to God*."[142] Lament is a cry for deliverance from suffering ("Save us, Lord"), but also from the threat of meaninglessness that the suffering brings ("Why have you let this happen?"). Lamentations does not turn its back on YHWH but clings to him at precisely this moment of Godforsakenness. This is exemplified best in the narrator's call to Lady Zion in 2:18b-19:

> Pour down tears like a torrent, by day and by night!
> Do not give yourself rest! Do not let the daughter of your eyes be still!
> Arise! Cry aloud in the night at the beginning of night watches!
> Pour our your heart like water in front of the presence of the Lord!
> Lift up your hands to him for the life of your children fainting from hunger on every street corner!

And Zion does pray (1:9c, 11c, 20-22; 2:20-22). Her prayer is honest about her sin and her pain. It is also angry and confused yet still looks to God for salvation. When all is said and done, Jerusalem's pain is simply too deep for human healing (2:13c). Some evils are *so* horrendous that the only hope for their ultimate defeat is the infinite goodness of YHWH.[143] So it is appropriate that the book of Lamentations climaxes in an extended prayer in which the pain is brought before God and he is asked to intervene (chapter 5).

Remembering God's Covenant Love

The suffering man in Lamentations 3 recalls, in the midst of his sorrow, YHWH's past acts of loving kindness and tender mercy. This recollection revives hope within his hopeless heart even before his situation sees any improvement (3:18-24). The practice of recalling God's past acts of mercy is crucial to empowering sufferers to face their situations with hope, and, for the Christian, the story of the cross, resurrection, and ascension will be at the heart of recollections of God's ḥesed. However, it is important to realize that, before the man could get to this "moment," he spoke very bluntly of God's mistreatment of him. We need to appreciate that Lamentations gives space for both phases of his response, and we should be careful not to rush with undue haste to remembrance.

---

142. Wolterstorff, "If God Is Good and Sovereign," 43.
143. See Adams, *Horrendous Evils.*

Repentance

The community is called to confess its sins (3:40-42), and Zion has a place in her prayer for confession of sin (1:18a). While confession of sin and repentance do not dominate Lamentations, they are practices affirmed in the book. In cases where the suffering is not related to the sin of God's people, then such a practice is not directly relevant.

Humble Submission to God

The location of the teaching of 3:25-39 in the canonical form of the book (its juxtaposition with texts that have other emphases) invites readers to ponder quite how it should be taken. The teaching on handling suffering in 3:25-39, while problematic for many modern readers, received a much more affirmative reaction in Christian history. The advice on the goodness of bearing the yoke *in youth* (3:27) is used by Methodius to support the need to cultivate virtue for childhood.[144] Jerome took 3:28-31 as a description of the vocation of anchorites, who go from the monasteries into the desert with nothing but bread and salt. He traces this vocation back through Paul the hermit, St. Anthony, and John the Baptist to those of whom "Jeremiah" spoke in Lamentations 3. These devout people bear the yoke, sit alone in silence, give their cheek to the one who strikes it, and so on.[145] In Letter XLIX.–L.4, Jerome takes "Jeremiah's" exhortation to bear the yoke and sit in silence (3:27-28) as wise advice for a wayward and argumentative monk who was troubling him. Theodoret, commenting on "Good is YHWH to those who hope, to the soul that seeks him" (3:25), writes, "Let us not murmur at the storm that has arisen, for the Lord knoweth what is good for us. . . . Let us then bravely bear the evils that befall us; it is in war that heroes are discerned; in conflicts that athletes are crowned."[146] Augustine plausibly sees Jesus' teaching in the Sermon on the Mount on turning the other cheek (Matt 5:38-39) as simply a reiteration of Lam 3:30, in which a man is praised for offering his cheek to one who would strike him.[147] In all these cases, the "wise" advice in Lam 3:25-39 is taken at face value — positive advice to be followed by the Christian.

144. *The Banquet of the Ten Virgins*, ch. 3. ANCL 14, 45.

145. Letter 22, To Count Ulpianus. NPNF² 3, 259.

146. Letter 78, To Eusebius, bishop of Persian Armenia. NPNF² 3, 274.

147. *Reply to Faustus the Manichaean*, Book 19.28. NPNF¹ 4, 250. Augustine's connection here is strengthened by the observation that Isa 50:6 seems to allude to Lam 3:30 (the Servant of YHWH offers his cheek to those who pulled his beard). For Christians, Jesus fulfills the role of the Servant of YHWH, and so a path can be traced through Scripture from the advice in Lamentations to Jesus and thus perhaps, as Augustine suggested, to his teaching on turning the other cheek.

The teaching is not encouraging passivity on the part of those who suffer (see next point). Rather, they are being invited to construe their suffering as a temporary chastening originating in God. This leads not to a perverse enjoyment of affliction, nor to acceptance of it as good, but rather to an attitude of humble and hopeful patience in the face of it.

Resistance to Suffering

Somewhat in tension with the previous point is the fact that lament in general, and Lamentations in particular, embodies a refusal to accept the current state of affairs. So the man in 3:48-51 declares that he will weep until God acts to save.

> My eyes will flow with streams of water,
> > on account of the destruction of the daughter of my people.
> My eyes pour down [tears] and will not stop,
> > without weakening,
> *until YHWH will look down and see*
> > *from heaven.*
> My eye[s] afflict me
> > because of all the daughters of my city.

He refuses to accept the way things stand. This is an important element for Christian spirituality. Brueggemann comments:

> The lament psalms, then, are a complaint that makes the shrill insistence that: 1. Things are not right in the present arrangement. 2. They need not stay this way and can be changed. 3. The speaker will not accept them in this way, for the present arrangement is intolerable. 4. It is God's obligation to change things. *But the main point is the first: life is not right.*[148]

Opposition to the Perpetrators of Suffering

While God is seen as ultimately responsible for the affliction, human enemies are the immediate cause. Lamentations is very clear in its condemnation of the evil inflicted by these enemies. To repeat a point made several times already, the fact that they are unwitting agents of God in no way mitigates their culpability (1:21-22; 3:58-66; 4:21-22). This gives the lie to the view that a strong doctrine of divine sovereignty necessarily undermines resistance to

---

148. Brueggemann, *The Psalms and the Life of Faith*, 105 (italics mine).

suffering and evil. While recommending submission to God's strange work through suffering, *Lamentations simultaneously advocates protesting against suffering and resisting that which brings suffering (even if that suffering originates with God).* The enemies are opposed in prayer and through the faithful recounting and exposure of their atrocities.

All of these practices have a place in Christian spirituality, and they are part of the gift of Lamentations to the church.

> Ah, my dear angry Lord,
> Since thou dost love, yet strike;
> Cast down, yet help afford;
> Sure I will do the like.
>
> I will complain, yet praise;
> I will bewail, approve;
> And all my sweet-sour days
> I will lament and love.[149]

Lamentations and Ethics

Lamentations 1 and 2 as Ethically Formative for Readers

We shall conclude these theological reflections on Lamentations by considering its possible contribution to ethical reflection.

Lamentations 1 is a poem that is crafted such that it draws out an ethical reaction from its audience. First of all, it provides some explicit and implicit ethical assessments of four sets of players: Zion, her enemies, her allies, and her God. The implied readers are expected to concur with these assessments (although the responses of actual readers are not so easy to control).

Both the narrator and Zion agree that she has sinned and is suffering for it. However, the focus of both is not her sin but her sorrow. Throughout the poem references to her sin by both the narrator and Zion are brief, general, and in contexts that focus on her pain — the point being that the intention is to elicit sympathy for Zion without portraying her as an innocent victim.[150]

---

149. George Herbert, "Bitter Sweet" (1633).

150. It is interesting that the rabbinic *Targum of Lamentations*, in its bid to make the book theologically safer for use in the synagogues and to vindicate God, uses a number of devices to place more emphasis on Israel's sin and God's justice in punishing it than the Hebrew original does. See Brady's excellent study, *The Rabbinic Targum of Lamentations*.

This in itself is theologically important. The biblical text is not seeking to elicit an attitude in which readers would gloat at the suffering sinner because she is getting what she deserves. On the contrary, without in any way seeking to justify her sin or undermine its seriousness, the poet still sees compassion rather than derision or indifference as the right response to her suffering. The ethical response would be to stand alongside her, to pray with and for her, to weep with her, to strengthen her, to resist the suffering and those who bring it. This chimes in perfectly with New Testament teachings about how God views sinful people: "But God shows his love for us in that *while we were yet sinners* Christ died for us" (Rom 5:8); "But God, who is rich in mercy, out of the great love with which he loved us, *even when we were dead through our trespasses,* made us alive together with Christ" (Eph 2:4-5). Hence, Lamentations is arguably seeking to facilitate *godly* reactions towards rebellious yet broken people.

Both the narrator and Jerusalem concur that Jerusalem's enemies, although God's unwitting agents, have acted despicably and deserve judgment for their behavior. This is implicit throughout but comes out most clearly in 1:21-22. This too is a theologically significant observation. In Old Testament literature, it is never the case that because God, in his providence, has brought about his purposes through a certain agent, this agent is not responsible for his or her actions. Humans are held fully responsible for their deeds, even though God is working to achieve his purposes through them.

It is also important to note that God's intention, which he brings about through the human agent, may not coincide with the intention of the human agent in performing the action. So, for instance, Joseph's brothers' intention in selling Joseph into slavery was to get rid of him, but God's intention brought about through their action was to save the whole family from a future famine. This distinction made in Old Testament texts between *God's* intentions and *human* intentions behind a single human action (or set of actions) allows Old Testament authors to consider a single human action (or set of actions) both as God's *righteous* action and as a human *evil* action. That was the case with Joseph's brothers' deed: *they* intended it for evil, but *God* intended it for good (Gen 50:20). This distinction is operating in Lamentations 1, and it allows Zion to declare that YHWH was behaving righteously when he punished her (1:18) *and* that her enemies were behaving wickedly, such that YHWH should punish them for their sin (1:21-22).

Now, the basic picture of divine sovereignty operating here raises all sorts of philosophical-theological questions. How exactly do the human freedom and responsibility that Old Testament texts clearly and consistently recognize work in conjunction with God's providence? The Bible never sets out to answer that question, but seeking to do so is a legitimate theological pursuit. In the history of theology, numerous attempts have been made to clarify the human freedom–divine sovereignty relation, and the results have been diverse indeed! There is no space here to explore the options, except to say that any satisfactory answer has to avoid two extremes: On the one hand, we must not embrace such a strong view of providence that human freedom is effectively denied. On the other hand, we must not embrace such a strong view of freedom that God is reduced to a helpless onlooker, swept along with the disaster that is history. Any suggested philosophical-theological solution to the problem, if it is to have any claims to being true to Scripture, must allow for the double-aspect accounts of single actions (or sets of actions) in which they can be described both as direct human and as indirect divine actions. The ethical implication is that just because God was using the Babylonians to punish Zion, it does not follow that Babylon was justified in its actions, nor that people should not condemn and resist Babylon.

Both the narrator and Zion agree that her allies have been treacherous and unfaithful. They failed to fulfill their treaty obligations, leaving Zion to face the storm alone, and now they look at her in disgust instead of acting to comfort her. This is also of theological interest because there is clearly one level in which Zion's relationship with her allies amounted to an abandonment of YHWH and an act of infidelity. Nevertheless, the allies are *still* expected to behave according to their covenants with Judah. They are *still* responsible to assist her when attacked and comfort her when she mourns, and that they do neither but instead mock and despise her is judged to be a treacherous response.

The assessment of YHWH is more complex and conflicted. For the most part, in Lamentations 1 the narrator and Zion agree that YHWH has acted righteously in punishing her. However, both the narrator (1:10) and Zion (1:12-16) have moments when they *implicitly* suggest that the punishment has not been appropriate. That implicit protest strand becomes much more dominant in the second poem. There the destructive activity of God is portrayed in very harsh terms (2:1-10), and the narrator breaks down in tears at Zion's affliction (2:11-13). Zion herself utters the most overt criticism of God in the entire book in 2:20, when she prays, "See YHWH, and observe who it is that you have dealt with severely here. Should women eat their offspring, the children of their care? Should priest and prophet be killed in the sanctuary of the Lord?" On the one hand, faith declares that YHWH must behave righteously, so his actions in Zion's case must be pure. On the other hand, it does not always *feel* or *look* that way, and the biblical lament tradition creates the space for such feelings to find voice in Israel's relationship with YHWH.[151]

---

151. See esp. Broyles, *The Conflict of Faith and Experience.*

So Lamentations 1 serves an ethical function by presenting ethical assessments of these four sets of characters. However, there is a second way, touched upon already, in which it, along with the rest of the book, serves to ethically shape readers: namely, the way in which the presentation of pain functions to elicit sympathy and compassion for Jerusalem. The narrator speaks directly to the implied readers and demands that they not look away from the grieving woman who sits alone. By his portrait of her sorrow, he seeks to draw readers to have compassion on this most broken of women. Zion speaks, not to the implied readers, but to other characters in her textual world: the passers-by (1:12a) and the nations round about her (1:18b). However, the implied and the actual readers will find it hard not to place themselves in the position of those passing-by on the road. As she speaks, the difference between those bystanders and the readers subtly collapses and the text makes readers feel that she is speaking to *them,* calling *them* to see her pain, drawing out *their* sympathy, inviting *them* to act as her comforter. In other words, the readers are invited to make an ethical response to this pain-sensitizing poem. Her gut-wrenching descriptions of abuse, her deeply felt expressions of emotion, and her incessant calls for help compel readers to face her tragedy. This poem does not allow readers to turn their eyes away from the lonely woman, for every part of the textual space is filled with her sorrow: to read *this* poem *is* to confront the pain.

However, while the narrator is clearly sympathetic towards Zion, there is a case for saying that in this first poem he does not have an *adequate* emotional appreciation of Jerusalem's pain. He *is* emotionally engaged with her, yet the reader cannot but notice that her words are much more passionate than his. She feels her pain from the *inside,* while he is looking on from *outside.* In the second poem, however, he has moved towards being much more emotionally sensitive to her suffering; indeed, he is overcome by sorrow and despairs that she is beyond healing (2:10-13). The emotional contrast between the narrator and Zion in poem 1 and between the narrator's words in poem 1 and poem 2 is one of degree, not of kind. However, the change in him between the first and the second poem alerts us to the need to read Lamentations 1 alongside Lamentations 2. So there is a development over the first two poems in his ethical-emotional appreciation of her pain, and the implied readers are invited on a similar journey of growing emotional perception.

The very existence and reading of the poem itself serve as an ethical response to Jerusalem's holocaust. The unknown author, by writing the poem, has made possible the ongoing remembrance of the calamity. The real readers in the Jewish and Christian communities that have preserved and used the text as Holy Scripture are led to pay attention to her. So the poem, *by its exis-*

tence, serves as an ethical response to this pain and, in its use, serves to elicit ongoing ethical responses from actual readers.

The ongoing use of the poem in subsequent generations invites the readers to engage it in the light of subsequent calamities and sufferings beyond the specific decimation described by the text itself. The experiences of later readers open up the text in new and unexpected ways and enable the sufferings of readers to be interpreted in fresh ways. Of course, readers will not feel obligated to see every aspect of their experience mirrored in the text. For instance, readers may not feel that their particular pain is a punishment for their sins in the way that Zion's was. Different readers will engage different elements of the poem as they set it in hermeneutical dialogue with their own situations.

> Lamentations is a potent work of art. To read it is to enter into a world apart, a world created by suggestion, image and metaphor. Because it is an imagined symbolic world, it can, like all good poetry, intermingle with our real worlds to reveal, mirror, and challenge them. In this conversation between worlds, it can help us see our pain, and, by reflecting it back to us, however indirectly, it has the potential to affirm our human dignity in a first step towards healing.[152]

YHWH as Ethical Reader of Lamentations

What commentators usually pass over in silence is *YHWH's* ethical reader-response to Lamentations. The *primary intended audience* of a lament was not the community, but *God.* Christians are used to thinking of God as the *inspirer* of Scripture and the one who *speaks through* Scripture, but to picture God as a *reader* of Scripture is not something that comes naturally. However, once we realize that the primary audience was YHWH, then we see that all the strategies employed by the author to draw the implied readers to comfort Zion were actually employed simultaneously to persuade *YHWH* to fulfill this role.

The one observation about God-as-reader of Lamentations that can be almost guaranteed to be made by commentators is the observation that God does *not* respond to Jerusalem's suffering in Lamentations. This is an impor-

---

152. O'Connor, *Lamentations and the Tears of the World*, 4. Interestingly, if Lamentations was written quite soon after the Babylonian destruction of Jerusalem, the original audience would have been fellow sufferers, yet the implied readers are onlookers *and not insiders.* Thus, the first *real* audiences of this poem were being drawn by the text into a different viewing position vis-à-vis *their own* sorrow.

tant insight that needs holding on to, for it preserves the view from below. However, for Jewish and Christian readers Lamentations has been framed within a bigger context, and this invites fresh perspectives on texts beyond those of implied authors.[153] Of special interest is the way in which YHWH in Second Isaiah explicitly picks up on the pleas of Lamentations and takes on the role of Zion's comforter. In Isa 54:11 he refers to her as "afflicted one, storm-tossed, *and not comforted*" before promising that she will be rebuilt with precious jewels. In 51:19-20 there is a clear echo of the calamity in Lamentations 1 when the prophet says, "Two things have befallen you — who will console you? — devastation and destruction, famine and sword; *who will comfort you?* Your sons have fainted, they lie at the head of every street like an antelope in a net; they are full of the wrath of the Lord, the rebuke of your God." YHWH immediately explains that Jerusalem's time of wrath is over (51:21-23). So YHWH recognizes that Jerusalem has indeed experienced terrible affliction at his hand, has lived for an awful period without any comfort, but now a new day is dawning. The comfort theme is a major motif throughout Isaiah 40–55, with YHWH himself coming to take on the role of the comforter. "For the Lord has comforted his people, and will have compassion on his afflicted" (49:13); "For the Lord has comforted Zion; he will comfort all her waste places, and will make her wilderness like Eden" (51:3); "I, I am he that comforts you" (51:12); "the Lord has comforted his people, he has redeemed Jerusalem" (52:9). We have already explored at length God's response to Lamentations in Isaiah 40–55 (pp. 162-68), and readers may refer back to that for further reflection.

However, YHWH's response to Zion's cries was a delayed response, and, by preserving the text of Lamentations in its Holy Saturday form, the Scriptures preserve the integrity of her dark night of the soul. Lamentations must be heard on its own before *and after* being held alongside Isaiah. But the canonical *context* of Lamentations also requires that we acknowledge that YHWH *had* in fact seen her suffering, *had* in fact heard her cries, and *would* act out of covenant faithfulness to restore her again.

Second Isaiah makes no attempt to deny that Israel's sufferings were indeed rooted in YHWH's wrath at her sin, just as Lamentations says. But the Isaiah scroll promises that wrath is not the last word: mercy is. The emphasis in

---

153. Pyper notes the way in which Lamentations, by virtue of the fact that it is a fixed text, "endlessly repeats the same words to its readers, frozen in the posture of abandonment. As a text, it cannot move to a point of new attachment"; "Reading Lamentations," 56-57. Thus, the textuality of Lamentations makes it not a text of mourning but of unrelenting, psychologically harmful melancholia. This is why it is so critical to appreciate that Jewish and Christian canons have framed the way the text has been read, and this is why the lack of resolution *within the book itself* does not degenerate into melancholia.

Lamentations on pain, sorrow, groaning, desolation, bereavement, wrath, and death is balanced in Isaiah with its emphasis on compassion, comfort, redemption, joy, and salvation. There is no suggestion in Second Isaiah that YHWH has behaved inappropriately in punishing Zion, but it is very clear that he is deeply moved by her suffering and passionately wishes to bring it to an end.

The Ethics of Prayers for Vengeance

One ethical issue raised by Lamentations for many readers is Zion's prayer for retribution on her enemies (1:21-22; cf. 3:64-66; 4:21-22). It sounds very nonredemptive, merely an expression of anger at those who have hurt her. Without doubt, this prayer is born of pain and anger, and at very least readers ought to acknowledge that Scripture allows space for wounded people to feel this way. However, there is more going on in this prayer than the gut instinct to want those who hurt us to be hurt. The prayer is predicated upon the beliefs that the behavior of the enemies was ethically wrong, and that it is ethically fitting that such behavior is punished in proportion to its seriousness. So, prayer for retribution is prayer for *justice* of a sort. In this case, proportionate punishment would be *harsh* punishment because the crimes stagger the imagination. Both of these ethical instincts are still widely shared today.

It is also important to appreciate that, for Zion, her own relief from suffering required the enemy to be removed, so the prayer for retribution is *simultaneously a prayer for liberation*. Beyond that, we also need to grasp that a prayer for harsh retribution was *not* a prayer for the annihilation of the enemy. Jerusalem herself had been harshly punished by YHWH, yet redemption was still a possibility for her. So also with her enemies. While Zion's prayer focuses on punishment, it does not exclude subsequent salvation (cf. Isa 19:22). From a Christian perspective, we might hope that, as Jürgen Moltmann says, "The message of the new righteousness which eschatological faith brings into the world says that in fact the executioners will not finally triumph over their victims. *It also says that in the end the victims will not triumph over their executioners.*"[154] Furthermore,

> It is important to recognize that these verbal assaults of imagination and hyperbole are *verbal*. They speak wishes and prayers. But the speaker doesn't *do* anything beyond speak. The *speech* of vengeance is not to be equated with *acts* of vengeance. This community which respected and

154. Moltmann, *The Crucified God*, 178, my emphasis.

greatly valued language encouraged speech, destructive as it might be, in the place of destructive action. So far as we know, even in the most violent cries for vengeance, no action is taken.[155]

Indeed, very typically for lament psalms, Zion passes the right to vengeance over to YHWH.[156] She does *not* ask YHWH for a situation in which *she herself could take revenge*. Instead, she asks YHWH to do it for her. "The assignment of vengeance to God means an end to human vengeance. It is a liberating assertion that I do not need to trouble myself with retaliation, for that is left safely in God's hands."[157] The New Testament takes a very similar approach towards vengeance, seen most clearly in Paul's admonition in Rom 12:17-19:

> Do not repay anyone evil for evil, but take thought for what is noble in the sight of all. If it is possible, so far as it depends on you, live peaceably with all. Beloved, *never avenge yourselves, but leave room for the wrath of God;* for it is written, "Vengeance is mine, I will repay, says the Lord."

Here divine vengeance is *not* a model for humans to imitate but *the exact opposite:* humans should avoid taking vengeance on their enemies *because that is God's prerogative*. This is the consistent message of the New Testament. (It is worth interjecting at this point that the asymmetry between divine and human action in the realm of vengeance is the grounds on which we can say that YHWH's violence against the sinful Lady Zion *must not* be seen to provide a theological justification for husbands to use violence against their wives.[158] God's action here is fundamentally *not* a model for human action.) Finally, before we dismiss Zion's prayer too quickly, we ought to note that in Isaiah 47, as we have already seen, *YHWH answers it* by dealing harshly with Babylon and, by so doing, liberating Zion. So, in Isaiah God did not think this prayer in Lamentations to be inappropriate.

Given all of this, we must ask whether a *Christian* can or should pray such a prayer. My answer is a cautious and highly qualified, "Yes." The Christian needs to allow the person of Jesus to act as a prism through which the light of Old Testament traditions can be shone. When those traditions are seen through Christ's prism, they can look quite different. Most relevant to our reflections here is Jesus' prayer from the cross, "Father, forgive them, for

155. Brueggemann, *Praying the Psalms,* 67. On vengeance, see Peels, *Shadow Sides.*
156. See Firth, *Surrendering Retribution in the Psalms.*
157. Brueggemann, *Praying the Psalms,* 70.
158. Understandably, this is one of Guest's concerns; "Hiding Behind the Naked Women," 431.

they do not know what they are doing" (Luke 23:34). This seems to reflect a radically different response to one's enemies than that exemplified by Zion in Lamentations. Jesus does not ask God to deal harshly with those who beat him, spat on him, mocked him, stripped him, humiliated, and crucified him. He exemplified his own teaching in the Sermon on the Mountain:

> You have heard that it was said, "An eye for an eye and a tooth for a tooth." But I say to you, Do not resist one who is evil. But if anyone strikes you on the right cheek, turn to him the other also. [an echo of Lam 3:30]
> You have heard that it was said, "You shall love your neighbor and hate your enemy." But I say to you, Love your enemies, and pray for those who persecute you so that you may be sons of your Father who is in heaven. (Matt 5:38-39, 43-45a)

So Jesus' response in his Zion-like crisis was to pray for the forgiveness of those who acted so wickedly towards him. Does this not require a rejection by Christians of Zion's kind of response? Not, I suggest, if Zion's response is reappropriated through a broader biblical-theological framework. Divine punishment of sin is a reality that Jesus himself clearly recognized and never attempted to dismiss. He regularly warned his audience to avoid acting in ways that would bring destructive judgment from heaven. Nevertheless, Jesus' focus was on God's breathtaking love, his staggering mercy towards rebellious people, his generous forgiveness of heinous sins, his astonishing grace, and his gentle acceptance of outcasts and sinners. God, as revealed in Christ, is seen to be preeminently one who desires to save people and one who is reluctant to punish (Lam 3:22-33).

I suggest that this framework of divine mercy can form the backdrop to understanding even God's punishment. Punishment is, in one sense, the opposite of mercy, but in a deeper sense may be seen as the long route towards mercy. The story of Israel itself illustrates this. God punished them because he loved them, and his punishment was never the end of their story but the difficult route towards eschatological mercy that was necessitated by their constant rebellions. Punishment had its place in their story, but that place was never at the end. The end of their story could only be saving, transforming grace. I suggest, first of all, that this theological plot needs to be firmly in mind if we are to reappropriate a prayer like Zion's. If we pray for God to punish our enemies, *it must be with their eventual salvation in mind.* I am not suggesting that Zion had this focus, but I am suggesting that such a prayer can only be a *Christian* prayer if it is a paradoxical form of blessing those who curse us.

Bibliography

Adams, Marilyn McCord. *Horrendous Evils and the Goodness of God*. Ithaca: Cornell University Press, 1999.

Albertz, Rainer. *Israel in Exile: The History and Literature of the Sixth Century B.C.E.* Studies in Biblical Literature 3. Atlanta: SBL, 2003.

Albrektson, Bertil. *Studies in the Text and Theology of the Book of Lamentations*. Studia theologica Lundensia 21. Lund: Gleerup, 1963.

Alter, Robert. *The Art of Biblical Poetry*. New York: Basic Books. 1985.

Anderson, Gary A. *A Time to Mourn, a Time to Dance: The Expression of Grief and Joy in Israelite Religion*. University Park: Pennsylvania State University Press, 1991.

Anderson, Kevin L. *"But God Raised Him from the Dead": The Theology of Jesus' Resurrection in Luke-Acts*. Milton Keynes: Paternoster and Eugene: Wipf & Stock, 2006.

Ansell, Nicholas John. *The Annihilation of Hell: Universal Salvation and the Redemption of Time in the Eschatology of Jürgen Moltmann*. Milton Keynes: Paternoster, forthcoming.

Bail, Ulrike. "Spelling Out No-Where. Lamentations as a Textual Space of Survival." www.lectio.unibe.ch/03_1/bail.htm.

Balthasar, Hans Urs von. *Explorations in Theology*. Vol 4: *Spirit and Institution*. Trans. Edward Oakes, S.J. San Francisco: Ignatius, 1995.

———. *Mysterium Paschale: The Mystery of Easter*. Edinburgh: T. & T. Clark and Grand Rapids: Wm. B. Eerdmans, 1990.

Barstad, Hans M. *The Myth of the Empty Land: A Study in the History and Archaeology of Judah during the "Exilic" Period*. Oslo: Scandinavian University Press, 1996.

Barth, Karl. *Church Dogmatics*. Vol. II/2: *The Doctrine of God*. Edinburgh: T. & T. Clark, 1957.

Beale, Gregory K. *The Temple and the Church's Mission*. Leicester: Apollos and Downers Grove: InterVarsity, 2004.

Bergant, Dianne. "The Challenge of Hermeneutics: Lamentations 1:1-11: A Test Case." *CBQ* 64 (2002) 1-16.

———. *Lamentations*. AOTC. Nashville: Abingdon, 2003.

———. "Violence and God: A Bible Study." *Missiology* 20 (1992) 45-54.

Berlin, Adele. *The Dynamics of Biblical Parallelism.* Rev. ed. BRS. Grand Rapids: Wm. B. Eerdmans and Livonia: Dove, 2008.

——————. *Lamentations.* OTL. Louisville: Westminster John Knox, 2002.

Berrigan, Daniel. *Lamentations: From New York to Kabul and Beyond.* Lanham: Sheed & Ward, 2002.

Bird, Michael F. *The Saving Righteousness of God: Studies on Paul, Justification and the New Perspective.* Milton Keynes: Paternoster, 2007.

Blenkinsopp, Joseph. "The Bible, Archaeology and Politics; or The Empty Land Revisited." *JSOT* 27 (2002) 169-87.

Boase, Elizabeth. *The Fulfillment of Doom? The Dialogic of Interaction Between the Book of Lamentations and the Pre-Exilic/Early Exilic Prophetic Literature.* LHB/OTS 437. New York: T. & T. Clark, 2006.

Boecker, Hans J. *Klagelieder.* ZBK 21. Zurich: Theologischer, 1985.

Boulton, Matthew. "Forsaking God: A Theological Argument for Christian Lamentations." *SJT* 55 (2002) 58-78.

Bozak, Barbara A. "Suffering and the Psalms of Lament: Speech for the Speechless, Power for the Powerless." *EgT* 23 (1992) 325-38.

Brady, Christian M. M. *The Rabbinic Targum of Lamentations: Vindicating God.* Leiden: Brill, 2003.

Brandscheidt, Renate. *Das Buch der Klagelieder.* Geistliche Schriftlesung, Alten Testament 10. Düsseldorf: Patmos, 1988.

Bretherton, Luke. "Valuing the Nation: Nationalism and Cosmopolitanism in Theological Perspective." In *Public Theology in Cultural Engagement,* ed. Stephen R. Holmes, 170-96. Milton Keynes: Paternoster, 2008.

Britt, Brian. "Unexpected Attachments: A Literary Approach to the Term חסד in the Hebrew Bible." *JSOT* 27 (2003) 289-307.

Broyles, Craig C. *The Conflict of Faith and Experience in the Psalms: A Form-Critical and Theological Study.* JSOTSup 52. Sheffield: JSOT, 1989.

Brueggemann, Walter. "The Costly Loss of Lament." *JSOT* 36 (1986) 57-71.

——————. "The Friday Voice of Faith." *Reformed Worship* 30 (2003) 25.

——————. *Praying the Psalms: Engaging Scripture and the Life of the Spirit.* 2nd ed. Eugene: Cascade and Milton Keynes: Paternoster, 2007.

——————. *The Psalms and the Life of Faith.* Ed. Patrick D. Miller. Minneapolis: Fortress, 1995.

——————. "Psalms and the Life of Faith: A Suggested Typology of Function." *JSOT* 17 (1980) 3-32.

Budde, Karl. "Die Klagelieder." In *Die Fünf Megillot,* ed. Budde, Alfred Bertholet, and G. Wildeboer, 70-108. KHC 17. Freiburg: Mohr, 1898.

——————. "Poetry (Hebrew)." In *A Dictionary of the Bible,* ed. James Hastings, 4:2-13. New York: Scribner's, 1902.

Calvin, John, *Commentaries on the Book of the Prophet Jeremiah and the Lamentations.* Trans. J. Owen. Grand Rapids: Baker, 1996.

——————. *The Institutes of the Christian Religion.* Trans. Ford Lewis Battles. LCC. Philadelphia: Westminster, 1960.

Cameron-Mowat, Andrew, S.J. "Lamentations and Christian Worship." In Parry and Thomas, *Great Is Thy Faithfulness?*

Chapman, Colin. "A Lament over Lebanon." http://www.fulcrum-anglican.org.uk/news/ 2006/docs.cfm?fname=20060724chapman&format=pdf&option=inline.

Clines, David J. A. *The Theme of the Pentateuch.* JSOTSup 10. 2nd ed. Sheffield: Sheffield Academic, 1997.

Coetzee, Johan H. "A Survey of Research on the Psalms of Lamentations." *OTE* 5 (1992) 151-74.

Cohen, Chayim. "The 'Widowed' City." *JANESCU* 5 (1973) 75-81.

Cohen, David J. "Getting to the Heart of the Matter — A Lamentable Situation." In *Text & Task: Scripture and Mission,* ed. Michael Parsons, 50-63. Milton Keynes: Paternoster, 2005.

———. "Towards an Appreciation of Lament Psalms in the Journey of Spiritual Formation." Unpublished paper. Tyndale Fellowship Conference, 2004.

Dahood, Mitchell. "New Readings in Lamentations." *Bib* 59 (1978) 174-97.

Dennison, James T. "The Lament and the Lamenter: Lamentations 3:1-23." *Kerux* 12/3 (1997): 30-34.

Dobbs-Allsopp, F. W. *Lamentations.* Interpretation. Louisville: Westminster John Knox, 2002.

———. "Linguistic Evidence for the Date of Lamentations." *JANESCU* 26 (1998) 1-36.

———. "The Syntagma of *bat* Followed by a Geographical Name in the Hebrew Bible: A Reconsideration of Its Meaning and Grammar." *CBQ* 57 (1995) 451-70.

———. "Tragedy, Tradition, and Theology in the Book of Lamentations." *JSOT* 74 (1997) 29-60.

———. *Weep, O Daughter of Zion: A Study of the City-Lament Genre in the Hebrew Bible.* BibOr 44. Rome: Pontifical Biblical Institute Press, 1993.

———, and Tod Linafelt. "The Rape of Zion in Thr 1,10." *ZAW* 113 (2001) 77-81.

Dormandy, Richard. "The Madness of St Paul." Unpublished.

Dumbrell, William J. *Covenant and Creation: An Old Testament Covenantal Theology.* Carlisle: Paternoster, 1984.

Eissfeldt, Otto. *The Old Testament: An Introduction.* New York: Harper & Row, 1965.

Evans, Craig A. "Jesus and the Continuing Exile of Israel." In *Jesus & the Restoration of Israel,* ed. Carey C. Newman, 77-100. Downers Grove: InterVarsity, 1999.

———. *Mark 8:27–16:20.* WBC 34B. Nashville: Nelson, 2001.

Fee, Gordon D. *God's Empowering Presence: The Holy Spirit in the Letters of Paul.* Peabody: Hendrickson, 1994.

Fichtner, Johannes. "ὀργή. III. The Wrath of God." *TDNT,* 5:395-409.

Fiddes, Paul S. *Participating in God: A Pastoral Doctrine of the Trinity.* Louisville: Westminster John Knox, 2001.

Firth, David G. *Surrendering Retribution in the Psalms: Responses to Violence in the Individual Complaints.* Milton Keynes: Paternoster, 2005.

Freedman, David Noel. "Acrostics and Metrics in Hebrew Poetry." *HTR* 65 (1972) 367-92.

———, and Erich A. von Fange. "Metrics in Hebrew Poetry: The Book of Lamentations Revisited." *CTQ* 60 (1996) 279-305.

———, and Jeffery Geoghegan. "Quantitative Measurement in Biblical Hebrew Poetry." In *Ki Baruch Hu: Ancient Near Eastern, Biblical, and Judaic Studies in Honor of*

Baruch A. Levine, ed. Robert Chazan, William W. Hallo, and Lawrence H. Schiffman, 229-49. Winona Lake: Eisenbrauns, 1999.

Garrett, Duane A. *Song of Songs;* Paul R. House, *Lamentations.* WBC 23B. Nashville: Nelson, 2004.

Gavrilyuk, Paul L. *The Suffering of the Impassible God: The Dialectics of Patristic Thought.* Oxford: Oxford University Press, 2004.

Gerstenberger, Erhard S. *Psalms, Part 2 and Lamentations.* FOTL. Grand Rapids: Wm. B. Eerdmans, 2001.

Gewaltney, W. C. "The Biblical Book of Lamentations in the Context of Near Eastern Lament Literature." In *The Context of Scripture.* Vol. 2: *Monumental Inscriptions from the Biblical World,* ed. William W. Hallo, 191-211. Leiden: Brill, 2000.

Goldingay, John. *Old Testament Theology.* Vol. 1: *Israel's Gospel.* Downers Grove: InterVarsity, 2003 and Milton Keynes: Paternoster, 2007.

Gordis, Robert. "The Conclusion of the Book of Lamentations (5:22)." *JBL* 93 (1974) 289-93.

———. *The Song of Songs and Lamentations.* Rev. ed. New York: Ktav, 1974.

Gottlieb, Hans. *A Study on the Text of Lamentations.* Acta Jutlandica Teologisk Serie 12. Århus: Det Lærde Selskab, 1978.

Gottwald, Norman K. "Lamentations." *Int* 9 (1955) 320-38.

———. *Studies in the Book of Lamentations.* 2nd ed. SBT 14. London: SCM, 1954.

Goulder, Michael. "Deutero-Isaiah of Jerusalem." *JSOT* 28 (2004) 351-62.

Gous, Ignatius G. P. "Exiles and the Dynamics of Experience of Loss: The Reaction of Lamentations 2 on the Loss of Land." *OTE* 6 (1993) 351-63.

———. "A Survey of Research on the Book of Lamentations." *OTE* 5 (1992) 184-205.

Gowan, Donald E. *Theology of the Prophetic Books: The Death and Resurrection of Israel.* Louisville: Westminster John Knox, 1998.

Grant, Jamie. "Psalm 44 and a Christian Spirituality of Lament." Unpublished paper. Tyndale Old Testament Lecture, July 2007.

Gruber, Mayer. "Introduction to Rashi's Commentary on the Book of Lamentations." In Parry and Thomas, *Great Is Thy Faithfulness?*

Guest, Deryn. "Hiding Behind the Naked Women in Lamentations: A Recriminative Response." *BibInt* 7 (1999) 413-48.

Guinan, Michael D. "Lamentations." In *The New Jerome Bible Commentary,* ed. Raymond E. Brown, Joseph A. Fitzmyer, and Roland E. Murphy, 58-62. Englewood Cliffs: Prentice Hall, 1990.

Gunkel, Hermann. *Einleitung in die Psalmen.* HKAT. Göttingen: Vandenhoeck & Ruprecht, 1933.

———. "Klagelieder Jeremiae." In *RGG,* 3:1049-52.

Gwaltney, W. C., Jr. "Biblical Book of Lamentations in the Context of Near Eastern Lament Literature." In *Scripture in Context.* Vol. 2: *More Essays on the Comparative Method,* ed. William W. Hallo, James C. Moyer, and Leo G. Perdue, 191-211. Winona Lake: Eisenbrauns, 1983.

Heater, Homer. "Structure and Meaning in Lamentations." *BSac* 149 (1992) 304-15.

Heim, Knut M. "The Personification of Jerusalem and the Drama of Her Bereavement in Lamentations." In *Zion, City of Our God,* ed. Richard S. Hess and Gordon J. Wenham, 129-69. Grand Rapids: Wm. B. Eerdmans, 1999.

Helberg, Jacob L. "Land in the Book of Lamentations." *ZAW* 102 (1990) 372-85.

Hiebert, Paula S. "'Whence Shall Help Come to Me?' The Biblical Widow." In *Gender and Difference in Ancient Israel,* ed. Peggy L. Day, 125-41. Minneapolis: Augsburg Fortress, 1989.

Hillers, Delbert R. "History and Poetry in Lamentations." *CurTM* 10 (1983) 155-61.

————. *Lamentations.* 2nd ed. AB 7A. Garden City: Doubleday, 1992.

Hoskins, Paul M. *Jesus as the Fulfillment of the Temple in the Gospel of John.* Milton Keynes: Paternoster, 2006.

Houk, Cornelius. "Multiple Poets in Lamentations." *JSOT* 30 (2005) 111-25.

House, Paul R. *Lamentations.* WBC 23B. Nashville: Nelson, 2004.

————. "Outrageous Demonstrations of Grace: The Theology of Lamentations." In Parry and Thomas, *Great Is Thy Faithfulness?*

Howard-Snyder, Daniel, ed. *The Evidential Argument from Evil.* Bloomington: Indiana University Press, 1996.

Hunter, Jannie H. *Faces of a Lamenting City.* BEATAJ 39. Frankfurt: Lang, 1996.

————. "How Can We Lament When We Are Glad? A Comment on Genre in Poetic Texts." *OTE* 5 (1992) 175-83.

————. "Tracing Lamentations 3: The Ideas of Individual Lament." *OTE* 12 (1999) 57-72.

Jahnow, Hedwig. *Das hebräische Leichenlied im Rahmen der Völkerdichtung.* BZAW 36. Giessen: Töpelmann, 1923.

Janowski, Bernd, and Peter Stuhlmacher, eds. *The Suffering Servant: Isaiah 53 in Jewish and Christian Sources.* Grand Rapids: Wm. B. Eerdmans, 2004.

Jervis, L. Ann. *At the Heart of the Gospel: Suffering in the Earliest Christian Message.* Grand Rapids: Wm. B. Eerdmans, 2007.

John of the Cross. *The Complete Works of Saint John of the Cross, Doctor of the Church.* Trans. E. Allison Peers. Wheathampstead: Anthony Clarke, 1974.

Johnson, Andy. "The 'New Creation', the Crucified and Risen Christ, and the Temple: A Pauline Audience for Mark." *Journal of Theological Interpretation* 1 (2007) 171-91.

Johnson, Bo. "Form and Message in Lamentations." *ZAW* 97 (1985) 58-73.

Joyce, Paul M. "Lamentations and the Grief Process: A Psychological Reading." *BibInt* 1 (1993) 304-20.

————. "Sitting Loose to History: Reading the Book of Lamentations Without Primary Reference to Its Original Historical Setting." In *In Search of True Wisdom,* ed. Edward Ball, 246-62. JSOTSup 300. Sheffield: Sheffield Academic, 1999.

Kaiser, Otto. *Klagelieder.* In Helmer Ringgren and Kaiser, *Das Hohe Lied/Klagelieder/Das Buch Esther,* 91-198. ATD 16/2. Göttingen: Vandenhoeck & Ruprecht, 1992.

Kaiser, Walter C., Jr. *Grief and Pain in the Plan of God: Christian Assurance and the Book of Lamentations.* Fearn: Christian Focus, 2004. 1st ed. *A Biblical Approach to Personal Suffering,* 1982.

Keefe, Alice. "Rapes of Women/Wars of Men." In *Women, War, and Metaphor,* ed. Claudia V. Camp and Carole R. Fontaine, 79-98. Semeia 61 (1993).

Keil, C. F. *Jeremiah, Lamentations.* Commentary on the Old Testament 8. 1872; repr. Grand Rapids: Wm. B. Eerdmans, 1980.

Kramer, Samuel N. *Lamentation over the Destruction of Ur.* AS 12. Chicago: University of Chicago Press, 1940.

Krašovec, Joze. "The Source of Hope in the Book of Lamentations." *VT* 42 (1992) 223-33.

Kraus, Hans-Joachim. *Klagelieder (Threni).* 3rd ed. BKAT 20. Neukirchen-Vluyn: Neukirchener, 1968.

Lanahan, William F. "The Speaking Voice in the Book of Lamentations." *JBL* 93 (1974) 41-49.

Lauber, David. *Barth on the Descent into Hell: God, Atonement, and the Christian Life.* Aldershot: Ashgate, 2004.

Lee, Nancy C. *The Singers of Lamentations: Cities Under Siege, From Ur to Jerusalem to Sarajevo.* Biblical Interpretation 60. Leiden: Brill, 2002.

Lewis, Alan E. *Between Cross and Resurrection: A Theology of Holy Saturday.* Grand Rapids: Wm. B. Eerdmans, 2001.

Linafelt, Tod. "Margins of Lamentation, Or, The Unbearable Whiteness of Reading." In *Reading Bibles, Writing Bodies: Identity and the Book,* ed. Timothy K. Beal and David M. Gunn, 219-31. London: Routledge, 1997.

———. "The Refusal of a Conclusion in the Book of Lamentations." *JBL* 120 (2001) 340-43.

———. "Surviving Lamentations." *HBT* 17 (1995) 45-61.

———. *Surviving Lamentations: Catastrophe, Lament, and Protest in the Afterlife of a Biblical Book.* Chicago: University of Chicago Press, 2000.

Lindsay, John. "Edomite Westward Expansion: The Biblical Evidence." *ANES* 36 (1999) 48-89.

Löhr, Max. *Der Klagelieder des Jeremia.* HKAT 3/2/2. Göttingen: Vandenheock & Ruprecht, 1906.

———. "Threni III. und die jeremianische Autorschaft des Buches der Klagelieder." *ZAW* 24 (1904) 1-16.

Love, Mark Cameron. *The Evasive Text: Zechariah 1–8 and the Frustrated Reader.* JSOTSup 296. Sheffield: Sheffield Academic, 1999.

Luther, Martin. *Luther's Works,* ed. Jaroslav Pelikan and Helmut T. Lehman. 55 vols. St. Louis: Concordia and Philadelphia: Fortress, 1955-1967.

Macchia, Frank. "Groans Too Deep for Words." www.apts.edu/ajps/98-2/98-2-macchia.htm.

———. "Sighs Too Deep for Words: Toward a Theology of Glossolalia." *JPT* 1 (1992) 47-73.

McConville, J. Gordon. *Judgment and Promise: An Interpretation of the Book of Jeremiah.* Leicester: Apollos and Winona Lake: Eisenbrauns, 1993.

McDaniel, Thomas F. "The Alleged Sumerian Influence upon Lamentations." *VT* 18 (1968) 198-209.

———. "Philological Studies in Lamentations I." *Bib* 49 (1968) 27-53.

———. "Philological Studies in Lamentations II." *Bib* 49 (1968) 199-220.

MacDonald, Gregory. *The Evangelical Universalist.* Eugene: Cascade, 2006 and London: SPCK, 2008.

Mackie, J. L. *The Miracle of Theism: Arguments for and against the Existence of God.* Oxford: Oxford University Press, 1982.

Mandolfo, Carleen R. *Daughter Zion Talks Back to the Prophets: A Dialogic Theology of the Book of Lamentations.* SemeiaSt 58. Atlanta: SBL, 2007.

Meek, T. J., and W. P. Merrill. "The Book of Lamentations." *IB,* 6:1-38.

Merwe, Christo H. J., Jackie A. Naudé, and Jan H. Kroeze. *A Biblical Hebrew Reference Grammar*. Sheffield: Sheffield Academic, 1999.

Michalowski, Piotr, ed. *The Lamentation over the Destruction of Sumer and Ur*. Winona Lake: Eisenbrauns, 1989.

Middlemas, Jill. *The Troubles of Templeless Judah*. Oxford: Oxford University Press, 2005.

———. "The Violent Storm in Lamentations." *JSOT* 29 (2004) 81-97.

Miller, Charles W. "The Book of Lamentations in Recent Research." *CurBR* 1 (2002) 9-29.

———. "Poetry and Personae: The Use and Function of the Changing Speaking Voices in the Book of Lamentations." Ph.D. diss., Denver, 1996.

———. "Reading Voices: Personification, Dialogism, and the Reader of Lamentations 1." *BibInt* 9.4 (2001) 393-408.

Mintz, Alan. *Ḥurban: Responses to Catastrophe in Hebrew Literature*. New York: Columbia University Press, 1984.

———. "The Rhetoric of Lamentations and the Representation of Catastrophe." *Prooftexts* 2 (1980) 1-17.

Moffitt, David M. "Righteous Bloodshed, Matthew's Passion Narrative, and the Temple's Destruction: Lamentations as a Matthean Intertext." *JBL* 125 (2006) 299-320.

Moltmann, Jürgen. *The Coming of God: Christian Eschatology*. London: SCM and Minneaspolis: Fortress, 1996.

———. *The Crucified God*. London: SCM and New York: Harper & Row, 1974.

Moore, Michael S. "Human Suffering in Lamentations." *RB* 90 (1983) 534-55.

Morse, Benjamin. "The Lamentations Project: Biblical Mourning through Modern Montage." *JSOT* 28 (2003) 113-27.

Moser, Barry. "Blood & Stone: Violence in the Bible & the Eye of the Illustrator." *Cross Currents* 51/2 (2001). www.crosscurrents.org.

Nägelsbach, C. W. Eduard. *The Lamentations of Jeremiah*. In J. P. Lange, *A Commentary on Holy Scripture*, 12. New York: Scribner, Armstrong, 1870.

Neusner, Jacob. *Introduction to Rabbinic Literature*. ABRL. New York: Doubleday, 1994.

———. *Israel After Calamity: The Book of Lamentations*. Valley Forge: Trinity, 1995.

O'Connor, Kathleen M. "Lamentations." *NIB*, 6 (2001) 1011-72.

———. *Lamentations and the Tears of the World*. New York: Orbis, 2003.

O'Donovan, Oliver. *The Desire of the Nations: Rediscovering the Roots of Political Theology*. Cambridge: Cambridge University Press, 1996.

Ogden, Graham S. "Joel 4 and Prophetic Responses to National Laments." *JSOT* 26 (1983) 97-106.

Olyan, Saul M. *Biblical Mourning: Ritual and Social Dimensions*. Oxford: Oxford University Press, 2004.

Owens, Pamela J. "Personification and Suffering in Lamentations 3." *Austin Seminary Bulletin* 105 (1990) 75-90.

Pao, David W. *Acts and the Isaianic New Exodus*. WUNT 130. Tübingen: Mohr Siebeck, 2000. Repr. Grand Rapids: Baker, 2002.

Parry, Robin A. "The Ethics of Lament: Lamentations 1 as a Case Study." In *Reading the Law: Studies in Honour of Gordon J. Wenham*, ed. J. Gordon McConville and Karl Möller, 138-55. LHB/OTS 461. London: T. & T. Clark, 2007.

———. "Prolegomena to Christian Theological Interpretations of Lamentations." In

Canon and Biblical Interpretation, ed. Craig G. Bartholomew et al., 393-418. Milton Keynes: Paternoster and Grand Rapids: Zondervan, 2006.

—————. "Reader-Response Criticism." In *Dictionary for Theological Interpretation of the Bible,* ed. Kevin J. Vanhoozer, 658-61. Grand Rapids: Baker, 2005.

—————. "Wrestling with Lamentations in Christian Worship." In Parry and Thomas, *Great Is Thy Faithfulness?*

—————, and Heath A. Thomas, eds. *Great Is Thy Faithfulness? Toward Reading Lamentations as Sacred Scripture.* Milton Keynes: Paternoster, forthcoming.

Peels, H. G. L. *Shadow Sides: The Revelation of God in the Old Testament.* Carlisle: Paternoster, 2003.

Pham, Xuan Huong Thi. *Mourning in the Ancient Near East and the Hebrew Bible.* JSOTSup 302. Sheffield: Sheffield Academic, 1999.

Plantinga, Alvin. *God, Freedom, and Evil.* Grand Rapids: Wm. B. Eerdmans, 1974.

Plöger, Otto. "Die Klagelieder." In *Die Fünf Megilloth,* ed. Ernst Würthwein et al.. 127-64. HAT 18. Tübingen: Mohr Siebeck, 1969.

Porteous, Norman W. "Jerusalem-Zion: The Growth of a Symbol." In *Living the Mystery,* 93-111. Oxford: Blackwell, 1967.

Provan, Iain W. *Lamentations.* NCBC. Grand Rapids: Wm. B. Eerdmans and London: Marshall Pickering, 1991.

—————. "Past, Present and Future in Lamentations III 52-66: The Case for a Precative Perfect Re-Examined." *VT* 41 (1991) 164-75.

—————. "Reading Texts Against an Historical Background: The Case of Lamentations." *SJOT* 1 (1990) 130-43.

Pyper, Hugh S. "Reading Lamentations." *JSOT* 95 (2001) 55-69.

Re'emi, S. Paul. "The Theology of Hope: A Commentary on the Book of Lamentations." In Robert Martin-Achard and Re'emi, *God's People in Crisis.* ITC. Grand Rapids: Wm. B. Eerdmans, 1984.

Reimer, David J. "Good Grief? A Psychological Reading of Lamentations." *ZAW* 114 (2002) 542-59.

Renkema, Johan. *Lamentations.* HCOT. Leuven: Peeters, 1998.

Resner, André, Jr. "Lament: Faith's Response to Loss." *ResQ* 32 (1990) 129-42.

Routledge, Robin. "*Hesed* as Obligation: A Re-Examination." *TynBul* 46 (1995) 179-96.

Rudolph, Wilhelm. *Das Buch Ruth, Das Hohe Lied, Die Klagelieder.* 2nd ed. KAT. Gütersloh: Mohn, 1962.

Sæbø, Mange. "Who Is 'The Man' in Lamentations 3.1?" In *On the Way to Canon: Creative Tradition History in the Old Testament,* 131-42. Sheffield: Sheffield Academic, 1998.

Salters, R. B. "Lamentations 1:3: Light from the History of Exegesis." In *A Word in Season,* ed. James D. Martin and Philip R. Davies, 73-89. JSOTSup 42. Sheffield: Sheffield Academic, 1986.

Sawyer, John F. A. "Daughter Zion and the Servant of the Lord in Isaiah: A Comparison." *JSOT* 44 (1989) 89-107.

Schopf, F. Jane. "Musical Responses to Lamentations." In Parry and Thomas, *Great Is Thy Faithfulness?*

Seerveld, Calvin. "The Meaning of Silence for Daily Life and Sunday Worship." In *In the Fields of the Lord,* ed. Craig G. Bartholomew, 294-307. Carlisle: Piquant, 2000.

Seow, C.-L. "A Textual Note on Lamentations 1:20." *CBQ* 47 (1985) 416-19.

Shea, William H. "The *qinah* Structure of the Book of Lamentations." *Bib* 60 (1979) 103-7.

Shoshana Pfau, Julie, and David Blumenthal. "The Violence of God: Dialogic Fragments." Cross Currents 51/2 (2001). www.crosscurrents.org.

Smend, Rudolf. *Die Entstehung des Alten Testaments.* Theologische Wissenschaft 1. Stuttgart: Kohlhammer, 1978.

Smith, Daniel L. *The Religion of the Landless: The Social Context of the Babylonian Exile.* Bloomington: Meyer Stone, 1989.

Smith-Christopher, Daniel L. *A Biblical Theology of Exile.* Minneapolis: Fortress, 2002.

Soll, Will M. "The Israelite Lament: Faith Seeking Understanding." *QR* 83 (1988) 77-88.

Sommer, Benjamin D. *A Prophet Reads Scripture: Allusions in Isaiah 40–66.* Stanford: Stanford University Press, 1999.

Spurgeon, Charles H. "A Message from God to Thee." Sermon, 16 November 1862. http://www.biblebb.com/files/spurgeon/0480.htm.

———. "Watch Night Service." Sermon, 31 December 1855. http://www.biblebb.com/files/spurgeon/0059.htm.

Stern, Elsie. "Lamentations in Jewish Liturgy." In Parry and Thomas, *Great Is Thy Faithfulness?*

Stern, Ephraim. *Archaeology of the Land of the Bible.* Vol. 2: *The Assyrian, Babylonian, and Persian Periods (732-332 BCE).* ABRL. New York: Doubleday, 2001.

———. "The Babylonian Gap: The Archaeological Reality." *JSOT* 28 (2004) 273-77.

Stevenson, Peter K. *God in Our Nature: The Incarnational Theology of John McLeod Campbell.* Carlisle: Paternoster, 2004.

Swinton, John. *Raging With Compassion: Pastoral Responses to the Problem of Evil.* Grand Rapids: Wm. B. Eerdmans, 2007.

Thomas, Heath A. "Aesthetic Theory of Umberto Eco and Lamentations Interpretation." Unpublished paper. International SBL, 3 July 2006.

———. "Current Trends in Psychological Analysis of the Book of Lamentations: Prospects and Pitfalls." Unpublished paper. SBL Annual Meeting, 2007.

———. "Feminist Interpretation(s) and Lamentations." In Parry and Thomas, *Great Is Thy Faithfulness?*

———. "Lamentations in Rembrandt van Rijn: 'Jeremiah Lamenting the Destruction of Jerusalem.'" In Parry and Thomas, *Great Is Thy Faithfulness?*

———. "The Liturgical Function of the Book of Lamentations." In *Thinking towards New Horizons,* ed. Matthias Augustin and Hermann Michael Niemann. BEATAJ 55. Frankfurt: Lang, 2008.

———. "Poetry and Theology in Lamentations: An Investigation of Lamentations 1–3 Using the Aesthetic Analysis of Umberto Eco." Ph.D. diss., Gloucestershire, 2007.

———. "Reading Lamentations with Daniel Berrigan, S.J." Unpublished paper. SBL Annual Meeting, 22 November 2008.

———. "Theology and Lamentations." Unpublished paper.

Tiemeyer, Lena-Sofia. "Geography and Textual Allusions: Interpreting Isaiah xl–lv and Lamentations as Judahite Texts." *VT* 57 (2007) 367-85.

———. "Lamentations in Isaiah 40–55." In Parry and Thomas, *Great Is Thy Faithfulness?*

———. "Two Prophets, Two Laments and Two Ways of Dealing with Earlier Texts." In *Die*

Textualisierung der Religion, ed. Joachim Schaper, 185-202. FAT 62. Tübingen: Mohr Siebek, 2009.

Torrance, Thomas F. "The Divine Vocation and Destiny of Israel in World History." In *The Witness of the Jews to God,* ed. David W. Torrance, 85-104. Edinburgh: Handsel, 1982.

―――. *Incarnation: The Person and Life of Christ.* Milton Keynes: Paternoster and Downers Grove: InterVarsity, 2008.

Turner, Mary D. "Daughter Zion: Lament and Restoration." Ph.D. diss., Emory, 1992.

Wagner, J. Ross. "The Heralds of Isaiah and the Mission of Paul: An Investigation of Paul's Use of Isaiah 51-55 in Romans." In *Jesus and the Suffering Servant,* ed. William H. Bellinger, Jr., and William R. Farmer 193-222. Harrisburg: Trinity, 1998.

Walker, Peter W. L. *Jesus and the Holy City: New Testament Perspectives on Jerusalem.* Grand Rapids: Wm. B. Eerdmans, 1996.

Wall, Robert W. "Reading the Bible from within Our Traditions: The 'Rule of Faith' in Theological Hermeneutics." In *Between Two Horizons: Spanning New Testament Studies and Systematic Theology,* ed. Joel B. Green and Max Turner, 88-107. Grand Rapids: Wm. B. Eerdmans, 2000.

Waltke, Bruce, and Michael O'Connor. *An Introduction to Biblical Hebrew Syntax.* Winona Lake: Eisenbrauns, 1990.

Watson, Wilfred G. E. *Classical Hebrew Poetry: A Guide to Its Techniques.* JSOTSup 26. Sheffield: JSOT, 1984.

Webb, Barry G. *Five Festal Garments: Christian Reflections on The Song of Songs, Ruth, Lamentations, Ecclesiastes, Esther.* Leicester: Apollos, 2000.

Weiser, Artur. *Klagelieder.* In H. Ringgren and Weiser, *Sprüche/Prediger, Das Hohe Lied/ Klagelieder, Das Buch Esther.* 2nd ed. ATD 16/2. Göttingen: Vandenhoeck & Ruprecht, 1962.

Wenham, Gordon J. "Sanctuary Symbolism in the Garden of Eden Story." *Proceedings of the World Congress of Jewish Studies* 9 (1986) 19-25.

―――. *Story as Torah: Reading the Old Testament Ethically.* Edinburgh: T. & T. Clark, 2000.

Wesley, John. "Lamentations." In *John Wesley's Explanatory Notes on the Whole Bible.* http:// www.searchgodsword.org/com/wen/view.cgi?book=la.

Westermann, Claus. *Lamentations: Issues and Interpretation.* Minneapolis: Augsburg Fortress, 1994. German ed. 1990.

Wiesel, Elie. *Night.* New York: Bantam, 1960.

Wiesmann, Hermann. *Die Klagelieder, übersetzt und erklärt.* Frankfurt: Philosophisch- theologische Hochschule Sankt George, 1954.

Wilcox, Pete. "John Calvin's Interpretation of Lamentations." In Parry and Thomas, *Great Is Thy Faithfulness?*

Willey, Patricia T. *Remember the Former Things: The Recollection of Previous Texts in Second Isaiah.* SBLDS 161. Atlanta: Scholars, 1997.

Wilshire, Leland E. "The Servant-City: A New Interpretation of the 'Servant of the Lord' in the Servant Songs of Deutero-Isaiah." *JBL* 94 (1975) 356-67.

Wolterstorff, Nicholas. "If God Is Good and Sovereign, Why Lament?" *CTJ* 36 (2001) 42-52.

―――. *Lament for a Son.* Grand Rapids: Wm. B. Eerdmans, 1987.

Wright, N. Thomas. "Adam, Israel and the Messiah." In *The Climax of the Covenant,* 18-40.

—————. *Christian Origins and the Question of God.* Vol. 1: *The New Testament and the People of God.* London: SPCK and Minneapolis: Fortress, 1992.

—————. *The Climax of the Covenant: Christ and the Law in Pauline Theology,* 18-40. Edinburgh: T. & T. Clark, 1991, and Minneapolis: Fortress, 1992.

—————. "Curse and Covenant: Galatians 3.10-14." In *The Climax of the Covenant,* 137-56.

Yoder, John Howard. "Trinity Versus Theodicy: Hebraic Realism and the Temptation to Justify God." http://theology.nd.edu/people/research/yoder-john/documents/TRINITYVERSUSTHEODICY.pdf. Unpublished, 1996.

Youngblood, Kevin. "The Character and Significance of LXX Lamentations." In Parry and Thomas, *Great Is Thy Faithfulness?*